History and Hermeneutics

History and Hermeneutics

Murray A. Rae

t&t clark

Published by T&T Clark
A Continuum imprint
The Tower Building, 11 York Road, London SE1 7NX
15 East 26th Street, Suite 1703, New York, NY 10010

www.tandtclark.com

Chapters 1 and 3 of this volume were published in an earlier form in *'Behind' the Text? History and Biblical Interpretation*, edited by Craig Bartholomew, C. Stephen Evans, Mary Healey and Murray A. Rae (Carlisle: Paternoster Press, and Grand Rapids: Zondervan, 2003). Used with permission.

British Library Cataloguing-in-Publication Data
A catalogue record for this book is available from the British Library

Typeset by Free Range Book Design & Production Ltd
Printed on acid-free paper in Great Britain by MPG Books Ltd, Cornwall

ISBN 0567081621 (hardback)
0567080927 (paperback)

For Edward, Micah and Luke

Contents

Introduction

This book is an enquiry into how theology and history may be thought together. It is not a forcing together of what should properly be kept apart, but an enquiry into the realities of God and of history and of their concurrence in Jesus Christ. Such an enquiry arises from and becomes in turn a prelude to the reading of the Christian Bible. The refusal to think theology and history together has been the cause of many hermeneutical false turns during the past four hundred years or so, beginning about the time that Descartes revived the ancient belief of the philosophers that the realms of history and of eternal truth were mutually exclusive. The Modern mind has been much enamoured with this view, sometimes asserting it in such a way that the study of history was considered to be of little worth (Descartes himself), while at other times insisting on studying history without reference to God (The 'Jesus Seminar' may serve as an example here). Whatever form the disjunction between theology and history has taken, however, the result has been a failure to comprehend aright the message of the Bible which has at its heart the proclamation that 'in these last days', and building on all that has gone before, 'God has spoken to us by a Son' (Heb. 1.2). The Bible proclaims that the eternal Word of God is sounded in our history, thus making it the realm in which God brings about his purpose for the world.

In his Bampton Lectures of 1992, subsequently published under the title *The One, the Three and the Many: God, Creation and the Culture of Modernity*, Colin Gunton contends that one of the characteristics of Modernity is disengagement.[1] Disengagement describes the propensity of the Modern mind to treat the world instrumentally, 'as a mere means of realising our will and not as in some way integral to our being'. 'Its other side', Gunton further explains, 'is that we do not seek in the world for what is true and good and beautiful, but create

1. Colin E. Gunton: *The One, the Three and the Many: God, Creation and the Culture of Modernity* (Cambridge: Cambridge University Press, 1993) 13–16. Gunton is following here the analysis of Charles Taylor, *Sources of the Self: The Making of the Modern Identity* (Cambridge: Cambridge University Press, 1989) 155.

our truth and values for ourselves.'[2] Whereas in Modernity it was expected that such creativity would, through the exercise of reason, produce consensus among all people,[3] those of Postmodern persuasion insist that we accept the relativity of all value and truth. What interests me here, however, is the assumption common to both that truth and value are of our own making and depend not at all on what is given in the world. Disengagement is apparent in relation to history too. Whether the appeal is to reason (as in Modernity) or to personal experience and intuition (as in Postmodernity), the quest for truth and value repudiates tradition[4] and refuses to accord authority to that which has taken place in the past. In the realm of theology, the Modern, as also the Postmodern, mind typically resists the Christian proclamation that it is through the particular history of Jesus of Nazareth, and not otherwise, that the Truth[5] is established and made known.

This book offers an examination of that resistance and of its damaging implications for biblical hermeneutics. It highlights in particular the impossibility, within the prevailing account of what history is, of believing what the Bible has to say. The historiography that has guided a great deal of biblical studies and theology during the course of the past four hundred years is inadequate to the task of apprehending the reality to which the Bible bears witness. In response to this situation I offer an account of history drawn from the Bible itself in which history is recognized as the space and time given to humankind to be truly itself as the covenant partner of God. Such an account will seek to give due recognition not only to the transcendence of God but also to his immanence in the history of Jesus of Nazareth and through the work of his Spirit. It will be argued, further, that the very idea of history requires both the biblical doctrine of creation, and a teleology, an account, that is, of the directedness of history towards some goal. It is within this framework of creation and divine promise that an account is given of what human history is. The book begins by tracing how, within the Western intellectual tradition,[6] the

2. Gunton: *The One, the Three and the Many*, 14.

3. Witness for example, Ernst Troeltsch's supposition that 'the essential uniformity of human nature provides a foundation for consensus in recognising supreme standards of value'. 'Historical and Dogmatic Method in Theology' in *Religion in History: Ernst Troeltsch* (Edinburgh: T&T Clark, 1991) 25.

4. Gunton, *The One, the Three and the Many*, 75.

5. Following the prologue to John's Gospel, I write Truth with upper case 'T' here to designate that Truth which concerns us ultimately and which provides the decisive clue to our understanding of the world as a whole. In Christian faith, of course, the Truth is identified with the One who proclaims himself to be the Truth.

6. I do not mean to suggest that disengagement from history is unique to the Western intellectual tradition; indeed it is evident too in all other Indo-European cultures, and most clearly so where it has not been tempered through an encounter with the contrasting Semitic view of history.

divorce between history and theology has come about. It then takes bearings from several more promising strands of recent theology before developing its own account of how history and theology may be seen together.

This book could, and possibly should, have been a much bigger one. There is a vast amount of literature that bears upon the topic that I have not engaged with. The book would no doubt be a better one had I done so. As it stands, however, the book sets forth a simple proposal that has merit, or not, regardless of how it might otherwise have been stated through more extensive engagements with the literature. The proposal will in the future course of my own work be tested through more thorough interaction with some whose work I have drawn upon all too briefly here. It will benefit too, I hope, from the process of critical scrutiny and response that readers will inevitably offer.

Not all who have helped to shape my thinking as this book developed are mentioned in its pages. Students and staff in the systematic theology research seminars at King's College London and St Andrews University deserve special mention as they responded to early drafts of parts of this work. My former colleagues at King's College London, the late Professor Colin Gunton, Dr Steve Holmes and Dr Douglas Campbell were constant partners in theological conversation as the ideas in this book were developed. I owe a huge debt to Professor Alan Torrance and to his wife Jane for their unfailing friendship, generous hospitality and regular invitations to join the theological conversations in St Andrews. I am grateful too for recent conversations with Dr John Stenhouse and Dr Tim Cooper at the University of Otago, both of them historians who are interested in how to think theology and history together. Finally, the project of the book itself began because of an invitation to take part in a meeting of the Scripture and Hermeneutics Seminar. I am grateful to Professor Craig Bartholomew for that invitation, and to all who gathered at Gordon College Boston in 2002 to consider the matter with which this book is concerned.

I am glad to offer this book as a gift to my sons, Edward, Micah and Luke, who, on account of my work, have tolerated less time with their father than they deserve.

Murray Rae

1

The Development of Modern Historiography

I — The Great Divorce

The Western intellectual tradition manifests an ambivalent relationship to the study of history. There is, of course, a great deal of historical scholarship undertaken, not least in the study of biblical texts, but as Colin Gunton has observed, the Western mind is curiously disengaged from history. That is to say, it does not expect to find that the truth, and meaning, and purpose of life have been disclosed through the particularities of human history. Truth, meaning and purpose are commonly thought in Modernity to be the fruit of rational analysis, untainted by the vagaries and contingencies of history. Or, as the Postmodern mind prefers, they are thought to be artefacts of our own making with local but not universal validity and significance. A consequence of this disengagement is that theology and history have been torn apart, especially so in biblical studies where the divorce between historical and theological study has done great violence to the integrity of the biblical texts.

The divorce between historical and theological study has taken two forms. The first seeks to protect theology from the alleged vagaries of history, while the second seeks to protect history from the allegedly ephemeral and speculative claims of theology. Both strategies are premised on the conviction that history and divine action are mutually exclusive categories and that it is improper, therefore, at least in academic circles, to speak of God's participation in the unfolding nexus of historical life. The first form supposes, therefore, that attention to the contingent realm of history is of little or no value in humanity's quest for truth. Truth, it is thought, belongs to the eternal realm of the divine and is not amenable, therefore, to historical mediation. History, on this view, is not a proper object of knowledge. The second form of incredulity concerning divine action in history is the more typically 'modern' form, and it proceeds under the assumption that both the integrity of historical enquiry, and the legitimacy of our claims to historical knowledge, must be safeguarded by resisting the utilization of theological categories in our accounts of what has taken place. Both attitudes have taken a heavy toll on biblical hermeneutics as will become apparent in the following consideration of Western historiography. The survey offered here is by no means comprehensive. It serves only to identify the problem and to give some account of its genealogy. The precise extent of the problem will be left for the reader to decide.

The first form of disengagement noted above, that of the disparagement of history in the name of theology, has its roots, as is well known, in the metaphysics of classical Greek philosophy. Illustrated by Plato's model of the cave, the life of human beings lived in the realm of space and time is recognized as a life of change and impermanence, and is, on this account, presumed to be alien to the truth which is, by definition, eternal and unchanging.[1] The material imperfections of the spatio-temporal world offer only a shadowy reflection of the unchanging perfection of the eternal. To consider that one might have knowledge of this ephemeral realm of human action was thought to be a contradiction in terms, 'an attempt to know what, being transitory, is unknowable'.[2] In the view of Plato, for instance, the world of change and decay

1. The Greek view of history and the inconsequence of historical events for the true understanding of reality is discussed by Wilhelm Dilthey in *Introduction to the Sciences of the Mind*. See *Gesammelte Schriften*, vol. i. (Stuttgart: Teubner, 1927) 329f.

2. R.G. Collingwood, *The Idea of History*, ed. T.M. Knox (London: Oxford University Press, 1946) 28. Despite the metaphysical bias against the study of history in the classical world, historical reconstruction as such was not completely unknown. Herodotus, the first advocate of historical reconstruction, opposed the dominant stream of Greek thought by setting out to develop a science of history. Herodotus proposed to preserve for future generations an account of what had taken place, and, more importantly still, to discern within the particulars of human action a rationally intelligible pattern of cause and effect. History became, under Herodotus, a proper object of human enquiry and knowledge, not because contingency and change were denied – these are the stuff of history – but because arbitrariness was. The variable particularities of history were thought by Herodotus to succeed each other according to intelligible relationships of cause and effect. In the historiography of Thucydides, however, who followed Herodotus in thinking history to be a worthy sphere of investigation, there is a retreat from this interest in particulars. Despite writing an account of history, most famously in his 'History of the Peloponnesian War', Thucydides was interested less in the events themselves and the causal connections between them than in the universal laws allegedly determining the events. His enquiry, anticipating Plato's theory of Forms, concerns the nature of the eternal and unchanging principles by which historical life is thought to be determined. Truth and meaning, for Thucydides, are vested not in the particulars but in the universal laws beyond the events themselves. In his conception, therefore, history takes on a deterministic character as events are understood to succeed each other in necessary conformity to those eternal laws. The freedom of the creation to be itself is thus brought under threat and the historic potential of all human action is undermined. For all his interest in history, Thucydides' recourse

was perceptible but not intelligible, and claims about what went on in history were matters of opinion (*doxa*) but not of knowledge (*episteme*). This dualism between the temporal and the eternal, between the *cosmos aisthetos* and the *cosmos noetos*, yielded, as R.G. Collingwood has put it,[3] an anti-historical tendency in Greek thought, and an account of truth from which all historical reference is excluded. It is for this reason that the Greek mind was not well disposed to the New Testament proclamation that the eternal Word of God had become flesh. The gospel of the incarnation –the supreme instance of God's involvement in history – appears, within this context, to be a form of intellectual foolishness, a kind of naive category mistake that, if not simply false, must be consigned to the realm of the mythological. The first four centuries of the Church's life are thus marked by a titanic struggle to counter the Greek incredulity, even as it sometimes occurred within the Church itself.

For a time it seemed that the Christian (and Jewish) view that God is indeed active in history would win out against the philosophical scepticism of the Greeks. Alan Richardson, for instance, claims that by the time of Augustine the Hebraic-Christian view of history had triumphed over the classical.[4] If it really was a triumph, it was not to be an enduring one, for with the rise of Modernity, the Western philosophical tradition began again to question whether truth and history could be regarded as coalescent terms.

It is with Descartes (1596–1650) that the problematic character of history begins to re-emerge. Echoing the scepticism of the Greek mind, Descartes asserted the impossibility of any knowledge being produced by historical enquiry. 'Even the most accurate historical accounts,' contends Descartes, 'while neither changing nor amplifying the value of things in order to make them more worth reading, at least almost always leave out the basest and least illustrious circumstances, with the result that *what remains does not appear as it really is*.'[5] In history we are dealing with the contingent and the uncertain, whereas knowledge and truth, according to Descartes, are characterized by necessity and indubitability. The Cartesian quest for truth eschewed the

to the concept of universal and eternal law meant that he did not finally break free from the ahistorical conception of truth and meaning which we have seen in Greek thought. For Thucydides too in the end, it was not in the immanent sphere of contingency and change but in the transcendent and unchanging realm of eternal forms that the truth of things was to be discovered.

3. Collingwood, *The Idea of History*, 29.

4. Alan Richardson, *History Sacred and Profane* (London: SCM Press, 1964) 59. The residual Platonic dualism in Augustine's thought along with the occasional tendency to disparage material reality qualifies Richardson's judgement a little.

5. Descartes, *Discourse on Method and the Meditations*, Discourse I, trans. F.E. Sutcliffe (Harmondsworth: Penguin Books, 1968) 31 (my emphasis).

contingent realm of history and sought satisfaction in the deliverances of human reason.

Descartes' view was soon to secure the support of Baruch Spinoza (1632–77) who argued that the study of history was not a science but a form of practical surmisal useful (as opposed to veridical) for political ends.[6] Truth along with divine purpose and will were thus rejected as categories that could be employed in the study of history. Abandoning his Jewish heritage, Spinoza's logic follows that of the Greeks: purpose, he argued, entails development and change through time, but what is eternal cannot change. To speak of divine purpose, therefore, is a compromise of God's eternal perfection. Truth, accordingly, is not to be found in claims of a historically mediated revelation but rather through the 'natural light' of reason that is common to all. Spinoza explains that knowledge of the Divine Law,

> does not demand belief in historical narratives of any kind whatsoever. For since it is merely a consideration of human nature that leads us to this natural Divine Law, evidently it applies equally to Adam as to any other man... Nor can the belief in historical narratives, however certain, give us knowledge of God, nor, consequently, of the love of God. For the love of God arises from the knowledge of God, a knowledge deriving from general axioms that are certain and self-evident, and so belief in historical narratives is by no means essential to the attainment of our supreme good.[7]

Spinoza, even more than Descartes, represents a fateful turn for Christian theology for it is under his influence that there arose in biblical interpretation a separation between history and faith. 'The point at issue [in the study of Scripture]', Spinoza explains, 'is merely the meaning of the texts, not their truth.'[8] Historical study of the texts seeks to uncover what the authors intended, to ascertain thus, 'the meaning' of the texts, but this ought not to be confused with 'truth of fact'.[9] Spinoza's utilization of historical criticism thereafter focuses not on the veracity of the texts with respect to the history they narrate, but rather upon the circumstances of their composition, 'the life character and pursuits' of their authors. The reference of the texts to that which has taken place apart from them fades into obscurity. Of interest, rather, is the 'meaning' of the text discernible through the natural light of reason. It is quite possible under Spinoza's scheme that the historical narratives be judged false, but this

6. The point is taken from David Novak, *The Election of Israel: The Idea of the Chosen People* (Cambridge: Cambridge University Press, 1995) 26.

7. Baruch Spinoza, *Tractatus theologico-politicus*, trans. Samuel Shirley (Leiden: E.J. Brill, 1991) iv, pp. 104–5.

8. Spinoza, *Tractatus*, vii, p. 143.

9. Spinoza, *Tractatus*, vii, p. 143.

is no threat to faith which is concerned principally with right conduct. Spinoza explains that 'the divinity of Scripture must be established solely from the fact that it teaches true virtue'.[10] And further: 'we can conclude that, with the help of such a historical study of Scripture as is available to us, we can readily grasp the meaning of its moral doctrines and be certain of their true sense.'[11] That is what the interpretation of Scripture apparently aims at. The history-like content of the biblical narratives, accordingly, serves only a pedagogical purpose and bears no essential relation to the content of Christian (or Jewish) faith. The Jewish and Christian faiths are thus dehistoricised. It is the abstract and universal *ideas* of the Bible that are to be reckoned with and not the history to which its narratives bear witness. The implication eventually to be drawn, not by Spinoza himself but by those who followed him, was that the historical narratives of the Bible should properly be regarded as mythical. To employ the terminology later to be used by Søren Kierkegaard in critique of this position, the 'Moment' of divine action in history is reduced to a vanishing point. History is no longer decisive.[12]

The distinction apparent in Spinoza between the realm of history and the concerns of faith was encouraged by the concurrent emergence of modern science. The spectacular success of scientific explanation, though arguably dependent, in part at least, upon a Judaeo-Christian worldview[13], was accomplished with less and less reference to God. While many scientists retained allegiance to Christian faith, their theology was very often deistic in character. The world was conceived as a closed causal nexus, intelligible without reference to God.[14] Under the influence of Isaac Newton, John Locke and David Hume, among others, historical explanation increasingly followed the natural sciences in seeking to account for things in these immanentist terms. Hume, for instance, writes,

> Would you know the sentiments, inclinations, and course of life of the Greeks and Romans? Study well the temper and actions of the French and English... Mankind are so much the same, in all times and places, that history informs of nothing new or

10. Spinoza, *Tractatus*, vii, p. 142.

11. Spinoza, *Tractatus*, vii, p. 154.

12. See Søren Kierkegaard, *Philosophical Fragments*, ed. and trans. Howard V. Hong and Edna H. Hong (Princeton: Princeton University Press, 1985).

13. For a proffering of that argument see, for example, Stanley L. Jaki, *The Saviour of Science* (Edinburgh: Scottish Academic Press, 1990); Christopher B. Kaiser, *Creation and the History of Science* (Grand Rapids: Eerdmans, 1991); and Harold Turner, *The Roots of Science: An Investigative Journey Through the World's Religions* (Auckland: DeepSight Trust, 1998).

14. Laplace's celebrated remark to Napoleon, 'I have no need of the God hypothesis', serves as apt illustration.

> strange in this particular. Its chief use is only to discover constant and universal principles of human nature, by showing men in all varieties of circumstances and situations, and furnishing us with materials from which we may form our observations and become acquainted with the regular springs of human action and behaviour.[15]

The quest for natural laws governing human behaviour allowed to historical enquiry a measure of epistemic legitimacy that had been denied to it in the first flowerings of the rationalistic spirit. If history too could be conceived as conforming to a pattern explicable according to a set of natural laws then it would regain credibility as a mode of scientific enquiry, albeit firmly set in its place by accounts such as Hume's.

It was inevitable that the deistic conception of the world and the thirst for immanentist explanation would eventually be brought to bear upon the account of history that is set forth in the Bible. It was the biblical critic Hermann Reimarus (1694–1768) who took up the task of applying the new wisdom of immanentist explanation to the biblical material, thus dealing a blow to the confidence that Christian truth was founded upon the solid rock of historical occurrence. The writings of the apostles, alleged Reimarus, cannot be considered as reliable historical testimony but add to Jesus' teaching a raft of erroneous 'mysteries' and 'articles of faith' that falsify their accounts of who Jesus really was. The explanatory power of the new historical science, able to sort the wheat of dominical teaching from the chaff of church dogma, allegedly reveals that Jesus was no divine saviour, but preached a simple message of repentance and the immanence of the 'kingdom of heaven'.[16] Such a kingdom was conceived of as a temporal kingdom presided over by a Messiah chosen, it was believed at the time, by God. Although Jesus himself expected to take on that role, he was frustrated in his plan. Sharing his frustration, the disciples fabricated stories of a resurrection in order to keep the dream alive.[17] Strangely, Reimarus thought it possible to salvage from the rubble of his immanentist explanations a form of Christian faith still worthy of our allegiance. His

15. David Hume, 'An Enquiry Concerning Human Understanding' in *Enquiries Concerning the Human Understanding and Concerning the Principles of Morals*, ed. L.A. Selby-Bigge (Oxford: Oxford University Press, 1962) 83.

16. See H.S. Reimarus, 'Concerning the Intention of Jesus and His Teaching', Part 1, §4, in *Reimarus Fragments*, ed. Charles H. Talbert (London: SCM Press, 1971) 65–7.

17. Reimarus takes the diversity of the gospels' testimonies concerning the resurrection to undermine their truth. 'The old Scripture evidence of the resurrection of Jesus', Reimarus alleges, 'never can stand proof before the judgement seat of sound reason, and only contains a miserable and palpable *petitionem principii per circulum*.' 'Concerning the Intention of Jesus and His Teaching', Part 2, §35, 210. Reimarus's account of the frustration of Messianic hopes appears in Part 2, §§37–45.

messianic delusions notwithstanding, Jesus' ethical teaching provided worthy guidance, it was supposed, for a life well-pleasing to God. The echo of Spinoza resounds clearly here; what Christian faith is finally concerned with in the biblical material is not the dubious historical claims but the teaching about virtue.

Although he had published the work of Reimarus and shared Reimarus' scepticism about basing one's Christian faith upon the historical testimony of the Bible, G.E. Lessing (1729–81) introduces a rather different anxiety to the task of reading the biblical narratives. Whereas Reimarus was sure that the Gospels' depictions of the life of Jesus were wilful fabrications, Lessing professed agnosticism about that, and contended instead that the increasing temporal distance between the events to which the Bible bears witness and those who read the Bible now undermines, for those readers, any epistemic confidence in the historical claims found there. Historical enquiry, in Lessing's view, can neither confirm nor deny the truth of the biblical witness. Lessing offers two reasons for this. First, the passing of time and the mediation of testimony itself erodes the epistemic value of historical testimony to the point that, in respect of the biblical narratives, we who stand so many centuries after the events are bound to remain agnostic about the veracity of the biblical testimony. 'Fulfilled prophecies, which I myself experience, are one thing,' Lessing says, 'fulfilled prophecies, of which I know only from history that others say they have experienced them, are another.' Likewise with miracles: 'Miracles, which I see with my own eyes, and which I have the opportunity to verify myself, are one thing; miracles, of which I know only from history that others say they have seen them and verified them are another.'[18] The difficulty, Lessing continues, is that reports of these things must pass through a medium, that of historical testimony, that 'takes away all their force'.[19]

It is true, as Lessing says, that the past is no longer the content of immediate experience, but it is by no means clear that it cannot therefore be the object of knowledge. The study of history may not yield absolute certainty, but perhaps the demand for such certainty derives from a wrong idea of what constitutes knowledge. We cannot here offer a philosophical defence of this suggestion,[20] but for the sake of our present argument the appeal to common

18. G.E. Lessing, 'On the Proof of Spirit and of Power' in *Lessing's Theological Writings*, ed. Henry Chadwick (London: Adam & Charles Black, 1956) 51–61, 51.

19. Lessing, 'On the Proof of Spirit and of Power', 52.

20. Though see, for example, the essays in *Christian Perspectives on Religious Knowledge*, edited by C. Stephen Evans and Merold Westphal. The suggestion is made by Evans and Westphal in the 'Introduction' to that volume that Enlightenment critiques of religious belief have been operating with 'the wrong idea of what it is to know something and how we know what we know', p. 2.

sense will suffice. In the course of our daily lives we claim knowledge of all sorts of things about which we cannot be absolutely certain. Even if only some of those claims are warranted then knowledge is not what Lessing thinks it is. It is not something from which every possible cause of doubt has been eliminated. Rather it applies to those things that we have 'good enough' reasons to believe. The question then arises, what might constitute good enough reasons to believe the narratives of history? May it not be that the contingent truths of history are reliably mediated to us through the faithful testimony of tradition? Hans-Georg Gadamer writes,

> The important thing is to recognise the distance in time as a positive and productive possibility of understanding. It is not a yawning abyss but is filled with the continuity of custom and tradition, in the light of which all that is handed down presents itself to us.[21]

Lessing need not be as sceptical as he is about the reliability of historical testimony. While it may not yield the absolute certainty he craves, historical testimony, where it is offered by trustworthy witnesses, might well give us good reasons to believe. It remains true, however, that the witness cannot remove from the believer the onus of personal judgement. The epistemic importance of testimony applies, as Iain Provan explains, not just to our reading of the biblical texts but equally to the vast proportion of what each of us claims to know about the world.[22] Lessing, however, thinks that belief in the Gospel narratives is a special case. He thinks so because what is required in Christian faith is the total commitment of one's life. Where absolute commitment is required, this must be founded, Lessing thinks, upon absolute certainty about the truths that Christianity proclaims. To make an absolute commitment on the basis of an uncertain knowledge would involve us, in Lessing's view, in an abdication of our responsibility as rational beings to seek the most stringent rational warrant for all our truth claims, with the aim of dispelling all doubt. Short of attaining such certainty, we must maintain a studied agnosticism. Because such warrant can never be offered in respect of the truths of history, Lessing, like so many before him and since, dismisses the notion that God's claim upon our lives is historically mediated. It must be rationally mediated instead. But again, it is not at all clear why absolute certainty should be required as a basis for Christian faith. The very fact that Christian discipleship has been regarded from the beginning as a matter of faith – even for those who

21. Hans-Georg Gadamer, *Truth and Method*, 2nd edn (London: Sheed & Ward, 1975) 265.

22. See Iain Provan, 'Knowing and Believing: Faith in the Past' in Craig Bartholomew, C. Stephen Evans, Mary Healey and Murray Rae, eds, *'Behind' the Text: History and Biblical Interpretation* (Carlisle: Paternoster Press, and Grand Rapids: Zondervan, 2003) 229–66. We will consider the importance of testimony in more detail in Chapter 6 below.

were eyewitnesses of Jesus' life – suggests a lack of embarrassment about the fact that Christianity is concerned with a truth that is contingent and thus always open to doubt. It is concerned with a truth, in other words, that does not permit of the kind of certainty that Lessing craves. Why should this be a problem? It did not trouble Jesus who appears consistently to suggest that the commitment of Christian discipleship has the character of interpersonal trust rather than rational certainty.

Lessing's second objection to the apologetic strategy that would seek to prove dogmatic claims on the basis of historical truths is that, even were we to be sure that the events reported in the Gospels had actually taken place, we would not be justified in concluding on the basis of them that Jesus was the Son of God or the Messiah, or any other such dogmatic claim. On this point Lessing is quite right; historical enquiry cannot establish the truth of the orthodox creedal claims about Jesus, not, however, because the claims themselves are false, but rather because historical enquiry does not have the competence to verify that about Jesus of Nazareth which is revealed not by flesh and blood but by the 'Father in heaven' (Matt. 16.17).

The question before us now is whether the historical claims of the Bible are therefore to be treated as incidental, as not belonging to the essence of Christian faith. This is the conclusion that Lessing draws. Christian faith, in his view, must find its sure point of reference elsewhere. Linking his concern to the dualistic metaphysics of Greek philosophy, mediated to him through Spinoza and Leibniz, Lessing famously remarked that 'accidental truths of history can never become the proof of necessary truths of reason'.[23] Again we may ask, however, whether the central truth claims of the Christian gospel are to be thought of as 'necessary truths of reason' and thereby as indubitable. On my reading of the text, the New Testament comes forth with the much more humble (and scandalous!) claim that God has entrusted his truth to the earthen vessels of historical circumstance. Blessed are those who take no offence at that (cf. Matt. 11.6).

Because it is a commonly repeated pattern, it is worth noting before we leave Lessing how his disparagement of historical testimony impacts upon his soteriology. If, so as to maintain our integrity as rational beings, the Christian life is to involve one's assent to rationally indubitable truth, salvation will likewise be conceived in terms of the autonomous exercise of our rational capacities. The truth to which Lessing turns is the truth of the law, the truths evident in the ethical teaching of Jesus. These truths are reducible in Lessing's scheme to the ethical injunction, 'love one another'. This is a good in which the rational person can believe, and, when the will is disciplined by one's reason, it is also a good that the rational person can accomplish. This then, is what Christian

23. Lessing, 'On the Proof of Spirit and of Power', 53.

faith amounts to, or reduces to, perhaps! Lessing's tract, 'On the Proof of the Spirit and of Power', published in 1777, closes with the words, 'I conclude, and my wish is: May all who are divided by the gospel of John be reunited by the Testament of John. Admittedly it is apocryphal this testament. But it is not on that account any less divine.'[24] The testament referred to here is, 'Little children, love one another.' This is the sum of Lessing's soteriological proposal. Jesus, and John too, are approved as good teachers of this wisdom, but – and here is the crucial point – the truth affirmed in this proposal bears no essential relation to Jesus himself. It matters not whether the narrative is apocryphal. Its meaning has saving power irrespective of whether it was taught by Jesus or not, and so, to employ Kierkegaard's terminology once more, the teacher, and all the historical particulars of Jesus' life, become a vanishing point. They have no soteriological significance. The person seeking the truth of Christian faith, therefore, has only to contemplate the truths of practical reason, as Kant calls them, and has no need to venture to the far side of that ugly ditch on which is found an uncertain testimony to the historical particularities of Jesus of Nazareth. Aside from finding in that testimony a happy agreement with what we have established ourselves through the power of reason, Christian faith, in Lessing's scheme, need take no account of such reports. The abandonment of history is complete.

Lessing's reduction of Christianity to a wisdom having no essential connection to Jesus himself sets a pattern that is replicated many times over among those who reject the decisive soteriological significance of Jesus' history, from Lessing himself, through Kant and Hegel and right up to the Jesus Seminar of our own day, whose members typically consider Jesus' 'theological' significance to consist in the wisdom of his teaching. Jesus is styled as a mere teacher, and perhaps exemplar, of a salvation that we are now responsible to attain for ourselves. That is also the pattern apparent in Postmodernism; Jesus is again styled as a good teacher, or perhaps, with even more appeal to the extreme individualism of Postmodernity, as some kind of personal guru fashioned, however, to suit one's own particular spirituality.[25] Modernity and Postmodernity converge upon the notion of a true humanity which is realized by every individual who works out her own salvation without necessary recourse to anything other than her own best insights.

The result of Reimarus' scepticism about the reliability of the Gospels as historical witness combined with Lessing's conviction that the passing of time

24. Lessing, 'On the Proof of Spirit and of Power', 56.

25. William Hamilton's *A Quest for the Post-Historical Jesus* (London: SCM Press, 1993) provides an example of a Postmodern 'Christology' that has no qualms about the fictional character of its portrayals of Jesus. The point of Christology is merely to fashion symbols of our current concerns.

is corrosive of any certainty we may aspire to concerning the events of history, has convinced many people that the truth of Christian faith ought to be established on grounds other than that of historical testimony. The scepticism is played out in the religious philosophies of Kant and Hegel, who, for all their differences, share the conviction that while the essence of Christian faith can be distilled from the reports of Jesus' life, that essence has no necessary connection to that historical life itself. What one finds in Jesus is the confirmation of a truth that can be established independently of him. For Kant the truth is ethical while, for Hegel, it is the pantheistic unity of Spirit and the coincidence in each one of us of true humanity and true divinity. In each case the supposed essential truth of Christianity depends not at all upon the fact and form of Jesus' historical existence. It merely finds confirmation there, albeit, in Kant's case, with rather grudging acknowledgement.[26] Faith has become dehistoricized. Its truth no longer depends on anything that has happened in history. Johann Gottlieb Fichte gives precise expression to this modern spirit: 'Only the metaphysical but not the historical contributes to our salvation,' he writes, 'the latter only makes it intelligible.'[27]

It might be doubted that Hegel is guilty of disparaging history. It is his philosophy of history, after all, that has impacted most forcefully upon modern thought, and it is through history itself, Hegel contends, that the truth of things is unfolded. And yet, despite his laying claim to the category of history, his account of things does not allow to the created order of space and time the freedom to be itself.[28] The truth may be worked out through the dialectical process of history, but its working out is shaped by the prior necessity of rational law. There is, Hegel argues, 'an *a priori* structure of history to which empirical reality must correspond'.[29] For Hegel, echoing Thucydides (see note 2 above), such *a priori* structures or laws may be identified as a matter of rational necessity in advance of historical enquiry itself. With respect to Christian faith, Hegel's early theological writings, written in Tübingen between 1795 and 1800, provide intimation of things to come. In his essay, 'The Positivity of Christian Religion', Hegel offers an account of Christian faith in

26. Witness Kant's refusal to speak of Jesus by name but to refer instead to the mere possibility that the 'archetype' of the truly moral life has appeared among us. See *Religion Within the Limits of Reason Alone*, translated with an Introduction and Notes by Theodore M. Greene and Hoyt H. Hudson (New York: Harper & Row, 1960).

27. Johann Gottlieb Fichte, *Die Anweisung zum seligen Leben*, ed. Fritz Medicus (Hamburg: Felix Meiner, 1954) 97.

28. We shall argue in Chapter 3 that precisely such freedom is required in order for human action to be considered historic.

29. G.W.F. Hegel, *Lectures on the Philosophy of World History*, trans. H.B. Nisbet (Cambridge: Cambridge University Press, 1975) 131.

which the positive elements of the biblical testimony – miracles, the resurrection, 'and so forth...were perhaps simply meant to awaken the attention of people deaf to morality...[As] contemporary ideas they do not belong to the content of religion, because any such content must be eternal and unalterable.'[30] In the later *Lectures on the Philosophy of Religion*, delivered in Berlin during the 1820s, it is evident that Hegel has abandoned the Kantian account of Christian faith as morality, but in representing Christianity as the 'religion of Spirit', he sets forth its essential elements in abstraction from the historical particularities of Jesus himself.[31]

It is not surprising to find also in Karl Marx, Hegel's intellectual heir, the conviction that history conforms to a pattern determined in advance of any particular actions or events. The moment in time, accordingly, can only instantiate the pre-ordained truth. It can never be the means of its establishment. In principle, therefore, the truth may be learned without reference to history. In Hegel and Marx, the great modern interpreters of history, we find the modern rejection of the decisiveness of the moment in full cry.

That is the position too of D.F. Strauss (1808–74) who applies Hegel's philosophy of history to the interpretation of the New Testament. With Strauss, the immanentist bias of Modernity finds expression in the quest for the historical Jesus, a Jesus stripped bare of the accretions of theological dogma. In his *The Life of Jesus Critically Examined*, Strauss argues that much of the testimony of the New Testament is not history but myth, the clothing of timeless religious truth in the dress of historical narrative. According to Strauss, it is not history, but timeless truth that is to be reckoned with. The particular truth with which the Bible is concerned is the synthetic unity of the divine and the human, that same truth that is given mature expression in the philosophy of Hegel. Jesus of Nazareth merely instantiates the ideal of humanity as it is present to human reason, so that his life has exemplary but not effectual soteriological significance.[32] We see in him what we could, in principle, just as well see without him.

30. G.W.F. Hegel, 'The Positivity of Christian Religion' in *Friedrich Hegel on Christianity: Early Theological Writings*, trans. T.M. Knox (New York: Harper Torchbooks, 1961) 67–181, 71.

31. See *Lectures on the Philosophy of Religion,* 3 vols, trans. P.C. Hodgson and R.F. Brown (Berkeley: University of California Press, 1984–6).

32. Strauss writes, for example, that 'Man being once mature enough to receive as his religion the truth that God is man, and man of a divine race; it necessarily follows, since religion is the form in which the truth presents itself to the popular mind, that this truth must appear, in a guise intelligible to all, as a fact obvious to the senses: in other words, there must appear a human individual who is recognized as the visible God.' *The Life of Jesus Critically Examined*, ET (Philadelphia: Fortress Press, 1972) §150.

It was suggested above that the disjunction between history and faith has taken two forms in the Western intellectual tradition. In the first form the disjunction has required that Christian faith be set free from the historical narratives of the New Testament. Its essence has been defined in such a way that it depends not at all on the truth or falsity of the New Testament's historical claims. In the alternative form of this disjunction, however, it has been supposed that history must be set free from faith. The historical narratives of the Gospels must be purged of their dogmatic content in order to lay bare the truth of who Jesus really was. We have seen that form anticipated in the work of Reimarus, and it is evident too in the nineteenth century in the historiography developed by Leopold von Ranke (1795–1886) who famously seeks to recover the past *wie es eigentlich gewesen ist* (as it really was). At the close of the nineteenth century that approach was taken further by the work of Ernst Troeltsch (1865–1923) who, in a famous essay written in 1898, distinguished between 'historical' and 'dogmatic' method in theology.[33] The historical method, which Troeltsch considered to be the only intellectually respectable option, treats the rise of Christianity merely as a cultural phenomenon. Just because it is a cultural phenomenon and is open, therefore, to historical investigation, Troeltsch supposes that God cannot be involved. But why is this so? The reason has been charted in all that we have said so far. Whether because of particular presuppositions about the eternal and unchanging nature of truth, or, in this case, because of the conviction that the world is a closed causal nexus explicable entirely within categories of immanence, divine action and human history are thought to be mutually exclusive categories. To be sure, Troeltsch does claim that something called the 'divine reason' is disclosed through history,[34] but it turns out that this divine reason is identical with the 'divine' depth of the human spirit. There is a resemblance here to Spinoza who similarly thought that divine reason was a phenomenon of the natural order. The adjective 'divine' in Troeltsch looks rather like a means of absolutizing the claim and power of reason as such.

With Troeltsch however, as with almost all thinkers who advocate the separation of historical and dogmatic method, the separation cannot finally be sustained. The method does not proceed in the absence of dogma but rather in the service of a dogma other than that of orthodox Christian faith. In seeking thus to defend the 'absoluteness of Christianity', Troeltsch fails to conform to his own methodological proposals. He insists, towards the beginning of the essay to which we have referred, that the Judaeo-Christian tradition must be 'resolutely subjected to all the consequences of a purely historical method', a central tenet

33. Troeltsch, 'Historical and Dogmatic Method in Theology'.

34. Troeltsch, 'Historical and Dogmatic Method in Theology', 27.

of which, according to Troeltsch, is the principle of analogy. The principle of analogy requires us to assess the probability of an event actually having happened by its agreement with 'normal, customary, or at least frequently attested happenings and conditions as we have experienced them';[35] ergo, nothing happens that is unique. And yet, later in the same essay, Troeltsch asks us to believe that '*at one point*' the usual limitations of the human spirit are broken through, namely in the person of Jesus. 'Here', Troeltsch explains, 'a God distinct from nature produced a personality superior to nature with eternally transcendent goals and the willpower to change the world.'[36] Troeltsch's own criteria, however, make it impossible to believe in such a unique manifestation of divine action. Troeltsch himself it was who laid upon us the obligation to do theology within the limits of historical reason alone, but these limits turn out to be so restrictive that they are violated as soon as Troeltsch begins to speak of God.

What we have seen manifest in Troeltsch, in a way typical of Modernity, is the prising apart of history and theology. The twin outcomes of Troeltsch's historiography is that history is thought to be explicable entirely within categories of immanence, on the one hand, and, on the other, Christian theology is cut loose from its moorings in the historical particularities of the life, death and resurrection of Jesus. It becomes impossible to do theology and history together as is the practice of the biblical authors, and as is demanded by the reality of God's presence in the midst of history itself.

II — History and Hermeneutics

While we have given indication at various points above of the impact upon biblical hermeneutics of the prevailing Western scepticism about the epistemic value of the historical narratives of Scripture, we turn now to give more explicit attention to that impact. The suspicion of history began, we noted, with classical Greek philosophy, and the roots of modern hermeneutics are also to be found there. Werner Jeanrond explains that in reading the Homeric epics, the *Iliad* and the *Odyssey*, two methods of critical reading developed, the grammatical and the allegorical. The first method seeks 'to reach the text's sense by studying the linguistic devices and connections within it', and the second 'looks for the hidden sense of a text with the aid of an interpretative key from outside it'.[37] 'This [allegorical] approach to the "sacred" texts', Jeanrond

35. Troeltsch, 'Historical and Dogmatic Method in Theology', 13–14.

36. Troeltsch, 'Historical and Dogmatic Method in Theology', 27.

37. Werner Jeanrond, *Theological Hermeneutics: Development and Significance* (London: SCM Press, 1994) 14.

further explains, 'allowed the reader to search for ways of understanding the meaning of these without being forced to dwell on their literal message...'[38]

While we do not wish to set a literal hermeneutic in opposition to an allegorical one as the simple alternatives in biblical interpretation, the preference in classical Greek thought for an allegorical approach diminishes or even precludes interest in the question of historical truth. It counts questions of historical fact as unimportant to the meaning of the text. That is surely appropriate in respect of *some* of the biblical material – not all forms of biblical writing belong to the genre of historical narrative – but the imposition of an exclusively allegorical approach upon texts that do intend an historical reference does violence to the integrity of the texts themselves.

Out of deference to the Greek view, and perhaps with the best of apologetic intentions, the allegorical approach to Scripture as a whole was promoted within Judaism by Philo, and gave rise to strident debate within Christian faith between the Alexandrian and the Antiochene Schools. Theodore of Mopsuestia was among those in the Antiochene School who alleged that the allegorical readings of the Alexandrians amounted to a denial of the biblical stories' actual historical reality.[39] The Antiochenes sought, in opposition, to preserve the reference of Scripture to God's action in the actual world of historical truths rather than merely to an ideal world of symbolic truths. While not entirely accurate in their assessment of Alexandrian hermeneutics,[40] the Antiochene critique may well be applied to the hermeneutics of Spinoza, Lessing, Hegel,[41] Strauss, and so on – the roll call of Modern, essentially docetic, interpreters could continue at length. Where such biblical interpreters proceed to offer an account of why the Jesus stripped of the falsifying dogma of the New Testament witness should be regarded still as worthy of our allegiance, then what is retained – as the essence of Christian faith – is typically reducible to a set of ideas: the wisdom of the wandering cynic, the insight of the great moral teacher, the revolutionary ethic of the inspired prophet. There is no necessary connection of this essence of faith to the person of Jesus himself.

38. Jeanrond, *Theological Hermeneutics*, 15.

39. On which, see Jeanrond, *Theological Hermeneutics*, 21, and Kevin J. Vanhoozer, *Is There a Meaning in this Text?* (Grand Rapids: Zondervan, 1998) 115.

40. Although the Antiochenes charged Origen with neglecting the historical reference of Scripture, Henri de Lubac has shown that the allegation against Origen himself is misplaced. See Henri de Lubac, *Medieval Exegesis*, trans. E.M. Macierowski (Grand Rapids: Eerdmans, 2000). I am grateful to Mary Healey for pointing out to me the common misrepresentation of Origen's position.

41. This attitude is especially evident in the early work of Hegel. See, for example, 'The Positivity of the Christian Religion' in *Friedrich Hegel on Christianity: Early Theological Writings*, trans. T.M. Knox (New York: Harper Torchbooks, 1961) 67–181.

While the disparagement of history is clearly evident in the theologians mentioned above, it is more common in our own time to discover that *theology* has been excluded from the consideration of the biblical texts. A prominent example is the work of the 'Jesus Seminar' which, following Troeltsch, insists that the dogmatic content of the New Testament must be abandoned in favour of a truth discoverable by historical enquiry alone.[42] The methodological weaknesses of the Seminar's deliberations have been well documented[43] and need not be repeated here, but it is of interest to highlight the conception of history that is operative in its work. For, again, it is supposed that God is not involved in human history. Like Troeltsch before them, the members of the Seminar apparently conceive the rise of Christianity as merely a cultural phenomenon, so that talk of God has no place in the retelling of that history except when referring to what some people apparently believed. The only 'defence' of this presupposition to be found in the Seminar's flagship publication, *The Five Gospels*, is that 'the Christ of creed and dogma... can no longer command the assent of those who have seen the heavens through Galileo's telescope'.[44] Quite apart from the fact that countless scientists well acquainted with Galileo's telescope do still believe in the Christ of creed and dogma, this explanation gives us no reason whatsoever to suppose that the truth about Jesus is discoverable through historical enquiry alone.[45] It is simply a statement of the dubious contention that we of the modern world are not naive as our forebears were.

A second feature of the method adopted by the Seminar is its devotion to a reductionistic account of history. It is supposed that the truth is arrived at by breaking the biblical texts into fragments and assessing the authenticity or otherwise of each fragment. This has resulted in the practice of dealing with individual sayings of Jesus in units not only of sentence length, but even of part

42. See, e.g., the claim that critical biblical scholarship was supported by other university disciplines that wanted to ensure that dogmatic considerations be not permitted to intrude into scientific and historical research, in R. Funk and R. Hoover, *The Five Gospels* (New York: Macmillan, 1993) 1; and the approving reference to Thomas Jefferson who wanted 'to separate the real teachings of Jesus, the figure of history, from the encrustations of Christian doctrine'. Funk and Hoover, *The Five Gospels*, 2–3.

43. See, for example, N.T. Wright, *Jesus and the Victory of God* (London: SPCK, 1996) 29–35, and 'Five Gospels but No Gospel: Jesus and the Seminar' in W.R. Farmer, ed., *Toward the Fullness of the Mystery of Christ: An Ecumenical Endeavor for a More Orthodox Christology* (Livonia, Mich.: Dove, 1995); Richard B. Hays, 'The Corrected Jesus', *First Things* 43 (May 1994) 43–8 .

44. See the 'Introduction' to Funk and Hoover, *The Five Gospels*, 2.

45. The claims of the Seminar about what the 'modern' mind can and cannot believe are just one more instance of the extraordinarily weak 'Force Majeure' argument that is critiqued by Alvin Plantinga in his *Warranted Christian Belief* (New York: Oxford University Press, 2000) 403–7.

sentences. The process further fragments the biblical witness by separating the sayings from the actions of Jesus and by considering their authenticity as historical data in isolation from one another. What remains after this process is complete is a collection of fragments of evidence isolated from the theological narrative of the Bible from which the evidence was plundered. It is important to recognize two questionable assumptions underlying this procedure. The first is that the New Testament evangelists are untrustworthy witnesses. Their interpretation of what has taken place is treated for the most part as false. It is important only to note here that, contrary to the Seminar's own claims, this assessment is not a *conclusion* of scholarly enquiry but is, rather, a dogmatic presupposition.[46] I do not for this reason demean the judgement; my point merely is that it should be called by its proper name. It can then be evaluated on appropriate terms. A second assumption is that only that counts as evidence which we deem to be absolutely certain. Here there is an echo of Lessing, and more broadly, of the epistemic predilections of modernity to which we have already referred. A striking parallel is also to be found in Fundamentalism. Both the Jesus Seminar and Fundamentalism share a view of knowledge in general and historical knowledge in particular, in which only absolute certainty will do. Fundamentalists secure certainty by their doctrines of biblical inerrancy and infallibility; the Jesus Seminar does so by stripping from their Jesus database anything deemed by them to be the least bit doubtful. Both, however, do violence to the Scriptures themselves, and fail to recognize, in contrast with Gadamer and Provan above, that the testimony of fallible human witnesses might also contribute to an epistemic warrant.[47]

46. Witness, for example, the following 'criteria' employed by the Seminar to determine the authentic words of Jesus. All are quoted directly from *Five Gospels*.

- Sayings and parables expressed in 'Christian' language are the creation of the evangelists or their Christian predecessors (24).
- Jesus' characteristic talk was distinctive – it can usually be distinguished from common lore. Otherwise it is futile to search for the authentic words of Jesus (30).
- Jesus' sayings and parables cut against the social and religious grain (31).
- Jesus does not as a rule initiate dialogue or debate, nor does he offer to cure people (32).
- Jesus rarely makes pronouncements or speaks about himself in the first person (32).
- Jesus makes no claim to be the Anointed, the messiah (32).

These criteria clearly fly in the face of the evangelists' testimony and might appear to have the form of conclusions arrived at after extensive research. They are all described, however, as 'rules of evidence'. They are the premises with which the Jesus Seminar sets to work. Clearly these 'rules' are nothing more than a means of ensuring that the Seminar will find what it is looking for.

47. I use the word 'contribute' deliberately here. The testimony of human witnesses constitutes only a part of the case for an assent to the witness of Scripture. The testimony of the Spirit is indispensable.

I have frequently cited the Jesus Seminar as representative of the problematic disjunction between theology and history. While other examples of what I believe to be a more widespread problem will be provided from time to time, the high profile of the Seminar warrants continuing critical attention to their work. More importantly, I acknowledge that the story told here has been one-sided. It does not chart the significant strands of Christian tradition that have been developed under the conviction that it is through the historic incarnation of the Word of God and second person of the Trinity, that the Truth is given to be known. It is the side of the story upon which we have concentrated thus far, however, that has dominated biblical hermeneutics in the recent past and that has generated the artificial distinction and uneasy relation between biblical studies and theology. It has been my contention so far that the heart of the problem is a faulty view of history, a view that supposes, for varying reasons, that history cannot be the medium of divine self-disclosure. Such a view has made it very difficult to do theology and history together, but that is the task required, I think, in order to read and understand the Christian Bible.

2

Theology and History

In Chapter 1 it has been argued that modern historiography is characterized by a determined separation of theology and history, a separation that has destructive consequences for biblical hermeneutics. In the present chapter I propose to prepare the way for a reappraisal of the relationship between history and theology by taking bearings from some of the leading figures in twentieth-century theology and biblical studies. Again, the survey will not be exhaustive. It aims only to identify the key landmarks in the debate, thus to chart a way forward in developing an account of how we may do theology and history together.

I — Martin Kähler

The nineteenth century ended with Troeltsch's call for the elimination of dogmatic considerations in theology and his advocacy of a theology based solely on the historical method. In the same decade, however, Martin Kähler (1835–1912) had come to quite different conclusions about the relation between theology and history. In an essay published in 1892 and subsequently translated into English as *The So-Called Historical Jesus and the Historic, Biblical Christ*, Kähler argued that the portraits of Jesus presented by historical-critical scholarship conceal from us the living Christ. The difficulty to begin with, Kähler explains, is that historians treat Jesus as a 'mere man' in just the same way that they treat any other significant figure from the past.[1] Precisely

1. Precisely the same complaint had been made earlier in the century by Søren Kierkegaard who comments trenchantly, 'Christendom has taken the liberty of construing the whole thing altogether historically, of beginning with letting [Christ] be dead.' See S. Kierkegaard, *Practice in Christianity*, ed. and trans. Howard V. Hong and Edna H. Hong (Princeton: Princeton University Press, 1991) 107. For further discussion of Kierkegaard's polemic against historical method in

in doing so, Kähler contends, they fail to understand 'the special nature of the problem and the peculiar significance of Scripture'.[2] The kind of 'modern biographical account' of Jesus' life that historians seek to piece together is simply not possible on the basis of the biblical material for 'the New Testament presentations were not written for the purpose of describing how Jesus developed'.[3] Kähler is particularly critical of the use made of the principle of analogy in the life of Jesus research he had seen in the nineteenth century. If historical judgements can proceed only by way of analogy, then the uniqueness of Jesus – that about him which is without analogy – is eliminated. This, says Kähler, brings us to the crux of the matter: '*Why* do we seek to know the figure of Jesus? I rather think it is because we believe him when he says, "He who has seen me has seen the Father" (John 14.9), because we see in him the revelation of the invisible God.'[4]

If it is true that Jesus is the one in whom the invisible God is revealed, then it follows that the truth about him will not be visible to the eye of the historian who is determined to work within the limits of Troeltsch's recommended method. God is not a possible subject of such enquiry. Kähler contends, therefore, that historical enquiry can never reveal the truth of Jesus. That truth is revealed in the *kerygma*, in the proclamation of the Church. Thus, says Kähler, 'it is impossible to reach a Christian understanding of Jesus when one deviates from the *total* biblical proclamation about him – his life as well as its significance'.[5] 'The risen Lord is not the historical Jesus *behind* the gospels', Kähler continues, 'but the Christ of the apostolic preaching, of the *whole* New Testament.'[6] And further, '*The real Christ is the Christ who is preached*.'[7] True though it may be, this claim is open to a misinterpretation that Kähler himself did not, perhaps, do enough to head off.[8] On the one hand, the true Christ is

Christology, see my article, 'The Forgetfulness of Historical-Talkative Remembrance in Kierkegaard's "Practice in Christianity"' in *International Kierkegaard Commentary: Practice in Christianity*, ed. Robert L. Perkins (Macon, Ga.: Mercer University Press, 2004) 69–94.

2. Martin Kähler, *The So-Called Historical Jesus and the Historic, Biblical Christ*, trans. Carl E. Braaten (Philadelphia: Fortress Press, 1964) 46.

3. Kähler, *The So-Called Historical Jesus*, 51.

4. Kähler, *The So-Called Historical Jesus*, 58.

5. Kähler, *The So-Called Historical Jesus*, 68.

6. Kähler, *The So-Called Historical Jesus*, 65.

7. Kähler, *The So-Called Historical Jesus*, 66 (italics original).

8. The danger is that the preaching will be cut adrift from history. I don't believe this to have been Kähler's intention but later exponents of the view that the true Christ is the preached Christ sailed much closer to this Scylla, thus prompting the concern expressed here by Gerhard Ebeling: 'If the person to whom the kerygma refers is in no way concretely definable in his historicity, if the reference of the kerygma to Jesus consists exclusively in assertions for whose understanding Jesus

revealed through the interpretive nexus of the New Testament and cannot be found by trying to go behind the text where a non-divine Jesus is allegedly to be found; Kähler is right about this. On the other hand, however, orthodox Christian theology, confessing as it does that the Word has become flesh, requires that the Jesus 'behind the text' – the one who went his way among us in the flesh – is one and the same person as the risen and ascended Lord whom the New Testament proclaims. Without that continuity the proclamation of the Church is simply false. While Kähler quite rightly insists that a true understanding of Jesus is to be sought through the witness of the community of faith,[9] that witness directs us to the Jesus of history, albeit the Jesus of history, through whom the Father is revealed, is not the same as the Jesus of the (Troeltschian) historians, by whom the Father is commonly obscured. With this qualification, we may interpret Kähler as saying that far from obscuring Jesus 'as he really was', the New Testament proclamation, which can be accepted only in faith, brings the facts about Jesus properly into view.

II — Rudolf Bultmann

Kähler's influence, combined with Albert Schweitzer's swingeing critique of the nineteenth-century 'Quest of the historical Jesus',[10] brought to an end, for a time, the enterprise of establishing Christology upon the foundations of historical enquiry. Kähler's protest against the Quest and reaffirmation of the authority of the biblical witness to Jesus was taken up in the twentieth century by, notably to begin with, Karl Barth (1886–1968) and Rudolf Bultmann (1884–1976). Both men accepted Kähler's view that historical research could not provide a foundation for Christian faith.

The chief reason for Bultmann's rejection of historical enquiry as a basis for faith is apparent in his critique of nineteenth-century liberal theology. 'The

himself is irrelevant, as merely a cipher that is accidental and in itself says nothing, then the kerygma – if it could be kerygma at all – would be pure myth.' Gerhard Ebeling, *Theology and Proclamation*, trans. John Riches (London: Collins, 1966) 64. Precisely the same concern lies behind Wolfhart Pannenberg's *Jesus – God and Man*, trans. Lewis L. Wilkins and Duane A. Priebe (London: SCM Press, 1968).

9. Wolfhart Pannenberg notes a similar point made earlier by Albrecht Ritschl: 'One can attain the full extent of this historic reality only out of the faith which the Christian community has in him.' Albrecht Ritschl, *The Christian Doctrine of Justification and Reconciliation* (Edinburgh: T&T Clark, 1902) 3. Cited by Pannenberg in *Jesus – God and Man*, 22n.

10. See Albert Schweitzer, *The Quest of the Historical Jesus*, translated from the 1906 German edition by W. Montgomery (London: A&C Black, 1954).

subject of theology is *God*,' Bultmann writes, 'and the chief charge to be brought against liberal theology is that it has dealt not with God but with man.'[11] This is a repetition of the complaint made against historical enquiry by Kähler; it cannot say anything of God, but only of Jesus as man. It is for this reason that Bultmann claims that 'the world which faith wills to grasp is absolutely unattainable by means of scientific research'.[12] It is Troeltsch who represents best, according to Bultmann, the fault of supposing that historical method can uncover the truth of Jesus Christ. Christianity is reduced to a 'phenomenon of this world'[13] and its truth is presumed to be exhausted within categories of immanence.

What does Bultmann propose instead? Like Kähler, Bultmann insists that it is the preaching of the New Testament, and, more particularly, the 'message of Jesus' presented in the New Testament that is the concern of Christian faith. Historians have little to contribute to our understanding of that message. Jesus' preaching of the coming reign of God, and the urgency of decision in favour of that coming reign,[14] presents itself to us without need of historiographical verification. The message floats free of the particular circumstances of its deliverance by Jesus which, in themselves, are merely incidental. 'Thus', remarks Bultmann, '*Jesus in his thought of God* – and of man in the light of this thought – "de-historized" God and man; that is, released the relation between God and man from its previous ties to history.'[15] Søren Kierkegaard once suggested of Luther that he had helped the world to climb back onto the horse of authentic Christian faith, only for it to fall off the other side.[16] The same appears true of Bultmann; he rightly insists that faith cannot rest on the deliverances of historical enquiry but now appears to dehistoricize faith altogether.

That history is incidental to Bultmann's account of Christian faith is especially apparent in his famed method of demythologizing. What parades as history in the New Testament turns out, in Bultmann's view, to be myth, an imaginative but outmoded vehicle for the transmission of Jesus' message but having no essential relation to the content of that message itself. 'Modern man',

11. Rudolf Bultmann, 'Liberal Theology and the Latest Theological Movement' in *Faith and Understanding*, 6th edn, trans. Louise Pettibone Smith (London: SCM Press, 1966) 28–52, 29.

12. Bultmann, 'Liberal Theology and the Latest Theological Movement', 31.

13. This was precisely the intention of the 'History of Religions' school, of which Troeltsch was a prominent member.

14. See Rudolf Bultmann, *Theology of the New Testament*, vol. i, trans. Kendrick Grobel (London: SCM Press, 1952) ch. 1.

15. Bultmann, *Theology of the New Testament*, vol. i, 25.

16. Søren Kierkegaard, *For Self-Examination;* and *Judge for Yourself!*, ed. and trans. Howard V. Hong and Edna H. Hong (Princeton: Princeton University Press, 1990) 24.

accordingly, is under no obligation, indeed is unable, to accept the New Testament's mythical view of the world as true.[17] We must confront, rather, the existential challenge of Jesus' message and reinterpret the mythical cosmology within which it is set. Bultmann is far too hasty, however. There is no sensible objection to be made to his claim that the world cannot be viewed any longer as 'a three storied structure with the earth in the centre, the heaven above, and the underworld beneath'[18] but it is quite another matter to dismiss the New Testament view that the world is 'the scene of the supernatural activity of God'.[19] Here we see repeated precisely the problematic historiography which was reviewed in Chapter 1 above. The world itself in its material and temporal constitution is thought to be a closed causal nexus impervious to the action of God. The christological implication, clearly enough evident in Bultmann, is that Christian faith is concerned essentially with Jesus' message and not with his person. Bultmann is alert to the problem, as the following passage indicates:

> But the New Testament speaks of an *event* through which God has wrought man's redemption. For it, Jesus is not primarily the teacher, who certainly had extremely important things to say and will always be honoured for saying them, but whose person in the last analysis is immaterial for those who have assimilated his teaching. On the contrary, his person is just what the New Testament proclaims as the decisive event of redemption. It speaks of this person in mythological terms, but does this mean that we can reject the kerygma altogether on the ground that it is nothing more than mythology? That is the question.[20]

Bultmann here identifies a fault with the 'older liberal theologians' – Harnack, for example – but can he avoid the same error? 'Is our re-interpretation of Christianity in existentialist terms open to precisely the same objection?', he asks.[21] Bultmann sees the problem with extraordinary clarity. What is at stake is whether human beings can achieve authentic Being by 'a mere act of reflection', as the existentialist philosophers of Bultmann's day would have it,[22] or whether, by contrast, our human predicament is such that 'deliverance can come only by an act of God'.[23] 'The crucial distinction between the New Testament and existentialism, between the Christian faith and the natural

17. See Rudolf Bultmann, 'New Testament and Mythology' in *Kerygma and Myth*, trans. Reginald H. Fuller (London: SPCK, 1953) 1–44, 3.

18. Bultmann, 'New Testament and Mythology', 1.

19. Bultmann, 'New Testament and Mythology', 1.

20. Bultmann, 'New Testament and Mythology', 14.

21. Bultmann, 'New Testament and Mythology', 23.

22. Bultmann offers Heidegger and Wilhelm Kamlah as examples.

23. Bultmann, 'New Testament and Mythology', 27.

understanding of Being', Bultmann continues, '[is that] the New Testament speaks and faith knows of an act of God through which man becomes capable of self-commitment, capable of faith and love, of his authentic life.'[24] The question arises, however, whether we can speak of an act of God in Christ, or does this language too belong to the realm of myth?[25] Bultmann responds:

> Now, it is clear from the outset that the event of Christ is of a wholly different order from the cult-myths of Greek or Hellenistic religion. Jesus Christ is certainly presented as the Son of God, a pre-existent divine being, and therefore to that extent a mythical figure. But he is also a concrete figure of history – Jesus of Nazareth. His life is more than a mythical event; it is a human life which ended in the tragedy of crucifixion. We have here a unique combination of history and myth. The New Testament claims that this Jesus of history, whose father and mother were well known to his contemporaries (John 6.42) is at the same time the pre-existent Son of God, and side by side with the historical event of the crucifixion it sets the definitely non-historical event of the resurrection.[26]

We see here the re-emergence of the problematic assumption that history is such that God cannot act within it. To claim that he does – by raising Jesus from the dead – is to speak the language of myth. The result, for Bultmann, is that we Moderns can leave the history-like content of such language to one side:

> We are compelled to ask whether all this mythological language is not simply an attempt to express the meaning of the historical figure of Jesus and the events of his life; in other words, [the] significance of these as a figure and event of salvation. If that be so, we can dispense with the objective form in which they are cast.[27]

This applies especially to the resurrection. To have faith in the resurrection is, for Bultmann, as we will see further in Chapter 4, 'the same thing as faith in the saving efficacy of the cross'. It follows then that,

> The real Easter faith is faith in the word of preaching which brings illumination. If the event of Easter Day is in any sense an historical event additional to the event of the cross, it is nothing else than the rise of faith in the risen Lord, since it was this faith which led to the apostolic preaching.[28]

Christian faith in the resurrection, on this account, involves the acceptance of a particular interpretation of the cross, but the resurrection cannot be, for

24. Bultmann, 'New Testament and Mythology', 33.
25. Bultmann, 'New Testament and Mythology', 33–4.
26. Bultmann, 'New Testament and Mythology', 34.
27. Bultmann, 'New Testament and Mythology', 35.
28. Bultmann, 'New Testament and Mythology', 42.

Bultmann, the inauguration of a new creation in which the material and temporal reality of the created order (to which human life belongs) in all its fallenness and alienation from God is reconstituted, made new, and set again on its path towards perfection in reconciled relation with God. Bultmann has claimed hitherto that redemption is an event of history, but here where it matters most, he loses his nerve. 'The historical event of the rise of Easter faith means for us', Bultmann says, 'what it meant for the first disciples – namely, the self-manifestation of the risen Lord, the act of God in which the redemptive event of the cross is completed.'[29] But what is it that is redeemed and given new life? If Jesus' body lies mouldering in the grave then it is something other than *human* life that is made new. For all that Bultmann wishes to restore the authority of the kerygma, he is unable, in the end, to affirm what the kerygma has to say.

III — Karl Barth

We will have more to say about Karl Barth's conception of history in Chapter 4 on the resurrection, but here I wish to begin an investigation of Barth's conception of the relation between revelation and history. We begin by noting Barth's agreement with Kähler that 'the real historical Christ is no other than the biblical Christ attested by the New Testament passages...'.[30] There is no question, for Barth, of a discontinuity between the historical reality of Jesus of Nazareth and the Christ of faith proclaimed in Scripture. But, and this is of crucial importance, the revelation of Christ cannot be read off from history. There is nothing to be observed in the history of Jesus of Nazareth that confirms him as the Son of God.[31] The reason for this, Barth explains, is that '*revelation is not a predicate of history, but history is a predicate of revelation*'.[32] The Word becomes historical flesh in the course of revelation not by virtue of some capacity in history itself, but by virtue of the capacity of the Word to

29. Bultmann, 'New Testament and Mythology', 42.

30. Karl Barth, *Church Dogmatics* I/2 (Edinburgh: T&T Clark, 1956) 64.

31. Lessing correctly makes the same point: 'If on historical grounds I have no objection to the statement that Christ raised to life a dead man; must I therefore accept it as true that God has a Son who is of the same essence of himself?... If on historical grounds I have no objection to the statement that this Christ himself rose from the dead, must I therefore accept it as true that this risen Christ was the Son of God?' Lessing, 'On the Proof of the Spirit and of Power', 54. Likewise Kierkegaard: 'Jesus Christ was a great man, perhaps the greatest of all. But that he was – God – no, stop; with the help of God that conclusion will surely miscarry.' *Practice in Christianity*, ed. and trans. Howard V. Hong and Edna H. Hong (Princeton: Princeton University Press, 1991) 26.

32. Barth, *CD* I/2, 58 (italics original).

make history. This history 'is what it is, entirely and altogether in virtue of the subject who acts there'.[33] We may say that the Word become flesh leaves its mark upon history, but the alterations to the fabric of history wrought by the incarnation are not unveiled as revelation except as the Spirit gives eyes to see and ears to hear. This is simply to follow the logic of the confession that 'God reveals himself'.[34]

In addressing the problem of the relation between revelation and history, Barth complains of a common 'failure to see that in answering this question we cannot start with the general phenomenon of time, or as it is preferably called, history. We cannot assume that we know its normal structure on the basis of comparative observation.'[35] This point is of the utmost importance and lies at the heart of my own project. We simply cannot proceed to investigate the Bible's witness to revelation by assuming that we know apart from revelation what history is. The order of knowing must be reversed. Only in the light of revelation itself can we properly know what history is. Only then can we see the fallenness of our own history in its alienation from God, and only then do we learn that as God makes time for us, our time is redemptively transformed.[36] Thus in Ephesians 1.9: '[God] has made known to us the mystery of his will, according to his good pleasure that he set forth in Christ, as a plan for the fullness of time, to gather up all things in him, things in heaven and things on earth.' Biblical hermeneutics must take account of this conception of history as destined to be gathered up into the headship of Christ. It will be the task of Chapters 3 and 4 in this volume to give a fuller account of history as it is here theologically conceived.

Barth notes secondly, 'a failure to see that the event of Jesus Christ as God's revelation can be found only when sought as such, i.e., when we are seeking what we have already found'.[37] Though 'apparently contradicting all honest investigation of the truth', this rule simply states that the revelation of God in Christ is invisible from within investigative paradigms that are antithetical to it. It is only as the reality with which we are concerned in revelation has taken hold of us that we may in fact see it. This matter too will be taken up in later chapters, particularly Chapters 4 and 5.

33. Barth, *CD* I/2, 60.

34. This is the confession guiding the whole of Barth's *Dogmatics*.

35. Barth, *CD* I/2, 56.

36. In putting the matter this way, I am not entirely in agreement with Barth who tends to emphasize the passing away or 'abolishment' of the old aeon rather than its transformation or renewal. The issue here is the same one posed by the question of the continuity of identity in the transformation of the old person to the new in baptism.

37. Barth, *CD* I/2, 57.

Especially germane to my purposes here, however, is Barth's judgement upon the misuse of historical-critical method. He writes:

> The so-called historico-critical method of handling Holy Scripture ceases to be theologically possible or worth considering, the moment it conceives it as its task to work out from the testimonies of Holy Scripture (which does ascribe to revelation throughout the character of miracle), and to present as the real intention, a reality which lacks this character, which has to be regarded as a reality otherwise than on the basis of God's free, special and direct act. This must be said of the gigantic attempt, (still as gigantic as ever) of the 'Life of Jesus research,' i.e., the attempt, made in every style from mildest conservatism to the most imaginative or else most unimaginative, 'hypercriticism,' to uncover out of the New Testament, by means of a series of combinations, restorations and also and particularly deletions, the figure of the mere man Jesus, the so-called 'historical Jesus' as he might have lived in the years 1–30.[38]

The enterprise is mistaken precisely by virtue of its supposition that the life of Jesus lacks the character of divine action, and that Jesus, accordingly, was 'mere man' – the same point in opposition to the 'Quest of the Historical Jesus' that we have seen in Kähler. If, therefore, there is to be an historical-critical method that is true to the reality of Jesus himself, then it must be one that submits itself to revelation, to what is given to be known only by God himself.

IV — Ernst Käsemann

Ernst Käsemann (1906–98) was, as is commonly observed, the student of Bultmann's who challenged the existentialist foundations of Bultmann's thought. Yet Käsemann retained some allegiance to Bultmann, not least the conviction that the truth of Christian faith is not immediately derivable from history.[39] It is founded rather, as Barth and Bultmann both insist, upon an act of divine revelation. Departing from Bultmann, however, Käsemann believed that the truth of faith should nevertheless be shown to have its proper grounding in the historical reality of Jesus. However much the kerygma is shaped by the interpretative concerns of the early Church, it is clear that the biblical authors themselves intended to tell the story of Jesus of Nazareth. They should not be understood as fabricators of a tradition that could be abstracted from Jesus himself. Käsemann thought it important, therefore, for historical

38. Barth, *CD* I/2, 64.

39. I take the point from Roy A. Harrisville and Walter Sundberg, *The Bible in Modern Culture: Theology and Historical-Critical Method from Spinoza to Käsemann* (Grand Rapids: Eerdmans, 1995) 238.

criticism to be able to show a degree of continuity between the preaching of the early Church and the figure of Jesus himself. Käsemann announced this departure from Bultmann in an essay of 1953 titled, 'The Problem of the Historical Jesus'.[40] Beginning with a brief outline of Bultmann's theological development Käsemann observes that in Bultmann's later work, Christian faith 'is being understood as faith in the exalted Lord for which the Jesus of history as such is no longer considered of decisive importance'.[41] Käsemann certainly acknowledges that 'the road of Liberalism', which Kähler, Barth and Bultmann rejected, 'had to be abandoned, because the hope of uncovering this "life story" [of Jesus] and of being able to correct the Church's dogma in the light of it proved a vain one',[42] yet, 'inasmuch as it is to the earthly Jesus that the Gospels ascribe their kerygma', the question of the continuity between Jesus and the kerygma remains of interest. Käsemann here anticipates a criticism of Bultmann made by Gerhard Ebeling a decade later. Ebeling writes:

> If we could ascertain nothing historically authentic concerning the person to whom the kerygma refers, then the relation of Jesus to the kerygma would consist in nothing more than a series of assertions for the understanding of which Jesus himself would have no more importance than that of a random and meaningless cipher. In this sense the kerygma – if such it could be called – would be pure myth.[43]

Käsemann goes on to explain that the story of Jesus in the Gospels is told in the light of Easter faith, and indeed of eschatology. That is clearly the case and is commonly recognized by New Testament scholars and systematic theologians alike. The question, however, is what is to be done with this observation. Are we to suppose that the backward reference of the Gospel writers to the earthly career of Jesus is of little value historically – that has been the view of many scholars – or might it be that the light of the resurrection and the eschatological reference illumines rather than conceals not only who Jesus really was and is, but also what history really is? Despite Käsemann's concern to investigate the continuity between the historical Jesus and the Jesus of the kerygma he is not optimistic about the historical worth of the Gospels.

40. First published in *Zeitschrift für Theologie und Kirche* 51 (1954) 125–53. Reprinted in Gregory W. Dawes, ed., *The Historical Jesus Quest: Landmarks in the Search for the Jesus of History* (Louisville: Westminster John Knox Press, 1999) 279–313.

41. Käsemann, 'The Problem of the Historical Jesus', 281.

42. Käsemann, 'The Problem of the Historical Jesus', 288.

43. Gerhard Ebeling, *Theology and Proclamation*, trans. John Riches (London: Collins, 1966) 64. At about the same time the identical concern motivated Wolfhart Pannenberg's attempt in *Jesus – God and Man*, trans. Lewis L. Wilkins and Duane A. Priebe (London: SCM Press, 1968), to establish on historical grounds a basis for the Christian kerygma.

> We have to ask at this point how this finding helps us to answer our particular questions. First, we have now come to see that our Gospels, with the necessary exception of Luke, are not in the least interested in the composition of a comprehensive biography of Jesus nor in investigating what has been reported about him to see how far it is reliable and how far it corresponds to historical reality... His historical existence is naturally presupposed and it enters the realm of the phenomenal to this extent, that his life on earth takes a human course. But as soon as he is portrayed as speaking and acting, this human course becomes an unbroken series of divine revelations and mighty acts, which has no common basis of comparison with any other human life and thus can no longer be comprehended within the category of the historical.[44]

It is necessary to qualify Käsemann's judgement by noting that Jesus can no longer be comprehended within the category of the historical *as it is comprehended by Troeltsch* and those who follow him. But that is to presume that history can be neither the locus of divine action, nor the terrain of anything that is utterly unique. Such a presumption is no more than a convention. So far as the Gospels are concerned it is a convention that is called into question by the reality of Jesus himself. Käsemann, it seems to me, is to be gratefully acknowledged for seeking to 'keep faith firmly tied to the life history of Jesus'[45] but precisely in doing that, faith may pose questions to the historical-critical method that its exponents, including Käsemann himself, have largely been unwilling to address. If we are to say with Käsemann that 'revelation invades human history and takes its course within it'[46] then, again, history as we thought we knew it cannot be left intact. Käsemann's recommendation that we embark again on a programme to distinguish authentic historical material in the Gospels from the theological interpretation of the early Church betrays his claim that in Jesus of Nazareth history and revelation are given together. History can no longer be understood, therefore, solely in terms of immanent causality, analogy, correlation and the like. Commenting on the Sermon on the Mount, Käsemann suggests that 'Jesus cannot be integrated into the background of the Jewish piety of his time. Certainly he was a Jew and made

44. Käsemann, 'The Problem of the Historical Jesus', 295.

45. Käsemann, 'The Problem of the Historical Jesus', 297. That is a concern that became quite widespread in the 1950s and 1960s. Alongside Käsemann, Gerhard Ebeling, Ernst Fuchs, Hans Conzelmann, Günther Bornkamm, James Robinson, Norman Perrin and Herbert Braun were leading proponents of the 'new quest' for the historical Jesus. The aims of this quest were not to write a biography of Jesus – that was not thought to be possible on the basis of the documentary sources – but rather to distil the authentic sayings and acts of Jesus from the kerygmatic material of the Gospels.

46. Käsemann, 'The Problem of the Historical Jesus', 297. In fact I would prefer to avoid speaking of an 'invasion' of history by revelation for, as Christ is both alpha and omega, history does not need to be invaded by God. It is already his.

the assumptions of Jewish piety, but at the same time he shatters this framework with his claim [to authority].'[47] I am suggesting that a further shattering of prior frameworks must take place where our understanding of history is concerned. We cannot presume that we know what history is in advance of the Lord of history disclosing its true nature to us.

V — Oscar Cullmann

Concurrent with Käsemann's renewal of interest in the relation between theology and history Oscar Cullmann (1902–99), first in *Christus und die Zeit* (1946)[48] and then again in his 1965 publication, *Heil als Geschichte: Heilsgeschichtliche Existenz im Neuen Testament*,[49] revived the proposal of J.C. Hofmann (1810–77) and the Erlangen School that the course of human history played host to a special divine history in which God brings about his purpose of salvation. Responding to Rudolf Bultmann, Cullmann complains of the dehistoricization of salvation in modern thinking. Fichte's dictum, 'Only the metaphysical, and in no way the historical, gives blessing; the latter only gives understanding',[50] is representative, observes Cullmann, of a widespread attitude that is in fundamental conflict with the message of the Bible.[51] Cullmann proposes, in opposition to this dehistoricizing trend, that the Bible is concerned with 'salvation history', that is, with the series of episodes in human history through which God works out his saving purpose for the world. The term 'salvation history' has been a controversial one for reasons recently summarized by Martin Hengel.[52] Cullmann himself acknowledges that the term 'salvation history' has not won much support among theologians,[53] and it seems to me

47. Käsemann, 'The Problem of the Historical Jesus', 303.

48. Published in English as *Christ and Time* (London: SCM Press, 1951).

49. Published in English as *Salvation in History* (London: SCM Press, 1967).

50. See Chapter 1, n. 27.

51. Cullmann, *Salvation in History*, 23.

52. See Martin Hengel, 'Salvation History' in David F. Ford and Graham Stanton, eds, *Reading Texts, Seeking Wisdom: Scripture and Theology* (Grand Rapids: Eerdmans, 2003) 229–44. Hengel notes the antipathy towards the term engendered by pietistic attempts to find in Scripture the stages of a universal and harmonious divine plan. Others have been critical of its incommensurability with the results of modern historical criticism (e.g Pannenberg). Some have argued that the notion of salvation history is in conflict with Paul's theology because Paul's account of salvation is punctiliar (e.g. Ulrich Luz). Still others reject the term because it suggests an objectification of the content of faith, whereas faith 'is an act of present day experience' (Heinrich Ott). This last objection tends toward the dehistoricization of the biblical message against which this book is arguing.

53. See the discussion in Cullmann, *Salvation in History*, 74–8.

too that it is not the most helpful term to use. Not least among the difficulties is the ambiguity of the term 'history' which can refer, on one hand, simply to the sequence of events in space-time, that is, to all the things that happen, while, on the other hand, it may refer to the account given of these events, the interpretative summations of the historian. This ambiguity plagues Cullman's account in my view, for it is not always clear, as it was not in Hofmann either, whether 'salvation history' refers to a series of events or to an interpretation of the events as divine history. For all the difficulties attending the term 'salvation history' itself, however, Cullmann does help to redress the problematic divorce between history and theology that has been characteristic of much biblical and theological scholarship. It is true, after all, that the biblical account of salvation, undoubtedly a theological matter, is 'bound up with history'[54] so, if we are not to reject or demythologize the biblical testimony, some account needs to be given of the relationship between the two.

It has sometimes been argued that the notion of salvation history applies well to the Old Testament but not to the New,[55] but Cullmann contends, correctly in my view, that 'the acceptance of the Old Testament by the New Testament writers indicates that early Christianity does not, like Gnosticism, preach ever valid truths in mythological garb, for the Old Testament reveals God's action in salvation history'.[56] And further: 'The acceptance of the Old Testament in the New is exceedingly important if it means that Christian faith is a faith in a divine salvation happening consisting in a sequence of events especially chosen by God, taking place within an historical framework.'[57] While it is important for Cullmann that the New Testament calls for a decision of faith and implies a new understanding of existence, as Bultmann contends, he argues that such decision cannot be abstracted from – indeed it presupposes – that a 'divine history' has occurred that is independent of and stands over against the believer. Faith, accordingly, means '*aligning our existence with this series of events* hic et nunc'.[58]

The 'divine history' of which Cullmann speaks is centred on Jesus Christ, the 'mid-point of history'. 'From this mid-point', Cullmann says, 'all history is to be understood and judged... This fact... is the final meaning and criterion of all history before and after it...'[59] That seems to me to be precisely the biblical view, as is evident in the way the New Testament writers craft their theological

54. Hengel, 'Salvation History', 232.
55. On which, see Hengel, 'Salvation History', 230.
56. Cullmann, *Salvation in History*, 24.
57. Cullmann, *Salvation in History*, 25.
58. Cullmann, *Salvation in History*, 12. (italics original).
59. Cullmann, *Christ and Time*, 20.

accounts of Jesus.[60] The process of interpreting history in the light of God's Word had already begun in the Old Testament of course. History was understood by Israel in terms of the divine economy even though the decisive clue to the meaning of the whole had yet to be revealed. These are themes that will inform my own account of the relation between theology and history to be developed in later chapters. Less satisfactory in Cullmann is the idea that salvation history is concerned essentially with a line of development plotted through and connecting a series of discrete events in human history. In this respect, Barth's caution in relation to the earlier proponents of salvation history is apposite in respect of Cullmann as well: salvation history for Barth is 'the ongoing crisis of all history, not a history *in* or *alongside* history'.[61] Martin Hengel comments in similar vein,

> Salvation history resists all harmonization; it is no 'self-contained' organism, but is full of oppositions, conflicts, bitter battles over the truth, tribulation and desperation. There is as much room in it for a poem like the book of Job as there is for a sceptical, 'enlightened' Koheleth. Here, too, time and again the *deus absconditus* appears, in the most terrifying way in the godforsakeness of Jesus between Gethsemane and his cry of prayer in Mk 15:34. All these texts combine testimony and confession with a dialogue between God and man within the people of God which God has chosen. Quite a number of 'mythical' constructions and accounts appear in it, above all in the histories of the beginning and the end, including the sagas and legends, historical narratives of terrifying profanity – and yet as a whole these texts are about God's *will for salvation in election, judgement and redemption*, and about the praise of his people in response.[62]

For all their diversity the texts narrate a story of history as the space and time in and through which God encounters his people and brings about his purpose. This emphasis of Cullmann's must be maintained but we shall seek in what follows to heed Barth's and Hengel's concern that salvation history not be treated as a special layer within general history. This will enable us to avoid

60. I have in mind, for example, the genealogies of Matthew (1.1–17) and of Luke (3.23–38) in which Jesus is shown to be the culmination of a long line of biblical figures in and through whom God had been at work. The commonly recurring efforts to link Jesus with the Old Testament story which is itself reinterpreted in the light of Christ provides another example, as does Paul's effort in Romans 9–11 to think through, in the light of Christ, God's dealings with Israel, and so on. That the light of Christ shines forward in history as well as backward is evident in the eschatological outlook of the New Testament writers, about which a great deal has been written in the past century. Even the book of Revelation with its many fantastic and non-historical elements is at root a christocentric account of *history*.

61. Barth, *Der Römerbrief*, 2nd ed (Munich: Christian Kaiser Verlag, 1922) 5. Cited in Hengel, 'Salvation History', 235.

62. Hengel, 'Salvation History', 239–40.

too the unfortunate suggestion that God is related to history only as one who may from time to time intervene.

VI — Wolfhart Pannenberg

Wolfhart Pannenberg (1928–) is perhaps the most prominent representative in recent years of the quest to think theology and history together. Two themes from Pannenberg's writings are of particular importance, first his determination that Christian theology must emerge from and be responsible to the historical reality of Jesus, and second, his insistence on the importance of eschatology.

Pannenberg's first explorations of the relation between theology and history took place in conversation with Rolf Rendtorff, Trutz Rendtorff and Ulrich Wilkins, from which emerged the volume *Offenbarung als Geschichte* (1961).[63] His position was then developed more fully in *Gründzüge der Christologie* (1964) and in subsequent publications culminating in his three-volume *Systematic Theology* (1988–93).[64] Focused particularly on Christology, Pannenberg's explorations of the relation between theology and history are shaped by the conviction that 'the character of the Christ event as revelation must be appropriate to what happened in Jesus of Nazareth as such if it is not just to be a subjective addition to our interpretation'.[65] The believer, Pannenberg writes, 'knows and believes that only the Christian way of speaking about Jesus is appropriate to the facts, or better, to Jesus' person. Such a claim must, however, be accounted for; it must show itself to be true, not primarily in the face of others' doubts, but to the satisfaction of the believer's own concern for truth'.[66]

This quite proper concern for continuity between the history of Jesus and theological witness echoes what we have heard from Käsemann and Ebeling and indeed from Kähler and Barth, but Pannenberg distances himself from these figures by insisting that the demonstration of this continuity must be open to the view of secular historians and must begin, therefore, not with the kerygma, but with the history of Jesus.[67] This 'Christology from below', says Pannenberg, is Christology which, 'rising from the historical man Jesus to the recognition of his divinity, is concerned first of all with Jesus' message and fate and arrives only

63. ET: *Revelation as History: A Proposal for a More Open, Less Authoritarian View of an Important Theological Concept*, trans. David Granskou (London: Macmillan 1968).

64. ET: *Jesus – God and Man.*

65. Pannenberg, *Jesus – God and Man*, 28.

66. Pannenberg, *Jesus – God and Man*, 19.

67. Pannenberg's agreement with Kähler and his critique appear in *Jesus – God and Man*, 22–3

at the end, at the concept of the incarnation'.[68] The question to be asked, however, is by what means is the theological significance of Jesus opened to view? Is it through the tools of historical research? Then they will have to be very different tools than those proposed by Troeltsch and latterly adopted by such as the Jesus Seminar. As we have seen, the presupposition governing the use of such historiography excludes God from the realm of historical life. Pannenberg shows no sign of being daunted by this difficulty.[69] He rejects the claim of Paul Althaus, for instance, that the character of the history of Jesus as revelation is 'not known by means of historical reflection or historical reasoning',[70] thus implying that the power to disclose the character of Jesus as revelation does indeed lie with historical reasoning. That could only be so if God were a category of historical explanation, but the historiography outlined in Chapter 1 denies precisely this. The methodological waters are muddied, however, when Pannenberg goes on to say, immediately following his critique of Althaus, that 'the task of *Christology* is to establish the true understanding of Jesus' significance from his history' (my emphasis).[71] Christology is a theological enterprise, as the name itself makes clear – Christology is the study of 'Jesus understood as God's Messiah'. It is not identical with 'historical reasoning' although it may not be exclusive of it. Although we cannot be satisfied with this lack of methodological clarity, there may be a positive result to be gleaned from it. If *Christology* rather than historical reasoning simpliciter is to be the means by which the true understanding of Jesus is to be established – although I would rather say, investigated – then the theological presupposition involved in such an enterprise combined with Pannenberg's quite proper focus on the historical reality of Jesus himself might well provide a means for thinking theology and history together. Support for such an approach is evident in the claim that, 'while Christology must begin with the man Jesus, its first question has to be that about his unity with God. Every statement about Jesus taken independently from his relationship to God could result only in a crass distortion of the historical reality.'[72] We must be clear, however, as Pannenberg, I think, is not, that the theological presupposition of such an enterprise will distinguish it from what the determined positivist historians will be prepared to allow.

68. Pannenberg, *Jesus – God and Man*, 33.

69. Pannenberg does offer a critique of Troeltsch in *Basic Questions in Theology*, vol. i (Philadelphia: Fortress Press, 1970) 53ff., but that critique is not brought to bear here where it is needed most.

70. P. Althaus, *Fact and Faith in the Kerygma Today* (Philadephia: Muhlenberg Press, 1959) 34. See Pannenberg, *Jesus – God and Man*, 30.

71. Pannenberg, *Jesus – God and Man*, 30.

72. Pannenberg, *Jesus – God and Man*, 36.

The ground of Jesus' unity with God is to be found, Pannenberg argues, in his resurrection, by which event Jesus' own claim to divine authority is confirmed by God. Although Pannenberg supposes that the resurrection is an event open to view by historical reasoning, much depends in discerning its significance upon a theological presupposition. Consider the following 'summary' points concerning the inherent significance of Jesus' resurrection.[73]

(a) If Jesus has been raised, then the end of the world has begun.
(b) If Jesus has been raised, this for a Jew can only mean that God himself has confirmed the pre-Easter activity of Jesus.
(c) Through his resurrection from the dead, Jesus moved so close to the Son of Man that the insight became obvious: the Son of Man is none other than the man Jesus who will come again.
(d) If Jesus, having been raised from the dead, is ascended to God and if thereby the end of the world has begun, then God is ultimately revealed in Jesus.

Confident that the hypothetical clauses are resolvable in the affirmative through historical investigation of the tradition surrounding the empty tomb and the appearances to the disciples,[74] Pannenberg thinks that the theological conclusions follow. But they don't, of course – at least, not straightforwardly. What may be said instead is that such conclusions are plausible *within a theological conception of what history is*. This means, however, that Pannenberg's method cannot really be understood as proceeding from below, not, at least, if proceeding from below entails setting one's theological presuppositions to one side.[75] The distinction between methods here is not between theological method on the one hand, and neutral or objective method on the other; it is rather between theology on the one side, and methodological atheism on the other. Both involve a presupposed framework of enquiry; since no enquiry can eliminate presuppositions altogether, the crucial question is, which framework gives better access to the truth?

A second problem of Pannenberg's christological method, again apparent in *Jesus – God and Man,* is the preoccupation with Jesus as a past figure. His

73. See Pannenberg, *Jesus – God and Man*, 67–9. I do not include all the summary points, merely those that make clear the theological presupposition.

74. See Pannenberg, *Jesus – God and Man*, 88–106. We will return in Chapter 4 to consider the merits of Pannenberg's study of the 'evidence' for the resurrection.

75. Pannenberg seems to acknowledge the point when he writes, 'The basis of the knowledge of Jesus' significance remains bound to the original apocalyptic horizon of Jesus' history, which at the same time has also been modified by this history. If this horizon is eliminated, the basis of faith is lost; then Christology becomes mythology and no longer has true continuity with Jesus himself and with the witness of the apostles. *Jesus – God and Man*, 83.

determination to accord primacy to historical investigation of the historical Jesus entails this preoccupation, of course. But Christian faith is faith in the one who now lives. Pannenberg is certainly concerned with the 'Jesus who is present today'[76] but it is difficult to see how, on the basis of historical investigation alone, he can claim that the present meaning of Christ is anything more than the continuing influence of a past historical figure, kept 'alive' by those who come after him. Pannenberg is much more sensitive to this concern in his later *Systematic Theology*. In this work he speaks of 'the pneumatological extension of the Christ event through time'.[77] This formulation recognizes that Christ is not simply a past historical figure but is raised and present now through the mediation of the Spirit. This has an important epistemological result however. If it is through the activity of the Spirit that the risen Christ is encountered and known, then the resources of flesh and blood, under which category we must place historical enquiry, are not of themselves sufficient to reveal who Jesus is.

Reservations about his methodological proposals notwithstanding, Pannenberg is undoubtedly right to insist that the proclamation of the Church must refer to the historical reality of Jesus of Nazareth. Christian faith cannot be detached from history. He is also correct, in my view, to focus on the resurrection, for it is true that in that event most especially there is an intersection of time and eternity, of the transcendent with the historical, that sheds light on the whole of Jesus' life. Here we come upon Pannenberg's focus upon eschatology, for the resurrection has to do with the end of the world: 'If Jesus has been raised, then the end of the world has begun.'[78] The implication is that in the resurrection of Jesus the end or *telos* of the world and of its history has been disclosed. The content of that end is new creation. This disclosure will be foundational for the theology of history to be offered in Chapters 3 and 4 below.

VII — Hans Frei

The Eclipse of Biblical Narrative is a landmark study by Hans Frei (1929–89) of eighteenth- and nineteenth-century hermeneutics through which Frei highlights what he considers to be a major false turn in biblical hermeneutics. The period under review had been preceded, Frei observes, by a developing trend to abandon literal-realistic readings of the Bible and to read it instead in ways that presumed 'a logical distinction and a reflective distance between

76. See e.g. Pannenberg, *Jesus – God and Man*, 21.
77. Pannenberg, *Systematic Theology*, vol. ii. See especially, 278–90.
78. Pannenberg, *Jesus – God and Man*, 67.

the [biblical] stories and the "reality" they depict'. There took place 'a detachment of the "real" historical world from its biblical description'.[79] As a result, the *meaning* of the text was increasingly detached from the specific story that it sets forth. 'The depicted biblical world and the real historical world began to be separated at once in thought and in sensibility, no matter whether the depiction was thought to agree with reality (Cocceius and Bengel) or disagree with it (Spinoza).'[80] This observation agrees with the survey we have conducted in Chapter 1. At the same time, however, figural reading too 'faded into oblivion as a means for relating the world of biblical narrative to present experience and to the world of extra-biblical events'.[81]

Frei's fundamental complaint is that in the eighteenth and nineteenth centuries there took place a reversal in the direction of biblical interpretation. Whereas in the biblical hermeneutics characteristic of earlier periods in Christian history the world rendered by the biblical narratives was 'the one and only real world' in light of which the experience of the present age and reader is to be understood, in the great reversal the task of hermeneutics was conceived to be a matter of fitting the stories and concepts of the text into a 'real world' discoverable apart from the text. Frei explains that for John Locke, 'The meaning of the stories is their ostensive reference or their failure to refer to certain events.'[82] They are true, moreover, if, and only if, the events they describe can be fitted into the world of the reader's own experience.

Biblical interpretation, accordingly, abandoned the task of 'incorporating extra-biblical thought, experience, and reality into the one real world detailed and made accessible by the biblical story'[83] and undertook to investigate instead whether 'the stories and whatever concepts may be drawn from them describe what we apprehend as the real world'.[84] It so happens that this reversal coincides with the Enlightenment project of describing the world without reference to God, with the result that the stories and theological concepts of the biblical narrative are rendered less and less applicable to the depiction of the world as it really is and survive only as a means of articulating ethical commitments and personal values.

The reduction of the narrative to a story about values and ethics is, as we have seen in Chapter 1, a prevalent consequence of the reversal that Frei

79. Hans Frei, *The Eclipse of Biblical Narrative: A Study of Eighteenth and Nineteenth Century Hermeneutics* (New Haven and London: Yale University Press, 1974) 4.

80. Frei, *The Eclipse of Biblical Narrative*, 5–6.

81. Frei, *The Eclipse of Biblical Narrative*, 6.

82. Frei, *The Eclipse of Biblical Narrative*, 99.

83. Frei, *The Eclipse of Biblical Narrative*, 3.

84. Frei, *The Eclipse of Biblical Narrative*, 5.

identifies. An alternative reaction to such reversal is naive literalism, or perhaps Fundamentalism as it is more commonly referred to. Such reading reacts to the perceived gap between the biblical narrative and the world as it really is by asserting an identity between the world of the text and the world *as it is thought to exist* apart from the text. This represents a failure to recognize that the world of the biblical text is genuinely different from the world perceived by the unbelieving eye and so is not apprehensible by the prevailing methods of scientific and historical-critical enquiry. Josh McDowell's *Evidence that Demands a Verdict*[85] is a popular and influential instance of this failure. The truth about the world as represented in Scripture is thought to be open to view without any need of God's help. Liberalism, however, makes exactly the same error. It too presumes that the stories of the Bible are true or not by virtue of their ostensive reference to events in the world as it is thought to exist apart from the text. Neither Fundamentalism nor Liberalism allow that the world as it is depicted in the Bible commands allegiance as the true depiction of the world as it really is in opposition to the depiction of the world arrived at through an a-theological reflection upon everyday experience.

The enormous value of Frei's work in identifying the reversal in hermeneutics which required the biblical world to be fitted procrustean-like into a view of the world arrived at apart from the Bible must be extended, I believe, into a critical assessment of what may count as historical. Frei notes that a realistic or history-like element is a feature of many of the biblical narratives. This is widely recognized, Frei says, but:

> commentators, especially those influenced by historical criticism, virtually to a man failed to understand what they had seen when they recognised the realistic character of biblical narratives, because every time they acknowledged it they thought this was identical with affirming not only the history-likeness but also a degree of historical likelihood of the stories. Those who wanted to affirm their historical factuality used the realistic character or history-likeness as evidence in favor of this claim, while those who denied the factuality also finally denied that the history-likeness was a cutting feature – thus in effect denying that they had seen what they had seen because (once again) they thought history-likeness identical with at least potentially true history.[86]

The question to be asked here is, how is 'true history' to be identified? Is it by the critical methods of Troeltsch and the like? Or is it by distilling from the various testimonial accounts of an historical event, some concatenation of data theoretically open to view by some eyewitness? Neither of these procedures will allow for the involvement of God in history and that is precisely the problem.

85. (San Bernardino: Campus Crusade for Christ International, 1972).

86. Frei, *The Eclipse of Biblical Narrative*, 11–12.

If 'true history' means 'that which has taken place', the question of God's involvement in what has taken place should not be excluded by virtue of a methodological decision about how the truth of history is to be discerned. 'True history' might better be told precisely through the narrative possibilities Frei goes on to explore. If we are to understand the world *as it really is* in the light of the text, rather than the text in the light of the world *as it is perceived to be*, then an important task upon which we ought to embark is a critique of the prevailing notions of what 'true history' is. In this regard, Frei, in *The Eclipse of Biblical Narrative*, is not critical enough.

To anticipate Chapter 4 for a moment, the biblical narratives about the resurrection, for prime example, are not to be treated as requiring accommodation within the prevailing conceptions of the world – this is Frei's point – but nor are they to be assessed against the prevailing conceptions of what true history is. They demand instead a reconsideration of how reality is constituted and thus also of how history itself is to be construed. It is in another work of Frei's, his essay 'Theological Reflections on the Accounts of Jesus' Death and Resurrection',[87] that we find hints of the reassessment of history that I think is required. Speaking of the manifestation of Jesus' identity in his resurrection, Frei writes,

> not only his own history but all of the past history of Israel receives its ordering by reference to his manifestation. The wheel has, in one sense, come full circle. Now that he is fully manifest in the absolute coincidence of his manifestation with his unsubstitutable individuality, the identity between him and the community is also restored. But whereas at the beginning, in the first stage of the account, it was the community which served to identify him, the reverse is now true. He, Jesus, provides the community and its whole history with his identity...[88]

Such is also true, I contend, of the whole of history. It is now to be understood as gathered into and reconstituted by the reality of Jesus himself.

The lack of critical attention to what history is in *The Eclipse of Biblical Narrative* is related, I think, to Frei's insistence in that work on the irreducibility of narrative. It may well be that one feature of the 'history-likeness' of the biblical narrative is that it invites readers to accommodate themselves to the world of the text rather than to accommodate the world of the text to their prior world-view, but if enquiry into the ostensive character of the biblical narrative is thought to involve an illegitimate reduction of the biblical narrative to some meaning distinct from the narrative itself, then the narrative does

87. Originally published by Fortress Press (1975). Reprinted in *The Identity of Jesus Christ* (Eugene, Oreg.: Wipf & Stock, 2000) 1–49.

88. Frei, 'Theological Reflections on the Accounts of Jesus' Death and Resurrection', 39–40.

indeed become detached from the world in just the way that Frei sought to avoid. The danger is evident in his apparent disinterest in the question whether 'the "essence" of Christianity depend[s] on maintaining that the veracity of a historical fact is indispensable for the salvation of mankind'.

It is no doubt true, as Frei points out, that 'empirical historical investigation into what most probably happened, together with supporting hypotheses and arguments, is a different enterprise from the endeavor to set forth a temporal world, which is the peculiar way in which realistic narrative means or makes sense',[89] but this observation fails to take seriously enough the intent and power of the narrative to disclose the true reality of what lies outside the text. Nor does it allow us to see the extent to which the biblical narrative about Jesus calls into question the deliverances of 'empirical historical investigation'.[90]

This weakness is apparent in *The Eclipse of Biblical Narrative* but, unlike Francis Watson,[91] I do not see it carried over into Frei's work on Christology. Watson observes that while Frei recognizes that the question of the factuality of a narrative is bound to arise, and legitimately so, 'he appears to have no means at his disposal whereby to reintegrate this question into the narrative framework'.[92]

The point at issue here is whether or not and in what way the biblical narrative can be said to be true. In other words, how does the narrative reveal what has taken place? This question need not be asked as an attempt to reintegrate the narrative back into the world as it is perceived to be apart from the text; it can instead be a means of enquiring about the way in which the narrative discloses how the world as we know it is in fact reconfigured and made new under the impact of the life, death and resurrection of Jesus. The sceptical request for a sign of the new reality sometimes invites rebuke from Jesus (See Matt. 12.38–9; 16.1–4; Mark 8.11–12; Luke 11.16, 29) but elsewhere he responds to faith's quest for a sign by indicating how the world is changed by his presence within it: 'Go and tell John what you hear and see: the blind receive their sight, the lame walk, the lepers are cleansed, the deaf hear, the dead are raised, and the poor have good news brought to them' (Matt. 11.4–5). If the world of the narrative is the real world, then we may expect it to become apparent to those who have eyes to see through, but nonetheless beyond, the text.

Although I am in sympathy with Watson's call for an account of how the factuality of the narrative is to be ascertained – of how we may have eyes to

89. Frei, *The Eclipse of Biblical Narrative*, 150–1.

90. See e.g 'Theological Reflections on the Accounts of Jesus' Death and Resurrection', 36; *The Eclipse of Biblical Narrative*, 150.

91. Watson's account is found in *Text, Church, and World: Biblical Interpretation in Theological Perspective* (Edinburgh: T&T Clark, 1994), 19–29.

92. Watson, *Text, Church, and World*, 25.

see – we do not in fact have any 'means at our disposal' for such a task. Having eyes to see is characteristically set forth in the New Testament as a gift from God. 'Seeing' the truth belongs within the event of revelation itself over which God himself is Lord. Whatever else might be the task of historical-critical method, therefore, it is not competent either to confirm or to deny what the Gospel narratives proclaim about the identity of Jesus Christ. Although this too may seem to be a 'mysterious affair'[93] Frei is nevertheless correct to insist that the risen Christ *manifests himself* as the one of whom the narratives speak. Frei insists that 'the resurrection must, in the eyes of those who believe, be a factual occurrence of a wholly unique kind, the conceptual content of which is the climactic establishment of Jesus' identity'.[94] This continues to be, however, the *veiled* action of God.[95] Precisely as God's action it does not become apparent by means at our disposal, but can be known only by virtue of a further episode in the divine economy of revelation and salvation. Frei cites Acts 10 in support of the point: 'God raised him on the third day and made him manifest; not to all people but to us who were chosen by God as witnesses' (Acts 10.40–1). 'It is necessary to say, with this passage from Acts, that, no matter what the logic of the Christian faith, actual belief in the resurrection is a matter of faith and not of arguments from possibility or evidence.'[96]

Frei's discussion lies within the tradition of Kähler's affirmation that the true Christ is the Christ of the Church's proclamation. It is clear too that Frei holds this preaching to be, not detachable from but rather a faithful representation of the actual history of Jesus, but he denies the propriety and indeed the possibility of going behind the narrative to investigate how the proclamation corresponds to particular empirical data. The risen Christ manifests himself as the one of whom the Gospels speak; he is not made manifest by the efforts of historical-critical enquiry.

VIII — N.T. Wright

A more optimistic account of the competence of historical enquiry has, in recent years, been set forth by N.T. Wright, who, in the course of a projected five-volume series, is embarked upon an historical investigation of the origins of Christianity. Wright's work is of particular interest and importance because of

93. See Watson, *Text, Church, and World*, 25.
94. Frei, 'Theological Reflections on the Accounts of Jesus' Death and Resurrection', 2.
95. See Frei, 'Theological Reflections on the Accounts of Jesus' Death and Resurrection', 38.
96. Frei, *The Identity of Jesus Christ*, 183.

his willingness to think history and theology together.[97] Hence the title of the five-volume project: 'Christian Origins and the Question of God'. Wright warns that to read the New Testament without attending to both theology and history risks doing violence to the text itself and precipitates errors that we have already come across. An exclusively historical reading, on the one hand, fails to recognise the 'authority' of the text for the Church or the world today, risks ignoring the theological import of the text, and may well succumb to the questionable assumption that we can get back to 'what actually happened', arriving finally at 'objective' historical truth. An exclusively theological reading, on the other hand, can avoid questions of history altogether thus relativizing a potentially 'normative' statement or a potentially 'historical' one into 'merely an aspect of Matthean theology'.[98]

Wright is also alert to questions posed by Postmodern critical theory; 'What are we doing when we are reading this text? What do I bring to the text by way of presupposition, and in what way am I changed through reading it?'[99] These are important questions but they too may be asked in such a way as to violate the integrity of the text, and effect a further disengagement from history. Wright insists, by contrast, that 'the rootedness of Christianity in history is not negotiable'.[100]

Athough I am in agreement with Wright's judgement in these matters I aim, nevertheless, to approach the question of the relationship between theology and history in a rather different way. Whereas Wright establishes base camp in the fields of historical enquiry, I set out from certain theological convictions about the self-revelation of God. Initial agreement on the need to think theology and history together, however, encourages me toward further exploration of Wright's work. It is not long, however, before I begin to have misgivings, particularly in considering passages such as the following:

> Looking next at the *historical* set of questions, we find the issues focused on Jesus, Paul and the gospels. (a) Who was Jesus, and was he in any sense responsible for the beginning of 'Christianity'? What were his aims, what did he hope to achieve, why did he die, and why did (what we now call) the church come into being? (b) Was Paul the real founder of 'Christianity', the corrupter of the original message, or was he the true interpreter of Jesus?...These are the questions...which, I suggest, must be looked at. They are open to any historian, of whatever ideological or cultural background...[101]

97. See Wright's programmatic discussion in the 'Introduction' to *The New Testament and the People of God* (London: SPCK, 1992) particularly 4–5.

98. See Wright, *The New Testament and the People of God*, 8.

99. Wright, *The New Testament and the People of God*, 9.

100. Wright, *The New Testament and the People of God*, 9.

101. Wright, *The New Testament and the People of God*, 11.

The emphasis demarcating these as *historical* questions is Wright's own, and here my worries begin. Is it proper to suppose that the questions 'Who was Jesus?' and 'Was Paul the true interpreter of Jesus?' are merely historical questions?[102] These look to me like questions that demand theological consideration as well. The New Testament writers, including Paul, of course, make theological claims about who Jesus was (and is!). Are we to suppose that historians alone, without assistance from theologians, are competent to pronounce upon whether or not these theological claims are true?[103] My worries are not assuaged by Wright's further claim that,

> It might in principle have been the case that we had excellent alternative records which would have enabled us to provide a thorough and adequate set of historical answers with only occasional recourse to the books written by Christians themselves. Some, of course, might want to object to this suggestion, and to insist that the events could only be understood through the eyes of faith, so that nothing short of the New Testament would do... I think this smacks of cooking the evidence in advance, but such a retort could only be properly made when the bulk of the work is done.[104]

That might be a valid point if in fact the testimonies of faith are false, or if faith contributes nothing essential to the understanding of Jesus, but that is not Wright's view. I am puzzled, therefore, that he should appear to have forsaken already the promise to integrate the questions of history and theology. He goes on: 'In a sense, the study of Jesus is first and foremost a matter of history, needing careful ancillary use of literary study of the texts and theological study of implications.'[105] Theology is thus put in its place! Historians – with some help from the literary scholars – will lay bare who Jesus was, while theologians are left to consider the implications. This is the kind of assumption that this book is written to oppose. If Jesus is properly to be understood as Lord, for example, or as the one through whom God addresses the world, then the discernment of this reality will not be achieved within the usual limits of historical research. Or to put it the other way around: a proper account of who Jesus 'was' cannot exclude his Lordship without falsifying the matter.

102. The assumption that the truth about Jesus is revealed through a consideration of who he *was* is itself questionable on account of its supposing his resurrection to have no bearing upon the question of his identity, but that matter will be discussed elsewhere.

103. I am convinced that even the efforts of historians and theologians together are not enough to settle the questions thus posed, although that is itself a theological judgement closely allied to Frei's claim noted above that the risen Christ *manifests himself* as the one to whom the New Testament bears witness.

104. Wright, *The New Testament and the People of God*, 11–12.

105. Wright, *The New Testament and the People of God*, 14.

Despite the less than helpful description of methodology here offered (which seems strangely in conflict with other aspects of his work), Wright knows that a dogma-free historiography is not attainable[106] and that one cannot proceed in the positivistic manner that historians still wedded to the Troeltschian ideal presume. This recognition, however, just makes Wright's earlier contention that we might just as well proceed without the insight of faith provided by the New Testament all the more puzzling. The important question to be considered is whether the faith or dogma informing the New Testament witness obscures or helps to reveal the reality with which we are concerned. Wright quite properly resists 'a slide into subjectivism' as also 'arrogant objectivism'. Both need replacement by an open acknowledgement that all judgements about 'the facts of the matter', including those of history, are personally involving; they cannot help but be informed, and in turn reshape, the things we believe about the world in which we live and its relation to God. Theology (or atheology) and history are already joined together, so that the effort to rend them asunder is bound to be forlorn. When Wright subsequently explains that '*the simple historical description* of early Christianity and its theology cannot by itself be a complete enterprise',[107] we should add that it is not even possible, if by 'a simple historical description' we mean something that is not already informed by particular theological commitments. The historical project must indeed 'broaden its horizons'.[108]

Having set out some guidelines for the historical task, Wright proceeds to offer some cautions to theology. Here I am in complete agreement, especially with his rejection of the notion that the isolation of timeless theological truths is the goal of biblical hermeneutics. Demythologization and form-criticism are singled out for criticism in this regard. Both are liable to relativize the historical events about which the New Testament speaks in favour of a timeless theology essentially unrelated to their historical mediation. 'This proposal', Wright says, 'is subject to the damaging criticism that it has not given to history, or creation, sufficient weight for them to be taken seriously within the reading of the New Testament, in which both seem to be enormously important.'[109] This observation is of the utmost importance. If Wright is correct, as I believe him to be, then the recovery of a proper conception of history and of creation is an essential and urgent task in the enterprise of biblical hermeneutics.

Despite my criticisms of some of the methodological claims made above, I believe Wright to be correct in suggesting that,

106. Wright, *The New Testament and the People of God*, 16.

107. Wright, *The New Testament and the People of God*, 18 (my emphasis).

108. Wright, *The New Testament and the People of God*, 18.

109. Wright, *The New Testament and the People of God*, 21.

> part of the wider task—which I believe faces modern Western culture in its entirety, not only other theologians or Christians—[is] to rethink a basic worldview in the face of the internal collapse of the one which has dominated the Western world for the last two centuries or so. And it is precisely one of the features of the worldview now under attack that 'history' and 'theology' belong in separate compartments.[110]

If it is true that the divine economy is irreducibly historical, if God's address to humankind and his purpose for the creation are worked out through the vicissitudes of history, then history is not what it is often thought to be. More particularly, it is not what historians who are wedded to the worldview now experiencing collapse present to us as the results of their enquiries. Contrary to the prevailing assumptions of historians, history is not impervious to divine agency, but is the very means by which God establishes the relation with his people for which they were created. What is needed, therefore, is a theological account of what history is. It is to that task that we now turn.

110. Wright, *The New Testament and the People of God*, 24. I have not paid any attention here to Wright's discussion of the role to be played in biblical hermeneutics by literary considerations and the insights of Postmodernism about reader response. My focus on history and theology is not meant to discount such considerations, but I will postpone my limited discussion of them until Chapter 7.

3

Creation and Promise

I — Towards a Theology of History

While the books of the Bible are clearly comprised of a great variety of literary genres, poetry, myth, prophecy, proverb, prayers, hymns, and so on, much of it also takes the form of historical narrative. The Bible tells the story of the history of Israel, a history set within the context of God's purpose for all nations. The telling of that story, furthermore, arises from the conviction that a true account of history will relate the involvement of God in the successive unfolding of events. Thus can Gerhard von Rad declare that '[a]ny study of the Old Testament that does not begin with its character as a witness to God's action in history is condemned to sterility because it does not take account of the facts'.[1] It is a mistake, therefore, to presume that the biblical writers, in the New as well as in the Old Testament, were not concerned with history and that they set out instead to construct a religious mythology, or that they chose, as a communicative strategy, to couch essentially spiritual or rational truths in the form of a fictional historical narrative. There can be no doubting that the writers of the historical narratives in the Bible intend to refer to the prior historical reality and, as Francis Watson has put it, whatever fictionalizing tendency may be present is always subordinate to the backward historical reference.[2]

We may say, therefore, that the Bible is a theological account of history. It is an account that is shaped by the conviction that all that takes place does so within the context of God's providential care for the created order. That it is a theological account, employing categories peculiar to its own concerns, does not

1. Gerhard von Rad, *God at Work in Israel*, trans. John H. Marks (Nashville: Abingdon Press, 1980) 154–5.

2. Francis Watson, *Text and Truth: Redefining Biblical Theology* (Edinburgh: T&T Clark, 1997) 33.

render it illegitimate as history, any more than a political history or an economic history should be called into question just because it is shaped by and seeks to explain the course of history according to a strictly defined interest. A distinction made by Hegel between history and chronicle is important at this point.[3] While chronicle is the mere recording of events without any attempt to discern or chart any relation between them, the writing of history is an undertaking that seeks and offers an explanation for the unfolding of events. As such, every telling of the story of history involves the selection and interpretation of evidence according to the historian's convictions about the meaning and purpose of the whole. There is no good reason to suppose that a purely secular account of history, in which divine action is dispensed with as an explanatory category, brings the historian closer to the truth. Western historiography, however, in most of its variant forms has typically been founded upon just this assumption. In quest of a status and supposed legitimacy comparable to that of the natural sciences, historical enquiry in the Modern era has been undertaken, as we have seen, without recourse to the 'God hypothesis'. For all the epistemological challenges involved in discerning the work of God in history, however, the truth or falsity in principle of theological versus secular accounts of history depends not at all on such difficulties as may be involved in a theological account, much less upon the agnostic or atheistic predilections of the age, but solely on whether God has or has not acted. There is no *a priori* basis upon which that matter can be determined. The conviction of Israel, therefore, that its own history as a people is inaugurated by God and is shaped throughout by God's action, is an account requiring to be reckoned with. It cannot be dismissed in advance!

There are two conditions, I think, that give shape to the Hebraic understanding of history. First is the creation of the world by God *ex nihilo*, and second is God's direction of history towards its goal. This second aspect will be discussed below under the rubric of divine promise. It is within this framework of creation and promise that human action can properly be conceived as historic.

II — The Doctrine of Creation

The disparagement of history described above is a symptom of the malaise identified by Colin Gunton as the neglect of the doctrine of creation.[4] In his

3. See Hegel, *Lectures on the Philosophy of World History*, 12.

4. This is especially true of Spinoza, who denies that God can be the creator of anything outside of himself. The extended and thinking things of this world are simply attributes of God or affections of God's attributes. See *Ethics*, trans. Andrew Boyle (London: J.M. Dent & Co., 1959) Part I, 14C2.

book *The Triune Creator*, Gunton outlines three aspects of the Christian doctrine of creation that are unique among the range of philosophic and religious accounts about how things came to be.[5] First is the notion of creation 'out of nothing'.[6] The import of this, Gunton argues, is that 'the creation is an act of divine sovereignty and freedom, an exercise of God's will that there be something other than himself. It further implies that the universe had a beginning in time; it is neither eternal nor infinite.'[7] Two things follow from this for our concern with history. Because, in contrast with the doctrine of *creatio ex nihilo*, the Greeks believed that the matter of the universe had always existed, that it 'just is', they presumed that it had no particular meaning, nor any purpose. That the world should be brought forth by God 'out of nothing', however, implies that God creates with some purpose in mind. The principle of *creatio ex nihilo* implies that the world is invested with a *telos*. There is a reason for its being, and history, in consequence, is to be understood as the space and time opened up for the world to become what it is intended to be.

Second, the idea of creation out of nothing means that the world is fully God's world. Unlike the demiurge in Plato's *Timaeus* who simply gives order to the matter that already is, the God testified to in the Christian doctrine of creation is not constrained in his creative work by some pre-existent matter. The world both in its form and in its matter is the outcome of the Creator's will. That means for our understanding of history, that history cannot be conceived along Manichean lines as a struggle between opposing forces. Everything is held in God's hands so that, even in the face of evil and sinfulness, it is possible to affirm, along with the biblical writers, that all things happen under the will and purpose of God. History may be confessed to have an overall coherence under the creative, providential and redemptive care of God.

This introduces us to the second unique aspect of the Christian doctrine of creation identified by Gunton. Taking his point of departure from the creedal confession – 'I believe in God the Father, Maker of heaven and earth' – Gunton points out that the doctrine is a matter of belief. It is to be distinguished, therefore, from something that is known intuitively, from something that reason shows us, or from something that is self-evident.[8] The corollary of

5. I am following the discussion in Chapter 1 of Colin E. Gunton's work, *The Triune Creator: A Historical and Systematic Study* (Edinburgh: Edinburgh University Press, 1998).

6. The doctrine of *creatio ex nihilo* is not universally accepted but there are good arguments for its acceptance within the Christian theological tradition. See, for prime example, Gerhard May, *Creatio ex Nihilo: The Doctrine of 'Creation out of Nothing' in Early Christian Thought*, trans. A.S. Worrall (Edinburgh: T&T Clark, 1994).

7. Gunton, *The Triune Creator*, 9.

8. See Gunton, *The Triune Creator*, 8.

this for our understanding of history is that the purpose of history is not given up to rational enquiry without recourse to revelation; nor is that purpose reducible to a set of laws so that everything must fall into analogous conformity with what has gone before. It is neither within the limits of reason alone, therefore, nor within the limits of historical enquiry alone that the purpose of history is disclosed. This has a decisive implication for all our efforts to investigate the historical reality of Jesus Christ. The reality of his person cannot be treated as nothing other than an object for human interpretation, a brute fact which it is our task now to interpret. The study of Christ cannot begin, as Kierkegaard nicely puts it, by letting him be dead. The fact of Christ is rather an event – and here I am in agreement with Wolfhart Pannenberg – which, in its pneumatological extension through time, itself gives rise to a community of interpretation, a body of faith and witness constituted by the headship of the risen Christ.[9] God himself, that is to say, is involved in our understanding of who Christ is. It is through the action of God in the community of faith that the true reality of Christ comes to light. The decisive mistake of those engaged in the nineteenth-century quest of the historical Jesus was to presume that the truth of the history of Jesus would yield itself up by means of a deliberate isolation of the enquirer from the pneumatological extension of this event in time through the faith and witness of the Church. That error is replicated on every occasion that biblical interpretation is thought to be the task of the academy in isolation from the community of faith.

The third aspect identified by Gunton as uniquely characterizing the Christian doctrine of creation is the creation of the world as the act of the triune God, Father, Son and Holy Spirit. Here again, there are important implications for our understanding of history. Gunton explains that

> [b]ecause [the doctrine of the Trinity] holds that God is already, 'in advance' of creation, a communion of persons existing in loving relations, it becomes possible to say that he does not need the world, and so is able to will the existence of something else simply for its own sake. Creation is the outcome of God's love indeed, but of his unconstrained love. It is therefore not a necessary outcome of what God is, but is contingent. This is important because it enables us to say that the world is given value in its own right.[10]

So, too, is human action given value in its own right. It is not simply the necessary unfolding of God's own being, as is seen both in Hegel and in various forms of process theology. Hegel's scheme renders the particulars of

9. See Wolfhart Pannenberg, *Systematic Theology*, vol. ii, trans. Geoffrey W. Bromiley (Edinburgh: T&T Clark, 1994) 437–41, especially 440.

10. Gunton, *The Triune Creator*, 9–10.

history of no account, for they are but the inevitable outworking of a process that is determined apart from them. In contrast with such views, God entrusts to the precarious stewardship of human beings a measure of responsibility for the way that history takes shape. Things are not simply the inevitable outcome of all that has gone before. Human response matters. It is in this way that human action can be genuinely historic – shaping the course of things in obedience to, or sometimes in defiance of, the guiding hand of God. History and human responsibility go hand in hand. One finds recognition of this point even in a writer like Jacques Derrida whose work is in other respects corrosive of the idea of history. Drawing upon the thought of Jan Patoçka, Derrida observes that the reluctance of historical man to admit to the historicity of our existence is a reluctance to accept responsibility. Responsibility is only accepted by the one who has faith that history matters.[11] The same point is apparent in Lucien Goldmann's claim that one can only answer the question, 'How ought I to live?' 'by situating one's life inside an eschatological or historical whole in which it inserts itself by faith'.[12] Human action, to make any sense and to be evaluated ethically, requires some notion of the purpose of history as a whole. Christian faith holds that it is within the framework of divine creation and promise and particularly within its christological articulation, that the true *telos* of history is disclosed.

The second crucial implication of a trinitarian account of God's creative action is that it defeats Deism. That the world is the creation not of the Father alone but also of the Son and the Spirit enables us to speak of God's continuing action in the world. Becoming incarnate in the midst of history, and pouring out his Spirit on all flesh, God confirms creation as his own project. It is not left to its own devices but is redemptively refashioned after the tragedy of human sin and is set again on its trajectory to fulfilment in reconciled relation with God. This action of the triune God enables us also to conceive how, under both christological and pneumatological description, the human agency in history upon which we have insisted can be directed toward the fulfilment of the divine purpose. We have observed above the biblical conviction that God enlists human participation in the working out of his purpose. Again, it is in Jesus Christ that such participation reaches its fulfilment – his human life of obedience to God, his death, his resurrection and his ascension, is the series of events that truly make history. It is through Christ that God restores the

11. See Jacques Derrida, *The Gift of Death*, trans. David Wills (Chicago: University of Chicago Press, 1995) 4–6.

12. Lucien Goldmann, *The Hidden God: A Study of Tragic Vision in the 'Pensées' of Pascal and the Tragedies of Racine* (London: Routledge & Kegan Paul, 1964) 264. Cited by Nicholas Wolterstorff in *Until Justice and Peace Embrace* (Grand Rapids: Eerdmans, 1983) vii.

world to its true purpose. By sending then his Holy Spirit, who bestows gifts and fruits for truly human life, Christ ensures that our own human action may become, under the impact and empowerment of that Spirit, a like participation in God's purpose.

Summarizing my argument, then, we have seen that the idea of *creatio ex nihilo* identifies the creation as a contingent act of divine will, gives to the created order its own being and integrity in distinction from God, and thus accords to human action a meaning and a value within the purpose of God. The trinitarian description of divine creativity adds to our conception of history the further insight that God does not abandon the world to its own devices, nor withdraws his promise, but involves himself in bringing creation to its goal.

III — God at Work in Israel: Promise and Fulfilment

The biblical account of Israel's history as a nation distinct from other nations begins with the story of Abraham and Sarah, and, as von Rad again points out, it is a measure of Israel's historical consciousness that Abraham does not descend direct from the heavens like so many mythical founders of cities or peoples, but emerges from the diverse array of nations described in Genesis 10, all of which are equally the creation of God. The readiness of Israel to see herself, 'quite unmythically, as belonging to the world of nations'[13] implies that God's purpose of salvation, as it is related in the biblical story, takes place *within* history, not apart from it. What follows, then, is that historical events are themselves decisive for the working out of God's purpose. So we read in Genesis 12:

> Now the Lord said to Abram, 'Go from your country and your kindred and your father's house to the land that I will show you. I will make of you a great nation, and I will bless you, and make your name great, so that you will be a blessing. I will bless those who bless you, and the one who curses you I will curse; and in you all the families of the earth shall be blessed.' (Gen. 12.1–3)

Whatever the provenance of this story may be, by recounting it as they do, the people of Israel seek an historical grounding for their present experience of God's blessing and guidance, and offer thereby a radically different conception of history than those adhered to by the surrounding cultures. In the words of Walter Eichrodt,

13. See von Rad, *God at Work in Israel*, 139.

> The Old Testament writers find in the self-disclosure of God the factor in world events by which individual events are placed in a spiritual connection, and which makes events meaningful; i.e. only through it can a chaos of changing and hurrying events become comprehensible as *real history*. Under the impression of this divine experience they cannot describe world events in any other way than as historical succession in which everything is united under God's leading, and moves to a definite objective.[14]

History is affirmed by the biblical writers as the *locus* of God's action ('I will show you a land, and make of you a great nation') and the terrain upon which his *purpose* is worked out ('and in you all the families of the earth shall be blessed'). It is the action of God, therefore, that is understood to give history its purpose and that directs it towards its goal. Only thus is the succession of events conceivable as 'real history'. Furthermore, it is God's enlisting of human participation – the address of his Word to humankind and the call for a response – that gives to human action its meaningful[15] and teleological character. Human action becomes 'historic'[16] in a way not thought of by surrounding peoples who typically saw history in cyclical terms, robbing it thus of its directedness towards a goal, and divesting human action of its capacity to contribute to a future that is new.

The importance of teleology for the idea of history is acknowledged in the theory recently espoused by Francis Fukuyama that with the arrival of Modernity and particularly of liberal democracy, history has come to an end; there is nothing else towards which we might be expected to evolve.[17] Contestable though Fukuyama's judgement is that we have now reached the end, the point is right that without any further purpose, without something new to be striven for or waited upon, there is no history. Western intellectual discourse about history is thoroughly permeated with teleology – as it must be if the idea of history is to be coherent – and yet it determinedly eschews reference to God who alone can credibly be thought of as bestowing a purpose

14. W. Eichrodt, 'Offenbarung und Geschichte im Alten Testament', *Theologische Zeitschrift* 4 (1948) 321–2 (my emphasis).

15. There is no space here to engage in philosophical debates about the meaning of meaning. My own view, stated briefly for the purposes of this chapter, is that the meaning of a thing refers to its place and role in a wider context, whether that be a word in a sentence, a sentence in a wider story, or an event in the course of history. Meaning refers to the way in which that thing, as part of something larger, contributes to and shapes the whole. See further discussion of this matter in Chapter 7.

16. The term 'historic' is used here to speak of those actions and events which contribute to the making of a new future, being as such, neither an endless cycle of recurring events, nor the necessary unfolding of an idea or principle that is transcendent of history and essentially unaffected by it.

17. Francis Fukuyama, *The End of History and the Last Man* (New York: Free Press, 1992).

upon history as a whole. That error is part of humanity's efforts to foist upon history a purpose of its own, and that, in turn, is what the Bible calls sin.

Without teleology, without the conviction that history has some purpose that can be either hindered or advanced by all that happens, history itself is rendered meaningless. It is simply, 'one damn thing after another' as Henry Ford once remarked of life in general, and all change is simply the same old thing in new constellations. The soteriological consequence of this cyclical and non-purposive view of 'history' found in the non-Semitic religions is that humanity's ultimate fulfilment or salvation is conceived in terms of an escape from the endless round of events, an escape from this historical life which can only frustrate our search for fulfilment and can never be the means through which our salvation is worked out.

In contrast with cyclical views of history in which the future is essentially no different from the past, it is emphasized in the biblical narrative that Abraham sets out in obedience to the divine command 'without knowing where he is going'. His lack of foreknowledge renders his action historic in the sense I have outlined above. What is yet to come is not simply the inevitable and necessary outworking of what has already come to be, nor is it the cyclical return of that which has already appeared before. Under the guidance and promise of God, Abraham is setting out on a new course, the outcome of which is unknown. Although he is motivated by the promise of God, Abraham's particular actions are not determined by God. Determinism too would rob human action of its historic character; Abraham's own action would no longer matter. But Abraham's action does matter. It is under the condition of his obedience that God chooses to see his promise through.[18]

A further feature of the biblical story of Abraham is that the *particular* events of Abraham's life are thought to be of *universal* significance. Under the condition of his obedience to God's promise, '*all* the families of the earth shall be blessed'. In the Hebrew view of things, historical events are not robbed of

18. It is important to head off the suspicion of Pelagianism here. Two things need to be said, more extensively no doubt than is attempted here. First, that God enlists Abraham's obedience to the working out of his promise is essential to the content of the promise itself, i.e that there shall be a covenant between God and his people. The promise is of a two-sided relationship. While it is true that the covenant is a unilateral covenant, initiated by God and sustained by God, its fulfilment requires human response. Unlike Pelagius, however, we shall not suppose that such response can have anything other than a christological ground. Jesus Christ, a 'son of Abraham', is the one through whom the human response is eventually brought to fulfilment. Second, we must speak of the Holy Spirit. For just as a theological account of human response requires Christology, so also it requires pneumatology. It is under the impact of God's Spirit that we are made one with Christ and share thus in his human response to the divine promise.

a wider significance simply by virtue of their particularity. It is rather the case that precisely through the particularities of time and place, God invests the whole of history with its meaning and purpose. It was not because of their particularity as such, therefore, that the events of Jesus' life, death and resurrection were said by Paul to be a stumbling block to the Jews. It is rather the Greek mind that baulks at the suggestion that through the particularities of Jesus' history the eternal truth of God is mediated once and for all time. In like manner, the discounting of particularity evident both in the Modernist tendency 'to suppress the particular through the universal and in postmodernism's homogenizing tendency to attribute to all particulars essentially the same value', as Colin Gunton has put it,[19] undermines the proclamation of God's self-disclosure in a particular time and place, and is nothing less than the abolishing of history itself. It is on these grounds that D.F. Strauss rejects the incarnational narrative of the New Testament. He writes,

> If reality is ascribed to the idea of the unity of the divine and human natures, is this equivalent to the admission that this unity must actually have been once manifested, as it never had been, and never more will be, in one individual? This is indeed not the mode in which Idea realizes itself; it is not wont to lavish all its fulness on one exemplar, and be niggardly towards all others – to express itself perfectly in that one individual and imperfectly in all the rest. ... Is not the idea of the unity of the divine and human natures a real one in a far higher sense, when I regard the whole race of mankind as its realization, than when I single out one man as such a realization? Is not an incarnation of God from eternity, a truer one than an incarnation limited to a particular point in time?[20]

As Søren Kierkegaard would make clear very soon after the first publication of Strauss's 'examination of the life of Jesus', this dehistoricizing inclination of the Western mind is opposed by the incarnational narrative of the New Testament.[21] That narrative has its place within Israel's doctrine of election. By this doctrine, found at the very heart of Jewish faith, it is confessed that, beginning with Abraham, God works out his purpose for the world through the election of a particular people and through the actions of particular individuals. For the Christian mind, this election is finally brought to fruition in Jesus of Nazareth, called a son of Abraham by both Matthew and Luke, and so implying both that God is at work again here, and further, that through *this* offspring of Abraham the promise of blessing to all the families of the earth

19. Gunton, *The One, the Three, and the Many*, 70.

20. D.F. Strauss, *The Life of Jesus Critically Examined*, ET (Philadelphia: Fortress Press, 1972) §151.

21. See Kierkegaard's *Fragments*, published in 1844, nine years after the first appearance of Strauss's Hegelian treatise on the life of Jesus.

is finally being fulfilled.[22] It is for this reason that Karl Barth makes the doctrine of election central to his theology and places it within his discussion of the doctrine of God. The electing grace of God, fulfilled in Christ, reveals at once both who God is: the one who determines to be none other than God for us; and what history is: the medium through which God works out his promise.[23]

The christological focus of the doctrine of election in Christian thought brings us to the heart of the Christian concern with history, namely, to the story told in the Gospels of God's redemptive participation in history by which history itself, turned away from God through human sin, is reoriented to its proper goal in the kingdom of God. Robert Jenson explains, however, that the incarnation is to be seen 'not merely as remedy, but as the provision of the very conditions for participation in the divine community, according to God's intention'.[24] The point is being made that redemption, reconciliation, the fulfilment of the divine purpose – all of these – take place not without but precisely through this set of historical particularities. I side here with the view of Duns Scotus that the incarnation is not a mere expedient consequent on the fall, but the outworking of God's purpose to enter into communion with his people. In the event of incarnation, God's purpose in creation is realized; the goodness of the created order is confirmed and its suitability as the medium for the working out of God's purpose is made clear. It is for this reason that the Gospel writers take care to locate historically their accounts of the things that have taken place concerning Jesus, including, quite crucially, the resurrection.[25] If the resurrection of Jesus is not an event located in (while not confined by) time and space, then we revert once more to the non-Christian idea that the fulfilment of human life and victory over death occurs 'outside' of the created order, thus casting aspersions on the goodness of creation itself. The Christian hope, rather, is for the resurrection of the body, the salvific transformation of *all* that makes us who we are.

The course of our lives, therefore, the historicity of our existence, is not to be disparaged. It is not to be left behind when the *dis*embodied soul returns or progresses to some spiritual realm after death. This is the Gnostic error that has been repeated all too frequently in the Christian tradition. The biblical view,

22. See also Paul's discussion of the same theme in Galatians 3.15ff.

23. See Karl Barth, *Church Dogmatics* II/2 (Edinburgh: T&T Clark, 1957) 3–506.

24. I am indebted here to Jeremy Ive for his comments on Jenson's theology. See Jeremy Ive, 'Robert W. Jenson's Theology of History' in *Trinity, Time and Church: A Response to the Theology of Robert W. Jenson*, ed. Colin E. Gunton (Grand Rapids: Eerdmans, 2000) 146–57, 147.

25. Luke's resurrection narrative in particular offers a sustained polemic against those who might have argued that the resurrection of Christ was an event in the minds of believers.

in contrast, consistently held throughout Old and New Testaments, is that not merely the human soul but also the material creation along with the whole course of history, has a future. The vision of the book of Revelation of a new heaven and a new earth summarizes the hope articulated throughout the Bible that, far from treating the material world and its history as a cast-off in the process of the human soul's redemption, God's purpose is to redeem the world as a whole, to gather the whole of our history into reconciled relationship with himself and thus to see to it that every tear will be wiped from our eyes.

This is the point of the incarnational narrative. In the incarnate life of Jesus Christ, the Word of God and second person of the Trinity graces our history with his own presence, thus confirming its goodness, and showing it to be the medium through which God's loving purpose is worked out. In Jesus Christ, God's relation to the world takes the form of his becoming a subject within it. The one through whom and for whom all things were created and hold together (Col. 1.17) renews through his presence that which human sinfulness had subjected to disorder and decay and 'reconstitutes it in its relation to God'.[26]

It is through Holy Week and Easter most especially that God's love for his creation is made apparent. Through the trials of Gethsemane and his death on the cross at Calvary, the Son of God, through whom all things were created and hold together, exposes himself to the reality of this world's dissolution, drains once and for all time the cup of bitterness that has been filled to overflowing with human treachery to God, and thus ensures that not even the worst that humanity does can thwart God's purpose of communion with all that he has made. If death means the same thing as a life alienated from God, then in submitting himself to that death the Son of God, by virtue of the fact that it is he who suffers these things, robs humanity of its power to render the world Godless and saves us thus from the dread consequence of our sin. Or to put it in the language of John's prologue, the term 'Logos', used there of Christ, signifies the reason and order of the universe. He is the world's reason for being and the one who gives it its order and purpose. That this Logos, therefore, should confront on the cross humanity's tragic efforts to foist upon the world an order and purpose of its own making and to wrest from God, by crucifying his Son, the prerogative to preserve the world and guide it to its fulfilment – that Christ should confront this evil at the greatest depths to which it may sink, establishes and confirms his sovereignty at the point of humanity's most profound rebellion against it. What this means is that the world and its history is not finally in our hands but in God's. This does not

26. Colin E. Gunton, *Christ and Creation* (Carlisle: Paternoster Press, 1992) 33.

mean that we have been absolved of that responsibility for history about which we have spoken above. But it is precisely response-ability, a responsive sharing in the purposes of God. The fact is we remain capable of abusing that trust. We remain capable of making a hell out of that which has been created for good. But we are not capable of defeating the steadfastness of God's love for the world, for, even where we do our worst, God is to be found there, in the crucified figure of Jesus, gathering together in himself all things in heaven and on earth, and preparing them for that day when all things will be completed and presented to the Father.

The distinctiveness of the Christian understanding of things is readily apparent here. The kingdom of God is not yet, and disbelief has evidence upon which it can base its claims. So the faith of which we have been speaking, as also the act of redemption itself, is yet an anticipation of things hoped for. The work of Christ does restore God's project, but it requires us still to wait for and work towards something that is not yet. Such hope and work is founded, however, upon that further aspect of Christ's encounter with evil, namely his resurrection and ascension. The victory over the disorder that humanity has wrought in history is not accomplished solely through the presence within it of the Logos himself, but also through God's raising to new life the one whose faithfulness to the world had taken the form of suffering love within it. The chaotic human arraying of things is robbed thus, not only of its Godlessness, but also, and concomitantly so, of its bondage to death. The resurrection of Christ, the *first born* of a new creation, is the beginning and condition of the transformation towards fulfilment of the whole of God's creation. And Christ's ascension to sit at the right hand of the Father in glory, confirms, once and for all, this Logos and not our own as the Word by which the world will be upheld.

We referred above to the claim of Alan Richardson that by the time of Augustine the Hebraic-Christian view of history had triumphed over the classical. That triumph comes about most especially, Augustine argues, because of the resurrection of Jesus Christ. Here in the midst of history itself, the *telos* of history is decisively revealed, and creation's bondage to decay, or otherwise to endless repetition, is defeated once and for all. 'Christ, being raised from the dead, will never die again; death no longer has dominion over him' (Rom. 6.9).[27] Richardson comments,

> The Christian experience of the conquest of death through Christ's resurrection brought to an end the classical view of history. The European mind was freed by the proclamation

27. See Augustine, *City of God*, trans J. Healey (London: J.M. Dent & Son, 1945) Book XII, 13.

> of God's saving act in history from the fatalistic theory of cyclical recurrence which had condemned Greek historiography to sterility.[28]

The resurrection of Jesus is the refutation, not only of the cyclical view of history, but also of the myriad ways in which history itself is devalued. The resurrection of Jesus from the dead is God's vindication of this man and his history as the means through which participation in his coming kingdom is opened up. We may say therefore that through the death and resurrection of Christ God's action makes history. It is through the series of events that make up the life of Jesus of Nazareth that creation's destiny is secured and its meaning revealed. Here the Truth is made known. This moment, of incarnation and death, resurrection and ascension is decisive. It is not lost. It is not a vanishing point of no eternal significance, but is the event in the midst of history that secures the fulfilment of God's promise and brings creation to its goal.

Without any such *telos* it is difficult to imagine what sense there could be in the unfolding of historical life. It could be, presumably, only a sense of our own making and not one that inheres in the events themselves. It is the theological framework of creation and promise, then, that provides a conceptual grounding for the meaningfulness of human life. Apart from these conditions the idea of a purpose in history, and thus of the historic character of human action, must be either abandoned or contrived.

This, it seems to me, reveals the plight of that form of biblical scholarship that we have seen represented in the Jesus Seminar. Rejecting the New Testament proclamation that God is working his purpose out in Christ, and rejecting thus the incarnational narrative which is intelligible only within such a view of history, the scholars have only a few scraps of data left. The task of understanding 'who Jesus really was' then becomes, very nearly, a feat of *creatio ex nihilo*, a kind of miracle, one might suggest, in which the power in which we are invited to trust is not that of the Holy Spirit, as the narrative itself commends, but of the biblical scholars themselves.

IV — History and Hermeneutics Revisited

We have traced the reasons for and the character of a fundamental resistance in the Western intellectual heritage to the historical mediation of truth and salvation. Identified by Christian theology as the scandal of particularity, this resistance takes offence at the proclamation of Christ crucified and raised from

28. Richardson, *History Sacred and Profane*, 60.

the dead as the decisive action of God in bringing about the reconciliation of the world with himself. The rejection of this historical mediation of truth and salvation has its roots, we have argued, in the devaluation of the realm of space and time in Greek thought, and has been allowed to flourish in the Christian theological tradition because of the neglect of the doctrine of creation. The soteriological consequence of this rejection of history is that, forsaking dependence upon what has taken place in Jesus, the individual finds within the self the resources of wisdom and insight to work out his or her own salvation. Our project has been to offer an alternative conception of what history is, a conception drawn from the Bible itself. I offer now, by way of conclusion to this chapter, an indication of how this biblical conception of history might impact upon the task of biblical hermeneutics.

1. The first point is straightforward: There is no good reason to decide as a presupposition of biblical hermeneutics that God is not involved in history. To do so is to set the biblical writings in a conceptual framework that is alien to them, and will, very likely, preclude our understanding them aright.

2. Just because the books of the Bible are theological documents does not mean that they are not also history. The only justification for such a claim would rest on God's certainly not being involved in history. If, on the other hand, God is involved in history, that would mean that there cannot be history without theology. History and theology, therefore, are not mutually exclusive by definition.

3. If God is active in history, guiding his people and bringing about his purpose of reconciliation with him, then it is reasonable to suppose that God is also involved in our apprehension of the events through which this purpose is worked out. Primarily, this means that God is involved in our understanding of Scripture. It is, at the very least, therefore, a regrettable impoverishment of that understanding, if not a falsification of Scripture itself, if we undertake to read while trusting in our own resources alone. We ought instead, to claim the promise that Christ will send the Holy Spirit to bear witness to himself and to guide us into all Truth.

4. Because the Spirit is a gift, not to individuals, but to a people gathered by God into the community of faith, the interpretation of Scripture under the guidance of God's Spirit is not primarily the task of individual scholars undertaken in the privacy of their own studies. First and foremost, it is the task of the Church in public acts of witness and worship. Biblical scholarship is done properly when it is put in service of that task.

5. The Church is a body extended through space and time. Every local gathering of the Church is bound in fellowship with the communion of saints. The apostolic witness, therefore, for all that it has been shaped by the cultural conditions of the first century, is not something from which we are separated by a 'broad ugly ditch'. The apostles

are not citizens of a world that we moderns no longer inhabit. They are part of the one community that is called into being and continues to be shaped by God to bear witness to the working out of his purpose. That christocentric and pneumatological reality overrides what differences there certainly are between Jew and Greek, male and female, ancient and modern, and thus enables the Spirit-inspired speech of the apostles to be heard 'in our own language'.

6. Because the central theme of the Bible is the action of God through history culminating in the life, death, resurrection and ascension of Jesus, then Jesus himself must be understood as the hermeneutical key to the biblical canon as a whole. The Bible is not to be treated as a disparate collection of texts with no intrinsic unity, but constitutes rather a consistent and coherent witness to Christ. To be sure, Christ is not explicitly known to the writers of the Hebrew Scriptures, but neither is he unknown. He is present rather as the Word of God throughout Israel's history, and shines his light backwards, as it were, when in incarnate form he makes himself known as the one to whom those Scriptures point.

7. Because Christian faith depends for its very essence and truth upon certain things that have taken place in history, that faith is not reducible to a set of abstract propositions recognized as necessarily true by the power of human reason. The truth with which we are concerned in Christianity, and which is proclaimed in the biblical writings, is contingent truth. It is simply not amenable, therefore, to the kinds of epistemic procedure that require an indubitable warrant for all truth claims. But then, very little of the truth we are most concerned with as human beings does fit that particular straitjacket. It is not for that reason untrue. This means for biblical hermeneutics that we should not be constrained by the demand for absolute certainty. Some things may be taken on trust, not because we have proven them beyond all doubt, but because they fit with what else we have learned of God's gracious accommodation to our human incapacity. That does not mean that we cannot know what took place in and through Jesus; it means, rather, that we know in part. That is a suitable kind of knowledge for human life, and is enough to be going on with until that day when we shall see face to face.

It is probable that these hermeneutical considerations will not satisfy those who are determined to read Scripture within the limits of historical-critical method alone. Be that as it may. I have tried to show what is involved in reading Scripture on its own terms, while at the same time arguing that there is no good reason why those terms should not also be our own.

4
Resurrection

In his account of the limitations of historical-critical method for understanding who Jesus is, Francis Watson writes that,

> Even Christian historians who at a personal level accept that Jesus is the Christ, will be subject to the constraints of this methodologically atheistic worldview – unless they are prepared to rethink what 'history' is, on the basis of theology.[1]

Rethinking what history is, on the basis of theology, was the task begun in Chapter 2, in which it was argued that the biblical notions of creation and promise provide the foundations of a theological conception of history. In the present chapter that theology of history will be brought to sharper focus by attending to the resurrection of Jesus Christ, the one who is the firstborn of a new creation, and in whom, as such, God's purpose for the whole creation is inaugurated and its fulfilment anticipated. I hope to contribute by this endeavour to what Watson calls 'a theologically informed approach to the "historical Jesus" that operates *within* the ideological perspective of the gospels, according to which Jesus is the Christ, the final meaning of history'.[2]

I want to explore two theses in this chapter. The first is that the resurrection is the key to understanding 'the Jesus of history'. The second is that the resurrection of Jesus reveals his history to be the key to the interpretation of history as a whole, bringing to fulfilment the Old Testament promise that through the descendants of Abraham all the families of the earth will be blessed, and inaugurating the new creation in which all things will be reconciled with God. In elaboration of these two themes, we shall also have to consider what kind of event the resurrection is and how it can be known.

1. Francis Watson, 'The Quest for the Real Jesus' in Markus Bockmuehl, ed., *The Cambridge Companion to Jesus* (Cambridge: Cambridge University Press, 2001) 156–69, 164.

2. Watson, 'The Quest for the Real Jesus', 164.

I — The History of Jesus

It is a common observation among biblical scholars that the New Testament is written from the perspective of those who believe that this Jesus who was crucified is no longer dead but has been raised by God. C.F. Evans thus writes,

> Of the synoptic gospels it would not be sufficient to say simply that they conclude with resurrection narratives, for it is only in the light of faith in the risen Lord that they were written at all...[3]

That observation is so far uncontroversial, but the implications of the observation do not remain so. What is to be made of this faith in the risen Lord? Does it render the reports of the evangelists unreliable, as is commonly alleged? Does such faith shift the balance of the Gospel accounts away from historical narrative and toward the genre of myth as Strauss, Bultmann and their like have argued? Do the Gospels reveal, therefore, a great deal about the religious convictions and interests of the early Church, and very little about Jesus himself as has sometimes been alleged in the recent history of biblical scholarship?[4] Pursuit of one or more of these suppositions has been widespread among scholars during the past two hundred years, or, more precisely, ever since Hermann Samuel Reimarus in the early eighteenth century first argued that stories of the resurrection were fabricated by the disappointed disciples who had given up all to follow Jesus in the expectation of worldly wealth and power. After the ignominious failure of Jesus' death, so Reimarus contends, the disciples sought to bring about the fulfilment of this expectation as best they could by fabricating the story of Jesus' resurrection.[5] The 'fictitious invention' of the resurrection legend, Reimarus further explains, continued with the evangelists who rewrote the history of Jesus and presented his whole life as a passage to this triumphant end. Although the efforts of historians and biblical interpreters willing to accept Reimarus' discounting of the resurrection have not produced any consistent picture of the Jesus 'behind' the text, it remains a widely accepted axiom of biblical interpretation that the 'bias' of resurrection

3. C.F. Evans, *Resurrection and the New Testament* (London: SCM Press, 1970) 4.

4. Donald L. Denton, Jr credits Strauss with 'shifting the focus in Jesus studies from the event narrated in the Gospels, to the account itself'. See Denton, *Historiography and Hermeneutics in Jesus Studies: An Examination of the Work of John Dominic Crossan and Ben F. Meyer*, JSNT Supplement 262 (London: T&T Clark, 2004) 103.

5. See discussion of Reimarus in Chapter 1 above, and for the point here see Reimarus, 'Concerning the Intention of Jesus and His Teaching', Part II §53, 242.

faith must be put to one side.[6] Even some Christian scholars who believe in the resurrection have been intimidated by such an axiom and have felt obliged to 'concede' the impact of resurrection faith upon the writings of the New Testament. Christopher Tuckett, for instance, writes:

> Virtually all the evidence we have has been preserved by Christians, all of whom clearly regarded Jesus in a positive light. That in turn makes for its own peculiar difficulties in handling the evidence, above all because it is potentially influenced by Christians' belief that the Jesus about whom they wrote had in some real sense been raised from death by God and was now alive in their present.[7]

Tuckett goes on to admit that 'accounts of Jesus by others may be equally affected by their authors' beliefs and attitudes!'[8] but by this time the aspersions have been cast – resurrection faith renders the evidence of the Gospels problematic in one way or another. Erosion of confidence in the historical value of the biblical testimony is apparent too in Amos Wilder's admission that, 'we concede that the picture of Jesus given to us in all four Gospels was shaped by the early resurrection faith rather than by an objective historical interest as *we* understand that'.[9] Wilder's words were formulated almost fifty years ago at a time when there was less awareness of the problematic nature of the claim to objectivity, and yet, as evidenced by Tuckett above, who is far from a thoroughgoing sceptic, the assumption remains widespread that belief in the resurrection gets in the way of a true account of the history of Jesus as it really was. It is clear enough, of course, that if the resurrection didn't happen, or if the accounts of the resurrection do not refer to something that happened to Jesus but describe, rather, a transformation in the minds of the first disciples, then the Gospels do falsify the history of Jesus. Wolfhart Pannenberg is correct in noting that 'only because of the resurrection of Jesus were the Synoptics able

6. Robert Funk and Roy Hoover, for example, speaking on behalf of 'The Jesus Seminar', consider it a 'rule of evidence' that the evangelists 'christianized' Jesus by making him conform to what they later came to believe. See *The Five Gospels*, 24–5. The 'rule' is used to deny the authenticity of any sayings placed on Jesus' lips which sound too much like what a Christian believes, and thus to uncover the real Jesus 'behind the Christian façade of the Christ' (2).

7. Christopher Tuckett, 'Sources and Methods' in Markus Bockmuehl, ed., *The Cambridge Companion to Jesus* (Cambridge: Cambridge University Press, 2001) 121–37, 122–3.

8. Tuckett, 'Sources and Methods', 123.

9. Amos N. Wilder, *Otherworldliness and the New Testament* (London: SCM Press, 1955) 80. Gerd Theissen similarly expresses the desire to 'get behind the Christian images of Jesus shaped by Easter and find the historical reality before Easter'. Gerd Theissen, 'Historical Scepticism and the Criteria of Jesus Research or My Attempt to Leap Across Lessing's Yawning Gulf', *Scottish Journal of Theology* 49.4 (1996) 147–76, 162.

to describe his earthly cause to be the cause of the Messiah or of the Son of Man'.[10] Without the resurrection, therefore, the theological claims of the Gospels must be discounted. The faith of the evangelists is in vain.

The alternative view, and the one I propose to explore here, is that far from falsifying the history of Jesus, the resurrection is that which enables us to see the history of Jesus aright. The resurrection is the light shone backwards on the career of Jesus that makes sense and reveals the truth of the whole. The principle at work here is evident in the claim of John 12.16: 'His disciples did not understand these things at first; but when Jesus was glorified, then they remembered that these things had been written of him and had been done to him.' Or, as the principle has been put more recently by Gerald Downing, 'It is only in the light of what happens next that you can hope to understand and explain what has been happening.'[11] Thus, according to Graham Stanton, the first followers of Jesus believed that 'only in the light both of Resurrection faith and of the gift of the Spirit was it possible to understand the full significance of the story of Jesus'.[12] The real Jesus of history, in other words, is to be sought and understood not apart from or behind but precisely through the testimonies of those who believe him to have been raised from the dead. Martin Kähler is in this respect correct: the real Christ *is* the preached Christ. It was the resurrection, Kähler argues, 'that first placed this earthly life in its proper perspective and gave it its implicit and appropriate content'.[13] The true content and import of the beginning and middle of the history of Jesus is disclosed through what happens at the end.[14]

But here we come to a difficulty. Is what is claimed about Jesus at the end itself true? Was Jesus raised from the dead? According to the view of history that has prevailed in Western thought, namely that history is a closed causal continuum impenetrable to the action of God, the resurrection is simply an impossibility – we *know* that dead men do not rise! The matter has been put

10. Wolfhart Pannenberg, 'Did Jesus Really Rise from the Dead?' *Dialog* (Spring 1965), reprinted in Richard Batey, ed., *New Testament Issues* (London: SCM Press, 1970) 102–17, 103.

11. F. Gerald Downing, *Cynics and Christian Origins* (Edinburgh: T&T Clark, 1992) 167. Cited in N.T. Wright, *Jesus and the Victory of God* (London: SPCK, 1996) 109n.

12. Stanton, *The Gospels and Jesus*, 299.

13. Martin Kähler, *The So-called Historical Jesus and the Historic, Biblical Christ*. Cited in Daniel P. Fuller, *Easter Faith and History* (London: Tyndale Press, 1968) 70.

14. This principle has recently been expounded by David C. Steinmetz in 'Uncovering a Second Narrative: Detective Fiction and the Construction of Historical Method' in Ellen F. Davis and Richard B. Hays, eds., *The Art of Reading Scripture* (Grand Rapids: Eerdmans, 2003) 54–65. Drawing an analogy between the reading of Scripture and the reading of a mystery or detective novel, Steinmetz suggests that the plots of both are understood aright only in the light of 'how things turn out'.

this way not only by incredulous historians but by theologians too. Rudolf Bultmann, to take only the most influential example, asserts that 'An historical fact which involves a resurrection from the dead is utterly inconceivable.'[15] But the question we have been exploring in this book is whether the prevailing Western view of history is adequate to the task of perceiving what took place in Jesus. Might it not be that what happened through and to Jesus requires a transformation of what we suppose is possible in this world? Such transformations are not unprecedented. Who would have supposed one hundred years ago, for instance, that one could see and talk to people in real time on the other side of the globe? Satellite technology has transformed our conceptions of what is possible in the world. The resurrection, similarly, brings about a new understanding of the way reality is constituted. If this is true, then the old paradigms of historical and scientific enquiry will be inadequate for the task of apprehending this reality. 'Seeing' the resurrection, therefore, is not possible within the prevailing canons of historical-critical enquiry, not, as we shall argue, because the resurrection is not an historical event, but rather because history itself has been misconceived by historians as a causal series from which God is necessarily excluded. In attempting to see history apart from the Creator and Lord of history, historians fail in important ways to see it all.[16] Within such constraints, it is true that dead men don't rise, just as it is also true that with the most powerful set of binoculars and a state of the art megaphone, I cannot converse with my friends on the other side of the world.

At this point, however, we must leave the analogy to one side. For, unlike the marvels of global communication, one's apprehension of the resurrection is not brought about by human ingenuity or by better procedural tools. The transformation in our 'seeing' takes place, rather, under the impact of the new reality itself, the reality of the risen Christ. It was Jesus' appearance to the disciples – not human testimony,[17] nor their own investigative efforts at the empty tomb[18] – that convinced them that he was alive. For the disciples in

15. Bultmann, 'New Testament and Mythology', 39.

16. I have adapted here the contention of Colin Gunton that 'in attempting to see creation apart from the Creator [Modern thinkers] fail in important ways to see it all'. Gunton, *The One, the Three and the Many*, 216.

17. See Luke 24.11, 'But these words [of the women] seemed to them an idle tale, and they did not believe them.' Compare Luke 24.21–5.

18. When Peter went to the empty tomb, he saw the linen cloths by themselves and, while this amazed him, he apparently did not yet believe. Instead, he simply went home! (Luke 24.12). John's Gospel offers a more ambiguous account of the disciples' visit to the empty tomb. At 20:8 we read, 'Then the other disciple, who reached the tomb first, also went in, and he saw and believed'. It is not clear what he believed, however, for we then read, 'for as yet they did not understand the scripture, that he must rise from the dead'. Did he believe, simply, that the tomb was indeed

Jerusalem and in Galilee, according to the gospel record, the appearances involved the bodily presence of Jesus, while for Paul on the road to Damascus the appearance took the form of a vision. In both cases, however, encounter with the risen Lord brought about the conversion of minds and hearts that is integral to one's apprehension of the resurrection itself. Such appearances could not be accounted for within any conception of history that the disciples had hitherto understood. That is why the women's testimony was not believed. It is the resurrection itself, revealed in and through the appearance of the risen Christ, that prompted in the disciples a new way of seeing and a new way of understanding what history really is – the terrain in which God's redemptive and re-creative purposes for the world are being worked out. Conversion to this new way of seeing cannot be engineered, nor contrived. It is made possible rather by grace, and is dependent upon the self-disclosure of the risen Christ himself. If an analogy from quotidian experience is needed, it is like learning that one is loved. That experience too has an epistemic dimension, but it yields knowledge that is not accessible to or verifiable within the usual canons of scientific or purportedly objective enquiry. I do not deny here the value of scientific enquiry, but rather its omnicompetence. The same is true of historical-critical investigation into the testimonies of the Bible. It is not that such investigation yields nothing of value – far from it,[19] but in the case of the resurrection, there is much more to the reality than can be revealed through historical enquiry alone.

So far I have simply offered a general statement of the position I am arguing. It is time now to support the position with some more detailed argument.

II — The Event of the Resurrection

It is necessary to consider, in speaking of the resurrection, what kind of event it was. Theologians of the modern era have been deeply divided on this matter. In a recent essay Carl Braaten suggests that 'the easiest way to characterize the debate is by using two familiar words: history and eschatology'.[20] Braaten explains that,

empty as Mary Magdalene had said? The words that follow suggest that this is not yet equivalent to the belief that Jesus had been raised.

19. There is a great deal of value for instance in the historical-critical work of N.T. Wright in his recent volume, *The Resurrection of the Son of God* (London: SPCK, 2003). Wright does not suppose, indeed, despite criticisms made earlier of some aspects of his methodology, he argues against the view that historical enquiry and the claims of faith are necessarily exclusive of one another.

20. Carl E. Braaten, 'The Reality of the Resurrection' in Christopher R. Seitz, ed., *Nicene Christianity: The Future for a New Ecumenism* (Grand Rapids: Brazos Press, 2001) 107–18, 111.

> [o]ne side of the debate will urge that the resurrection is indeed a historical event. The name of Wolfhart Pannenberg is typically associated with this position. The other side speaks of the resurrection as an eschatological event. Karl Barth and Rudolf Bultmann, as different as their positions finally came to be developed, are often attached to this eschatological view.[21]

There is a further division, however, between those who hold the resurrection to be an historical event apprehensible through historical-critical enquiry, and by those who claim it as an historical event but argue that it may be known only through faith. Braaten offers Pannenberg as a representative of the first view, and Walter Künneth as representative of the second. While this is somewhat misleading in respect of Künneth's view, this need not concern us here.[22] My interest rather is in Pannenberg who for his part insists that, 'whether or not a particular event happened two thousand years ago is not made certain by faith but only by historical research, to the extent that certainty can be attained at all about questions of this kind'. And further: 'The only method of achieving at least approximate certainty with regard to the events of a past time is historical research.'[23] While, for the first disciples the apprehension of the resurrection was contingent upon their being encountered by the risen Christ himself, for us, apparently, it is not. As we saw in Chapter 2, the tools of historical enquiry are deemed by Pannenberg to be adequate to the task. As it turns out, however, Pannenberg's own faith commitments are as evident in his enquiries as are the a-theological faith commitments of secular historians in theirs.[24] Pannenberg recognizes, for example, that 'the possibilities [the historian] can consider... will depend upon the understanding of reality that [s]he brings with [her/]him to the task'.[25] But this is precisely the problem. The 'understanding of reality' represented in the historiography we have surveyed in Chapter 1, and which dominates both historical and biblical studies, deems the resurrection an impossibility. Only a theological understanding of reality, such as I have offered in Chapter 3, and which is itself formed in the light of the events with which we are concerned, affords understanding of those same events. Both cases, however, involve commitments of faith. When Pannenberg

21. Braaten, 'The Reality of the Resurrection', 111.

22. Künneth takes pains at the beginning of his book to stress 'the untenability of the thesis of the "historicality" of the resurrection of Jesus'. Walter Künneth, *The Theology of the Resurrection*, trans. James W. Leitch (London: SCM Press, 1965) 29–33.

23. Pannenberg, *Jesus – God and Man*, 99.

24. Stephen Davis has recently noted that 'The modern study of history requires a methodological commitment to atheism or at least some version of deism.' Stephen T. Davis, *Risen Indeed: Making Sense of the Resurrection* (Grand Rapids: Eerdmans, 1993) 29.

25. Pannenberg, *Jesus – God and Man*, 97.

requests, therefore, 'that an element of truth be granted to the apocalyptic expectation with regard to the hope of resurrection',[26] he is asking that one faith commitment be adopted, and another one relinquished. There is simply no way to exclude faith altogether.

On the other side of the debate cited by Braaten above, are those who deny that the resurrection is an historical event at all. The resurrection is not an historical but rather an eschatological event, and belongs as such above and beyond the realm of historical investigation. The two representatives of this view referred to by Braaten offer rather different accounts of what this means. Rudolf Bultmann, on the one hand, describes the resurrection as an eschatological event and means by this that nothing, as such, happened three days after Jesus' crucifixion. Instead, as we saw in Chapter 2, the resurrection is considered by Bultmann to be an interpretation of the significance of the cross itself, 'as annihilating death's power in general'. 'Faith in the resurrection is really the same thing as faith in the saving efficacy of the cross.'[27] The resurrection is not, therefore, something that happened to Jesus, but something that happens in the minds of those who accept and participate in the new existential situation brought about by Jesus' death. It is not therefore a proper object of historical investigation, for it is not properly thought of as an event that happened in the past.

Karl Barth, on the other hand, also proclaims that the resurrection is not an historical event but means by this that it is not an event that is accessible to historical enquiry. This is closer to my own view, but I am not willing to concede that the resurrection cannot therefore be called historical. My argument, rather, is that we need a more generous account of what is historical. Historical events are those that take place in space and time – on the third day after the crucifixion, for instance, and, in and around Jerusalem and Galilee. There are no grounds to suppose that God could not be the cause of such events, although it is true, as Barth recognizes, that God's involvement would render them inaccessible to any form of historical enquiry that refuses to countenance that God is active in the world.[28] Barth contends, indeed, that

> it is sheer superstition to suppose that only things that are open to 'historical' verification can have happened in time. There may have been events which happened far more

26. Pannenberg, *Jesus – God and Man*, 97–8.

27. Bultmann, 'New Testament and Mythology', 41.

28. Thus Barth writes, 'We may well accept as history that which good taste prevents us from calling "'historical' fact", and which the modern historian will call "saga" or "legend" on the ground that it is beyond the reach of his methods, to say nothing of his unavowed assumptions.' Karl Barth, *Church Dogmatics* III/2, 446.

> really in time than the kinds of things Bultmann's scientific historian can prove. There are good grounds for supposing that the history of the resurrection of Jesus is a pre-eminent instance of such an event.[29]

I differ from Barth here, only in being unwilling to concede to the superstitious historians exclusive title to the term historical. I want historical to mean what it properly means, namely, that which has taken place within the created order, while acknowledging also that the created order belongs to God and is in process of being redeemed and perfected by God. The resurrection, along with the whole career of Jesus, is on this account a transformative event, an event, that is to say, through which God's redemptive and perfecting work is done, and in the light of which our understanding of history is transformed. This is also the sense in which the historical event of the resurrection is an eschatological event. The eschatological reality of the created order, perfected and made new, is made present in the midst of history as a foretaste of what is to come. It is for this reason that Jesus is spoken of as the firstborn of creation and the firstborn from the dead (Col. 1.15, 18). His perfection and life with God is the *telos* of creation as a whole. That *telos* is articulated in the further claim of Colossians 1 that 'through him God was pleased to reconcile to himself all things, whether on earth or in heaven' (Col. 1.20).

To make this claim, however – and this is where the point is right that the resurrection is not apprehensible just like any other event in history – is to recognize that the resurrection bursts the bounds of the present order. That the risen Jesus walks through locked doors and mysteriously appears and disappears, might suggest a mythical embellishment of the stories of his appearances to the disciples, but it might be, instead, a portent of the new heavens and a new earth in which the old order has passed away and all things are made new. We are not presently in a position to conceive that adequately, as Paul makes clear in 1 Corinthians 15, and so we should not insist, therefore, upon construing the new reality of Christ's resurrection body within the conceptual resources of the old order. The best Paul can do is to offer suggestive but nevertheless inadequate metaphors of the transformation wrought in the making of all things new. He confesses, however, that he speaks of a mystery to be revealed in its fullness only when the last trumpet shall sound.

It is therefore not wrong to say, as do Barth and others, that the resurrection is not an historical event if by that it is meant that the resurrection is an event of the new order rather than the old, but in my view, this statement on its own gives inadequate recognition to the tangibility of Christ's presence as he walked on the road to Emmaus, and showed Thomas his wounds, and ate fish on the

29. Barth, *CD* III/2, 446.

lake shore in Galilee. Somehow in the resurrection of Jesus, the new order intersects with the old, so that the creation as it is presently configured cannot any longer be thought to exclude the transforming presence of God. Creation, that is to say, and history along with it, isn't quite what we thought it was, where 'we' here means the citizens of the modern, Western world. The tapestry of space and time is open-textured. The creator continues his work with it, weaving in the threads of new life so that at the last we will see the creation brought to its full perfection and the glory of the Lord revealed.

This means that Barth doesn't get at the whole truth by asserting that the resurrection is not an historical but an eschatological event, while Pannenberg, on the other hand, obscures the transformative character of the resurrection in insisting that it be investigated with the resources of the old order alone. The threads of the old order do not remain unmoved by this irruption of the new order – the stone is rolled away, the tomb is left empty and there is indeed someone present with the disciples in the room – but these threads do not disclose their meaning in and of themselves, not even within the broader context of Israel's apocalyptic hope.[30] Flesh and blood can apprehend these alterations to the fabric of the old order – it can run to the tomb and see – but the revealing of the Truth here is in the Father's gift, the gift we otherwise know as the Holy Spirit of God.

The question of the historicity of the resurrection has been the subject of recent debate between Pannenberg and Jürgen Moltmann. Pannenberg, on the one hand, insists on the historicity of the resurrection – it is a spatio-temporal event – whereas Moltmann, in *The Way of Jesus Christ*, contends that 'Anyone who describes Christ's resurrection as "historical", in just the same way as his death on the cross, is overlooking the new creation with which the resurrection begins, and is falling short of the eschatological hope.'[31] Moltmann is right that the resurrection is an event of the new order, and this means, against Pannenberg, that it eludes the grasp of historical-critical enquiry as it is presently undertaken. In Pannenberg's favour, however, the resurrection is correctly described as historical, but only under a new *theological* description of what history is. Pannenberg comes close to recognizing this when he writes,

> In the case of the resurrection of Jesus, all Christians must realize that the facticity of the event will be contested right up till the eschatological consummation of the world because its uniqueness transcends an understanding of reality that is oriented only to the

30. Recall here the Barthian claim adduced in Chapter 2: 'Revelation is not a predicate of history, but history is a predicate of revelation.'

31. Jürgen Moltmann, *The Way of Jesus Christ: Christology in Messianic Dimensions*, trans. Margaret Kohl (London: SCM Press, 1990) 214.

> passing world and because the new reality that has come in the resurrection of Jesus has not yet universally and definitively manifested itself.[32]

Exactly! But this means, as Pannenberg does not himself appear to see, that a new description of history, and thus a new historiography is required, precisely on the basis of the resurrection itself. The old historiography, formulated by Ernst Troeltsch, and espoused still by many historical critics, is on this account inadequate to the reality of history itself.

Let me re-gather the argument as I have developed it so far. We began by recalling the observation commonly made that the New Testament record of Jesus' earthly career is profoundly shaped by its authors' belief that Jesus was raised from the dead. We then considered the claim that this renders the Gospel records an unreliable source for the understanding of who Jesus really was [*sic*]. This matter has not been resolved yet, but by offering, as we have, an account of what kind of event the resurrection is, we are better placed now to consider whether it is true that resurrection faith obscures the figure of Jesus as he really was.

The claim that the true story of Jesus is the prerogative of historians to tell, rests upon the supposition that they know best what history really is, and that they have the appropriate tools to uncover what has happened in the past. The tools of historical-critical enquiry, however, such as were laid out by Troeltsch, presume concerning the past – presume, but cannot show – that God was not involved. Thus, the claim that resurrection faith falsifies the story of Jesus is not itself an historical-critical judgement but merely a reiteration of the presumption that the story of history can be told without reference to God. That is why Barth abandons the tools of history and has recourse to theology instead, and it is also why Pannenberg's reliance on these tools of historical enquiry simply will not do. What is needed rather is a reconsideration of the nature of history itself, and, in the first instance, an openness to the possibility that history is not a tightly woven causal continuum that is exclusive by definition of the operations of God. That in turn would allow for the possibility that the Jesus of history, rather than the historians' Jesus, *is* the Christ of faith. Such openness would mean further that the Gospel accounts of Jesus, shaped as they are by resurrection faith, are legitimately to be reckoned with as witness to the truth. Such openness is encouraged by Richard Niebuhr who asks, 'Might not the standpoint of the Christian community afford insight into the structure of concrete historical reality equal to, or even superior to, that given by the natural sciences?'[33]

32. See Pannenberg, *Systematic Theology*, vol. ii, 360–1.

33. Richard R. Niebuhr, *Resurrection and Historical Reason: A Study of Theological Method* (New York: Charles Scribner's Sons, 1957) 117.

It remains possible, of course, that belief in the resurrection is mistaken and the perspective of the Gospel writers does indeed mislead. Then it would be true, as Paul says, that Christian faith is in vain. My plea simply is that we recognize clearly what is at stake here. The resurrection, indeed the whole life of Jesus, cannot be examined as just another configuration of historical data in a world that otherwise remains unchanged. Francis Watson puts it thus: 'The life of Jesus is not a piece of history like any other, for this life, uniquely, is the act of God…'.[34] And further, 'this is not one historical event among others but the particular history in which the goal and meaning of history is disclosed'.[35] The resurrection, on this account, is believed in or not as the inauguration of a newly ordered world – call it eschatological if you will – and as a reconfiguration of history itself under the impact of the redemptive and re-creative love of God. That is the claim to be examined, and not the question whether the resurrection can be found credible within a worldview determined by the presumption that God cannot be involved. We already know that the answer to the latter question is No!

III — The Jesus of History is the Christ of Faith

It is the resurrection in particular, that confirms the history of Jesus – his conception and birth, his ministry, his death, his resurrection and ascension – as the τέλος and turning-point of the world, and it is in the light of the resurrection therefore – retrospectively, that is to say – that the story of Jesus of Nazareth is told. As we have noted, however, this perspective of the New Testament writers is taken sometimes as a reason to doubt the veracity of their reports. The New Testament writers present the 'Christ of faith', it is claimed, whereas historians set out to recover from behind the distorting and falsifying testimony of faith the 'Jesus of history' as he really was.[36] The alternative view – that of Christian faith – is that it is precisely in the light of the resurrection, and not otherwise, that the truth of Jesus' history may be told. Here it is that

34. Francis Watson, 'The Quest for the Real Jesus' in Markus Bockmuehl, ed., *The Cambridge Companion to Jesus* (Cambridge: Cambridge University Press, 2001) 156–69, 160.

35. Watson, 'The Quest for the Real Jesus', 165.

36. Graham Stanton explains in relation to this development that the Gospels 'were said to be so strongly stamped with the Easter faith of the early church that their value for the student of the life and teaching of Jesus was strictly limited.' See Graham Stanton, *The Gospels and Jesus*, 2nd ed (Oxford: Oxford University Press, 2002) 27. Stanton later reflects that while the Gospels certainly are shaped by the Easter faith, 'there is no need to insist that the early church was not interested in setting out the "past" of the life of Jesus' (29).

Wolfhart Pannenberg's work has been most helpful, not in supposing that the resurrection itself may be established by historical enquiry, but in explaining that the resurrection is the decisive clue to the understanding of who Jesus is. This does not simply mean, however, that the resurrection reveals what was true of Jesus anyway; the resurrection is itself constitutive of Jesus as the Messiah – constitutive of Jesus as the one in and through whom God brings about his new creation. Without the resurrection Jesus would not be this one, even were every other aspect of his career the same. Thus, says Pannenberg,

> The Easter event certainly shed a new light on the death of Jesus, on his earthly ministry, and therefore on his person. But that does not mean that even without the event of the resurrection these would have been what they are when seen in its light. We depreciate the Easter event if we construe it only as a disclosure or revelation of the meaning that the crucifixion and the earthly history of Jesus already had in themselves. Only the Easter event determines what the meaning was of the pre-Easter history of Jesus and who he was in relation to God.[37]

This means, crucially for New Testament interpretation, and especially so for the so-called 'quest of the historical Jesus', that we cannot decide upon who Jesus is simply on the basis of his career up to the point of his death and burial. If the resurrection merely *reveals* who Jesus is rather than belonging to the essence of who he is, then his reality as Messiah, as prophet, as teacher, or even as the only-begotten Son of God who is of one being with the Father, would remain the same even were he not raised. That would entail, in turn, that the truth of Jesus could be told without reference to the resurrection. It is precisely this assumption, however, and not resurrection faith, that obscures the reality of Jesus himself. Here again Pannenberg is right: Only in the light of the resurrection can it be seen that 'the kingly rule of the Father was indeed present in Jesus'. Pannenberg explains:

> The divine confirmation of Jesus in the Easter event extends also to his earthly ministry and on this basis to his proclamation of the divine rule and of its coming with himself. The implied claim of Jesus for his own person – namely, that the future of God is present in and by him – no longer seems to be human arrogance in the light of the Easter event. The resurrection of Jesus now gives confirmation that already in his earthly ministry he acted on the Father's authority, so that the kingly rule of the Father was indeed present in him.[38]

37. Pannenberg, *Systematic Theology*, vol. ii, 345.

38. Pannenberg, *Systematic Theology*, vol. ii, 365. Despite Pannenberg's attempt to justify it, it seems to me to be misleading rather than helpful to say, as he continues to do immediately after the cited passage, that Jesus is 'instituted' into sonship by the resurrection. The adoptionist overtones are not removed by Pannenberg's claim that the institution has retroactive force.

Here we see again the principle adduced earlier: it is in the light of what happens at the end that the true nature and content of the Gospels' story is revealed. Here, fundamentally, is why any hermeneutic of the New Testament and any quest for the real Jesus, that does not begin with the resurrection, is bound to fail in its goal of discovering the truth of who Jesus was and is.

IV — The Resurrection as Centre and Goal of History

The centrality of the resurrection to Christian faith is famously remarked upon by the apostle Paul: 'If Christ has not been raised, your faith is futile' (1 Cor. 15.17). But the resurrection is not simply the centre of Christian faith; it is also the centre and the goal of creation and thus of history itself. It is in this sense that the resurrection of the crucified one is an eschatological event. The new life to which creation is directed and which was intended by God from the beginning is made present in Christ. The *telos* of history is manifest in the midst of time. As we have put the matter in Chapter 3, the resurrection of the crucified Christ is the beginning and the condition of the transformation towards fulfilment of the whole of God's creation. To put it in Pauline language, Jesus Christ is both the one in and through whom all things are created and now also the firstborn from the dead (Col. 1.16, 18). Through him God reveals his plan for the fullness of time (Eph. 1.10). 'The fullness of time' is an expression designating both the end of history and the gathering up of all time into the purpose of God. It refers to the *telos* of history as a whole. The resurrection, on this view, 'signals in advance the end of the story'.[39] All of this is illuminated by seeing it against the background of Jewish eschatological belief. According to Christopher Tuckett, 'many Jews believed that the events of the end-time would include the resurrection of the dead'. Thus, Tuckett further explains, 'any claims that the events of Easter were a "resurrection" carried with them the implicit claim that the events of the end-time had already started. (This is indeed Paul's argument in 1 Corinthians 15.20ff.)'[40] As Jean Daniélou has put it in his book, *The Lord of History*:

39. I take the expression from Watson, *Text, Church, and World*, 291.

40. Christopher Tuckett, *Reading the New Testament: Methods of Interpretation* (London: SPCK, 1987) 46. See also Veselin Kesich, who writes, 'The message of Easter is that the end is already here, the Messiah has come. The new humanity has been inaugurated with his coming and resurrection.' Veselin Kesich, *The First Day of the New Creation: The Resurrection and the Christian Faith* (Crestwood, NY: St Vladimir's Seminary Press, 1982) 37.

> He [Jesus Christ] is the culmination of the Old Testament, but also the First-born of the new creature; not only ἀρχή and τέλος, alpha and omega, but also, from another point of view, the τέλος—ἀρχη, the end of one world and beginning of another, the turning point of history. This pattern is another of the distinguishing marks of a Christian theology of history. It is prefigured in the story of Noah, who represents both the judgement and destruction of the old world and the inauguration of a new. It is finally worked out in the mystery of the passion and resurrection of Jesus Christ, when the old world came to an end and the new creation was brought into being, both alike in the one divine person.[41]

Jesus Christ is to be understood, in virtue of his resurrection, as the one in whom history has its meaning and its goal, and through whom history itself is being brought to its fulfilment. On this point modern theology owes a considerable debt to Jürgen Moltmann's *Theology of Hope*. More consistently than in *The Way of Jesus Christ*, Moltmann, in *Theology of Hope*, brings both the 'history-making' and the eschatological character of the resurrection to the fore. Earlier Dogmatics in the Modern period had de-historicized the resurrection, being cowed by the historians' claims about what real history is, and had agreed, in consequence, that the resurrection is an event somehow distinct from history. Even Barth capitulated to this view by insisting, as we have seen, that the resurrection is not an historical event. Moltmann, however, preserves both aspects of the matter, the historical and the eschatological. The resurrection is to be regarded, Moltmann writes, 'as a "history-making event" in the light of which all other history is illumined, called in question and transformed'.[42] And further:

> The raising of Christ is then to be called 'historic' not because it took place *in* the history to which other categories of some sort provide a key [cf. the categories of Troeltsch], but it is to be called historic because, by pointing the way for future events, it *makes* history in which we can and must live. It is historic because it discloses an eschatological future.[43]

The future to which the whole of history is directed is revealed in the crucified and risen Christ to be the transformation of creation and new life in communion with God. That is the *telos* of history and the context in which the whole of our life now is to be lived and understood. The author of 1 Peter can thus write, 'Blessed be the God and Father of our Lord Jesus Christ! By his great mercy he has given us a new birth into a living hope through the resurrection of Jesus

41. Jean Daniélou, *The Lord of History*, trans. Nigel Abercrombie (London: Longmans, 1958) 195.
42. Jürgen Moltmann, *Theology of Hope*, trans. James W. Leitch (London: SCM Press, 1967) 180.
43. Moltmann, *Theology of Hope*, 181.

Christ from the dead' (1 Pet. 1.3). Christian life is lived in hope, a hope grounded in the resurrection of Christ – but it is, as yet, 'hope'. The resurrection provides a foretaste of what is not completed yet. There is more yet to be said and done, before God will be all in all. Here again we must take issue with Barth, who recognizes that the resurrection is *the* centre and meaning of history but articulates this in such a way that the future is collapsed into the resurrection. 'Nothing which will be', Barth says, 'has not already taken place on Easter day'.[44] This formulation points to the resurrection as the centre and goal of all history, and yet, paradoxically, renders of no account all subsequent historical life. Barth's pneumatological weakness is evident again here, I suspect. For it is the Spirit who unites us with Christ and enables our life now to be a participation in the making of history. The history that we now live matters because if lived in the power of the Spirit, or not, it is gathered, or not, into that final consummation of all things that is the kingdom of God. Barth, to my mind, does not allow sufficient space for the historic character of all human action. We must rather say, along with Gerald O'Collins, that 'the goal of the resurrection is nothing less than that of moving the whole of creation to participate as fully as possible in the life of God'.[45] 'Participation' here does not take place whether we like it or not, as one sometimes suspects with Barth, but as we are enabled by the Spirit to respond to the risen Christ in faith and in hope.

V — Something about Epistemology

Although it will be considered more extensively elsewhere in the book, it is necessary to say something briefly here about epistemology. The claim that the resurrection is the centre and goal of all history is a claim of faith. I have denied that this truth of the resurrection gives itself up to the interrogations of an allegedly faith-free historical-critical enquiry. So how then can this truth be known? My basic answer is, 'by faith', but we have Pannenberg to contend with here, who says that

> if... historical study declares itself unable to establish what 'really' happened on Easter, then all the more, faith is not able to do so; for faith cannot ascertain anything certain about events of the past that would perhaps be inaccessible to the historian.[46]

44. Barth, *CD* III/2, 489.

45. Gerald O'Collins, 'The Resurrection: The State of the Questions' in Stephen T. Davis, Daniel Kendall and Gerald O'Collins SJ, eds, *The Resurrection: An Interdisciplinary Symposium on the Resurrection of Jesus* (Oxford: Oxford University Press, 1997) 5–28, 23.

46. Pannenberg, *Jesus – God and Man*, 109.

Pannenberg's assertion must be countered by considering what is designated by the phrase, what 'really' happened. I suspect that Pannenberg, along with all those who stand in the tradition of Leopold von Ranke's quest for history *wie es eigentilich gewesen ist* (as it really was), mean something like what the video camera might have recorded had there been one present. But this is naive. If what really happened is that God raised Jesus from the dead, what photographic evidence could be supposed to verify that fact? Suppose that CCTV was hidden in the tomb, and that the transition from dead body to empty grave clothes was captured on film. What evidence could possibly have been recorded that would establish God as the agent of this event? Even if the event were recordable by this method, any number of interpretations might be and have been offered. One well known interpretation has it that Jesus didn't really die but was simply revived in the tomb. When his strength was sufficiently restored, he simply got up and left. Could a video camera distinguish that occurrence from the Christian account of the matter? Quite possibly not. Other factors must therefore be brought into play if we are to 'discern' what really happened, and those other factors are matters of faith, the faith that the risen Christ has appeared to the disciples and to us, for example; or, on the other side, the faith that reality is configured in such a way that precludes resurrection from the dead, the faith that the events of history conform without exception to the patterns of immanent causality, or indeed the faith that human epistemic resources are sufficient to the task of revealing all truth. These are competing frameworks of meaning and truth that cannot be excluded from our apprehension of what 'really' happened, but which yield radically different accounts of what took place. An account needs to be given, therefore, of how we come to know that Jesus has been raised from the dead. This includes, I shall argue, a role for faith in discerning what has taken place in history.

Faith itself is a relation. It is not a matter of gritting one's teeth and believing what cannot be proven, but rather of being drawn into relation with God through the mediation of his Son and Spirit. In this sense the risen Christ is the agent of his own revelation. He is the one who in the power of the Spirit and sent by the Father, discloses himself to us as the risen one. This is precisely what happens in the apostolic apprehension of the risen Christ. We could trace this through the various Gospel accounts, but the Lukan story of the resurrection illuminates the matter particularly well.

Luke's account of the resurrection begins as it does in all four Gospels with the discovery of the empty tomb.

> On the first day of the week, at early dawn, [the women who had come with Jesus from Galilee (Luke 23.55)] came to the tomb, taking the spices that they had prepared. They

> found the stone rolled away from the tomb, but when they went in, they did not find the body. While they were perplexed about this, suddenly two men in dazzling clothes stood beside them. The women were terrified and bowed their faces to the ground, but the men said to them, 'Why do you look for the living among the dead? He is not here, but has risen. Remember how he told you, while he was still in Galilee, that the Son of Man must be handed over to sinners, and be crucified, and on the third day rise again.' Then they remembered his words, and returning from the tomb, they told all this to the eleven and to all the rest. (Luke 24.1–9)

Much has been written about how improbable it would have been at the time the Gospels were written to rest a fabricated narrative on the authority of women. N.T. Wright for example cites Josephus on the law of witnesses: 'From women let no evidence be accepted, because of the levity and temerity of their sex.'[47] Luke, in contrast, strengthens the authority of the women's witness by his mention of the women at two previous stages of the unfolding drama. They 'followed' Jesus as he made his way to Calvary. Luke highlights their presence by having Jesus single the women out from the crowd in order to address them. An extended discourse ends with the words that the women should not weep for him but for themselves (Luke 23.27–31). The women we are thus told were present at Jesus' passion; they saw Jesus die. That is important because it has subsequently been suggested that Jesus did not die but merely fainted and was later resuscitated. Luke insists, however, that the women saw Jesus die. What is more, they followed Joseph of Arimathea to the tomb and were witnesses of the burial. Luke reports that 'The women who had come with him from Galilee' – who were not prone to have mistaken Jesus' identity therefore – 'followed, and they saw the tomb and how his body was laid' (Luke 23.55). Luke's careful attention to the women as witnesses to the death, to the burial and eventually to the empty tomb is not simply incidental. It is a deliberate emphasis upon the body of Jesus. Resurrection is not merely about what happened to the disciples, a revival of faith after Jesus' death. Resurrection is about what happened to Jesus, and this means, for Luke, what happened to Jesus' body. This series of events, including the resurrection, has an historical reference. It is about what has taken place in time and space, and is not merely something in the minds of his followers.

I am not suggesting here that just because the Bible says so, this settles the matter of whether or not Jesus underwent some sort of bodily resurrection. My point rather, is that whether or not there are aspects of the resurrection beyond the scope of historical enquiry, Luke means us to understand that in at least

47. Wright, *The Resurrection of the Son of God*, 607–8, note 55. The quote from Josephus comes from *Antiquities* 4.219.

one important respect the resurrection is an event on the same plane of history as the crucifixion. Luke did not think that he was writing in the genre of myth.

Let us look further at how Luke emphasizes the material and historical reality of the resurrection of Jesus. The women who saw Jesus crucified and saw his body laid in the tomb went again to the tomb on the first day of the week, taking with them the spices they had prepared. When they got there, however, they reportedly found the stone rolled away. They entered the tomb and found that the body was gone. At this stage the women are said to be perplexed. Seeing his tomb empty does not of itself entail that Jesus had been raised. Taken by itself, the reality of the empty tomb is simply perplexing and can lead to a range of different interpretations. One such interpretation is clearly acknowledged in Matthew's recognition that a stolen body could equally account for the tomb being empty (Matt. 28.13).

Two men then appear who ask the women, 'Why do you seek the living among the dead?' The men mildly rebuke the women for not remembering that Jesus had spoken of his death and had promised that he would rise from the dead. The women then went and told all this to the other disciples. The word ἔλεγον used at Luke 24.10 is the imperfect indicative active form of the verb and indicates that the women do not simply tell once, but rather that they went on telling. They kept repeating their story.[48] One can well imagine that the news was greeted with disbelief and so had to be repeated again and again. We can imagine too that every last detail was enquired after and clarified through incessant questioning. Disbelief is the most natural immediate reaction. What the women are saying is very much out of the ordinary. It is something much harder to swallow than the relatively inoffensive suggestion that Jesus' influence will somehow carry on. Thus in verse 11 we read that the words of the women seemed to the disciples to be an idle tale, and they did not believe them. Luke makes no attempt to disguise the fact that what he is trying to tell us is very hard to believe.

At this stage of the narrative it is not yet clear that anyone believes that Jesus is alive, including the women themselves. They were simply amazed at the sequence of events and, as yet, as far as we can tell, they do not know what to make of it. Peter, who rushed to the tomb as soon as he had heard the women's testimony, is also reported to have been amazed (Luke 24.12) but, again, his sighting of the empty tomb is not enough on its own to convince him that Jesus has been raised.

48. Thus Fitzmyer translates: 'they and the others *kept repeating* these things to the apostles' (my emphasis) Joseph A. Fitzmyer, *The Gospel According to Luke X–XXIV* (Garden City, NY: Doubleday, 1983) 1532.

This uncertainty in the face of the empty tomb, an event easily verifiable by eye-witnesses but by no means easily understood, is borne out by the subsequent story of the disciples on the road to Emmaus. They have heard the women's story and convey it to the stranger whom they meet on the road: 'Some women of our group astounded us. They were at the tomb early this morning, and when they did not find his body there, they came back and told us that they had indeed seen a vision of angels who said that Jesus was alive' (Luke 24.22–3). Clearly, however, this testimony is not yet convincing. The two disciples, far from being jubilant at Jesus' resurrection, are still sorrowing over his death (v. 17). They are clearly unsure what to make of the women's testimony. Luke again makes it clear that what he is trying to tell us is not easy to believe. It is something much more momentous than a renewal of faith in the disciples. Of crucial importance here is that, on Luke's account, the resurrection of Jesus is an event that is *independent* of a renewal of faith in the disciples. Jesus is risen, but even though they have the evidence of something accessible to (their)[49] historical reason – the empty tomb – none of the disciples can yet believe it.

What then does generate belief? Luke has set this up very carefully, and here we come to the crucial point. It is encounter with the risen Lord himself. The testimony of the women is not enough on its own. Nor is the evidence of the empty tomb. Rather, it was the appearance of Jesus in person that led to the disciples' belief. For the two disciples who had gone to Emmaus, it was the breaking of bread – the evidence establishing a continuity between the risen one and the one who had died – that convinced them that Jesus was alive in their presence. When those two disciples rushed back to Jerusalem to tell the others, they were greeted with the news that in the meantime Jesus had also appeared to Simon, thus enabling the Jerusalem group also to say, 'The Lord has risen indeed' (Luke 24.34). There had been evidence available earlier, but only through encounter with the risen Jesus himself were the disciples able to understand what the evidence entailed. Luke's purpose here seems to be to insist that the resurrection has at least some of the characteristics of an historical event and that it happens independently of the beliefs of the first disciples. It is not a story that was fabricated in consequence of a renewal of the disciples' faith, but explains rather why that faith was renewed. Faith is not to be understood therefore as an epistemic tool already in the possession of the disciples.

49. It is not a straightforward matter for subsequent generations to verify that Jesus' body had gone from the tomb in which it had been laid, but if the disciples, or anyone else in Jerusalem at the time, wanted to see for themselves the reality to which the women testified, they could surely do so.

It is engendered rather by the presence of the risen Christ himself. It is Christ's giving of himself in the power of the Spirit, therefore, and the relation of faith established by that action that enables the disciples to know the truth.

As the Emmaus disciples recount their story to the others, Jesus appears once again in their midst. At this point Luke contends with another possible reaction to the news of the resurrection. Some of the disciples apparently thought that they were seeing a ghost (Luke 24.37). Why does Luke mention this? It is because he wants to refute the view that the resurrection appearances were merely visions, or even illusions. For the same reason he goes on to report that Jesus offers his hands and his side so that the disciples could touch him. Furthermore, Jesus asks the disciples for something to eat. They give him a piece of fish, and Jesus, Luke reports, ate it in their presence. It is true, apparently, that the appearance of Jesus can seem like a spirit or ghost, but the difference is stated in the most emphatic terms.

What is apparent here is that Luke deliberately counters the view that these stories are only mythical fabrications. The resurrection is not the product of the disciples' faith or wishful thinking as some would allege, but rather the very basis upon which that faith is founded. Luke openly acknowledges that it is very difficult to believe what he is trying to tell us. He also acknowledges that alternative explanations will be sought, but he particularly emphasizes that the resurrection of Jesus is to be understood as something that happened to Jesus independently of the disciples' faith, that it is to be understood as involving some sort of physical body, and that it takes place on the same terrain of historical occurrence that historians typically investigate. What will not do, however, is the prevailing assumption of secular historiography that that same terrain cannot be the locus of the action of God. We must also insist, on the evidence of Luke's Gospel at least, that the New Testament writers did not think that they were engaging in the genre of myth. They intended their witness to refer to things that have taken place. Should we Moderns choose to understand their testimony as myth, we are not preserving the essence of their Gospel while abandoning a supposedly naive cosmology; we are falsifying what they intended to say. Allegations of a naive or primitive cosmology cannot be allowed as an excuse for the semantic vandalism involved in the modern dehistoricizing of the New Testament accounts. In the matter of Jesus' resurrection from the dead, the first hearers of that news were, on Luke's account at least, no less disbelieving than we. Their worldview was called into question just as is ours. The news of the resurrection, as Luke presents it, is either to be rejected, or it calls for a new conception of history and of God's involvement in our world.

5

Seeing and Believing

I — On 'Seeing' the Truth

We will be concerned in this chapter with how one is to tell the truth about what really happened in the past. Or, putting it in the celebrated words of Leopold von Ranke, how is one to relate history *wie es eigentlich gewesen ist*.[1] The assumption often accompanying such a concern, particularly among naively literalistic readers of the Bible – though aided and abetted by the insistence of positivist historiography that all knowledge be based on directly observable phenomena[2] – is that telling the truth about what really happened is much the same thing as giving an account of what we would have seen had we been there. T.F. Torrance explains that, 'historical science, as we have developed it in the West, is dominated by the primacy of vision, as our word

1. I take the point of Colin Brown that von Ranke's plea for a recovery of history *wie es eigentlich gewesen ist* was not a statement of presumption about the capacities of historians to tell the simple unadulterated truth, but rather a statement of modesty in resisting a tendency to assign to history 'the office of judging the past and instructing the present generation for the benefit of future ages'. 'The present attempt [at history writing]', Ranke continues, 'does not aspire to such high offices: it merely wants to show how it actually was.' The citation from von Ranke's *Geschichte der romanischen und germanischen Völker, 1494–1535* (Berlin: Reimer, 1924) appears in Colin Brown's essay, 'History and the Believer' in *History, Criticism and Faith*, ed. Colin Brown (Downers Grove: Intervarsity Press, 1976) 147–218, 177.

2. Robert Funk and Roy Hoover writing on behalf of the Jesus Seminar represent, yet again, this naive historiography. They write that 'to be a *critical* scholar means to make empirical, factual evidence – evidence open to confirmation by independent, neutral observers – the controlling factor in historical judgements'. *The Five Gospels*, 34. Roy Harrisville comments in response that 'The assumption that neutral observation of data allegedly perceptible to the senses determines what is historical and what is not hides a staggering naïveté.' Roy A. Harrisville, 'The Loss of Biblical Authority and its Recovery' in Carl E. Braaten and Robert W. Jenson, eds, *Reclaiming the Bible for the Church* (Edinburgh: T&T Clark, 1996) 47–61, 56–7.

history (ἱστορία [to see/visit a person or object of importance] shows – the way of thinking it involves can be described as *controlled and tested observation*'.[3] In response to the primacy of vision in historical science I have two aims in this chapter; the first is to challenge the view that telling the truth about history is a matter of reporting what would have been apparent to the naked eye, and the second is to advance an account of 'seeing' that has less to do with ocular perception and more to do with *comprehending* what has taken place.

In his well known critique of historical arguments for the truth of Christianity, to which we have referred in Chapter 1, G.E. Lessing appears, at least for the sake of argument, to pay high regard to the epistemic power of visual perception. He writes:

> Miracles, which I see with my own eyes, and which I have the opportunity to verify for myself, are one thing; miracles, of which I know only from history that others say they have seen them and verified them are another.
>
> That surely, is beyond controversy? Surely there is no objection to be made against this.[4]

And further,

> if even now miracles were done by believing Christians which I had to recognize as true miracles: what could prevent me from accepting this proof of the spirit and of power, as the apostle calls it.[5]

Lessing offers an endorsement here of the principle, 'seeing is believing'. The evidence of his own eyes in respect of miracles, or, we might say, in respect of divine action, has a higher authority than the testimony of others. He seems to contend, furthermore, that such evidence would be sufficient to verify *for him* the claims of Christian faith. Lessing, however, is bluffing, and he knows that his bluff will not be called. There is no way now, eighteen hundred years later – as it was when Lessing wrote – that he can see with his own eyes the events of Jesus' career. The Gospel narratives and the historical claims therein are irretrievably beyond the reach of sensate perception and thus also of the kind of verification to which Lessing refers. Of course, we could appeal to the phenomenon known as 'secondary seeing'[6] in which, sitting at the breakfast table, I may remark, 'I see that Manchester United have been beaten again'

3. T.F. Torrance, *Theology in Reconstruction* (London: SCM Press, 1965) 21. Italics original.

4. Lessing, 'On the Proof of the Spirit and of Power', 51.

5. Lessing, 'On the Proof of the Spirit and of Power', 52.

6. On which, see, for example, Fred Dretske, *Seeing and Knowing* (London: Routledge & Kegan Paul, 1969) 153–68.

when my claim to see is founded, not upon my having seen the football match with my own eyes, but upon the testimony of the sports writer in *The Times*. The matter of testimony, however, and Lessing's distrust of it, is one to which we shall return in the following chapter.

Lessing, we noted, was bluffing when he said that the evidence of his own eyes would be sufficient warrant to accept the claims of the New Testament concerning Jesus, for he goes on to acknowledge that visual perception could not in fact confirm the theological claims that the New Testament makes about Jesus.[7] 'If on historical grounds I have no objection to the statement that Christ raised to life a dead man', Lessing writes, 'must I therefore accept it as true that God has a Son who is of the same essence as himself?'[8] And in the same vein: 'If on historical grounds I have no objection to the statement that this Christ himself rose from the dead, must I therefore accept it as true that this risen Christ was the Son of God?'[9] Such inferences, Lessing contends, would amount to a μετάβασις εἰς ἄλλο γένος, a leap over a 'broad ugly ditch' from one kind of truth to another, from historical truth to theological truth. I agree, contra Wolfhart Pannenberg, that theological claims, like the one that Christ was the Son of God, cannot be set forth as straightforward deductions from observable historical events.[10] Discerning the truth about history is not guaranteed to those who were there to watch. Such discernment requires, rather, a sophisticated conceptual apparatus that gives the lie to the slogan, 'seeing is believing'. There is a vast difference between seeing a phenomenon and knowing what to make of it. This is true even for Thomas who famously demanded to see and touch the risen Christ before he would believe (John 20.24–9). The epistemic gain for Thomas was not independent of an array of background beliefs, nor, we shall argue, of Christ's initiative in making himself known.

For Thomas, in the situation John describes, there is more to the truth of the matter than the sensate data can tell. The conjecture that Jesus had not really died on the cross, as has been proposed by some, could equally well account

7. For a helpful discussion of this point, see C. Stephen Evans's account of Lessing's problem in 'Empiricism, Rationalism and the Possibility of Historical Religious Knowledge'. Evans shows that Lessing does not in the end suppose that religious truths are of an empirical kind, for which incontrovertible historical evidence would suffice as proof, but are rather of a rationalist kind, upon which historical evidence of any kind can have no bearing. See Evans's essay in C. Stephen Evans and Merold Westphal, eds, *Christian Perspectives on Religious Knowledge* (Grand Rapids: Eerdmans, 1993) 134–60, especially, 143–4.

8. Lessing, 'On the Proof of the Spirit and of Power', 54.

9. Lessing, 'On the Proof of the Spirit and of Power', 54.

10. There are questions to be asked, of course, about the 'perceptibility' of the resurrection, but for now we will simply go along with the terms of Lessing's own argument.

for the reality that Thomas now sees with his own eyes. His confession instead that the one standing before him is 'My Lord and my God', is not given *simpliciter* with the sensate data itself but is informed by all that Thomas has seen and heard and only half comprehended during his companionship with Jesus prior to the crucifixion, and by the Jewish scriptural account of God's dealings with the world. To be sure, this is a moment of conversion as well, a moment in which Thomas sees everything in a new light, but the point for our purposes here is that the sense data in and of itself does not compel recognition of the truth. Alternative explanations are available; the data can be pieced together differently under the impact of all else that we believe, so that, presuming only one explanation is true (let us suppose it is that the one who was crucified now encounters Thomas as the risen Lord), those other things that we believe can either enable or preclude our seeing the reality aright.

While we shall in due course discuss some aspects of Thomas's confession that are unique to the case of seeing the risen Jesus as both Lord and God,[11] the hermeneutical character of historical perception and its dependence on belief is a feature of all cases in which the realities of history are truly perceived. As with Thomas's perception of Jesus as Lord and God, there are dimensions of all historical reality that cannot be 'seen', in the literal sense of the word. The truth of history, in other words, is not reducible to the raw data of perception. The eye-witness, accordingly, is not necessarily in the best position to 'see' the truth. There is a distinction common in philosophical accounts of perception between 'seeing things' and 'seeing that' or 'seeing as'. 'Seeing things' refers to the mere reception of incoming sense data, to the proper functioning of the ocular apparatus of the eye and the reflection of light rays from the object seen to the retina. 'Seeing that' or 'seeing as', on the other hand, refers to the interpretative activity by which a seasoned observer makes a judgement about what is seen, and determines, for example, that what is seen is an apple rather than an orange, or that the two yellow lines running along the road beside the kerb (in the United Kingdom) mean that I cannot park my car there. More complexly, I might see that player A holds a winning position in a game of chess, or that the destruction of the World Trade Centre on 11 September 2001 led to the invasion of Iraq in 2003, despite the testimony of many, which I also believe, that Iraq bore no direct responsibility for the attacks of 9/11. This last judgement is, of course, an historical judgement that is not dependent on visual perception, although we generally accept the validity of the metaphor of 'seeing' for the judgement here made. This judgement happens to be quite a complex one. As David Hume famously argued, I cannot

11. These unique aspects require a pneumatological account of Thomas's seeing.

see, just by looking, a causal connection between event A, the destruction of the twin towers, and event B, the invasion of Iraq, but I make the judgement of a causal connection by piecing together into a coherent pattern a range of information that I glean from numerous sources.[12] Among these sources are the judgments and authority of others who offer testimony concerning the complex array of events that constitute in my view a causal relationship.[13] This 'piecing together' is undertaken, moreover, within a framework of beliefs I hold about the way the world is configured.

That there is some causal connection between the events of 9/11 and the invasion of Iraq is probably not very contentious, although some have argued that President Bush was set on invading Iraq for the sake of securing access to Iraq's oilfields and that 9/11 merely provided a pretext. The political leaders responsible for the invasion have, at different times, offered several 'justifications' for their action, including the alleged need to remove the threat of weapons of mass destruction, the need for regime change in Iraq in order to secure the well-being of the Iraqi people, and the need to show that the resolutions of the United Nations are not to be flouted. There are vast complexities, therefore, in the historical judgement of a causal connection between 9/11 and the invasion of Iraq. Those complexities have occasioned much public debate and there is no definitive statement yet available on the causes of the war. Perhaps there never will be. Historical judgements are complex, approximate and provisional, and, even in respect of events with which we are contemporary, such judgements rely on a much more sophisticated process of discernment than is afforded merely through our being there to see for ourselves.

It has frequently been claimed by President Bush, Tony Blair and other advocates of the war that the invasion of Iraq was necessary in order to reduce the threat of terrorism. It is my belief, ten months on from the invasion as I write this chapter, that precisely the opposite will be the case. In my view, the flames of terrorist activity have been fuelled rather than doused by the invasion

12. Historical causality is, of course, quite a complex notion. Some causal relationships are much more strictly determined than others. When I strike the keys on the keyboard of my computer, for instance, I set in train a causal series that, assuming the proper functioning of my computer, cannot but lead to the appearance of the corresponding characters on my screen. To speak of a causal relationship between 9/11 and the invasion of Iraq, however, does not indicate the instigation of a fully determined causal series. President Bush could certainly have reacted in other ways to the events of 9/11. To speak of causality, therefore, is to propose, with a lesser degree of certainty, that without 9/11, Iraq would not have been attacked. This supports my point, however, that historical judgement is a complex hermeneutical activity.

13. The matter of testimony will concern us more fully in the following chapter.

of Iraq. That too is a judgement about history, but it cannot claim the warrant of empirical verification. It may never be able to claim such a warrant. Even if there is an escalation of terrorism in years to come, it will always be a matter of personal judgement whether the Iraq war contributed to that escalation, or whether, as Blair and Bush would have us believe, the terrorism would have been even worse without the war. It should be becoming more obvious now that our judgements about historical realities are shaped by our beliefs about the world. If, for example, I shared the belief of Thomas Hobbes that the state of nature is a state of war, then I would be inclined to the view that terrorism is best eradicated by a show of superior force. If, on the other hand, I happened to agree with John Locke that the state of nature is men and women living together according to reason, then I would place less trust in military solutions and be more inclined to the promotion of negotiation and the diplomatic resolution of human conflicts. Or, if I believed that forgiveness of one's enemies holds more promise for peace than retaliation and revenge, I would favour a political ethic that eschewed the use of force wherever possible and encouraged reconciliation between enemies. The beliefs I hold on these matters will shape, in turn, my judgement about whether the Iraq war will curb or encourage terrorism. Some will say, indeed have said, that such judgements as these are *merely* opinions. It is true that they are personal judgements that show clear traces of belief, but such is true of almost everything that we human beings claim to know. Our judgements are not rendered false on account of their being personal and belief-laden. The truth or falsity of one's judgements is a function of their correspondence to what is the case, not of how they were formed.

Several features emerge from this account of a particular set of historical judgements that are crucial for our understanding of what is involved in making historical judgements generally. First, historical judgements are selective, approximate and provisional. This does not mean that they cannot be true, or that they cannot succeed in providing reliable witness to the past. Truth and reliability in this context do not, however, denote absolute certainty. Achieving only a high degree of probability in historical judgement nevertheless means achieving a *good enough* account of the past to be going on with. Second, historical judgements are conditioned by one's background beliefs about the way the world is constituted. Or to put it otherwise, sound historical judgements are the fruit of wisdom, not merely of the accumulation of data.

Discerning what happens in history, on this account, is not simply a matter of determining what the eye-witness would have seen. The truth of the matter is seldom available to the naked eye. It is deeply problematic, then, to suppose that the historical reality of Jesus can best be discerned by eradicating from our judgements all personal beliefs or, to put it as one enquirer into the history of

Jesus has done, that 'historians have the right and duty to pursue their research independent of belief'.[14] Immediately following this claim, Geza Vermes, its author, writes, 'Research has to be restricted to Mark, Matthew and Luke and to exclude John because, despite the occasional historical detail it contains, its Jesus portrait is so evolved theologically as to be wholly unsuitable for historical investigation.'[15] This is a statement, not of 'objective fact' but of Vermes's own belief that theological categories shed no light on history, or, to put it more plainly, that God does not act in the world. It is a belief he is entitled to, but it gives the lie to his claim that historians should proceed independently of belief. One might make the case that Vermes *qua historian* is obliged to restrict himself to presenting the bare historical data while leaving the judgement of the final significance of Jesus to others. 'Presenting the bare historical data', however, is itself a problematic notion, for historians always sift and organize the data according to their own belief-laden conceptions of what is going on. Quite apart from that, however, Vermes and others like him, who claim independence from belief, never do leave it to others to pronounce upon who Jesus is. Thus Vermes offers us the inevitably *a-theological* judgement that Jesus was 'a charismatic prophetic teacher and miracle worker, the outstanding "Galilean Hasid"'.[16]

Vermes here opposes the judgement of a number of eye-witnesses to the events of Jesus' career who reputedly claimed that he was a blasphemer who needed to be executed (John 10.33), or of others still who, as witness to the same events, confessed that this man was the Son of God (Mark 15.39). We can agree, for the sake of argument,[17] that all three judgements are made by people who witness the same events – though Vermes's witness is not, of course, first hand – yet each comes to a different conclusion about what is to be made of the events. They piece together the evidence in different ways, again suggesting that the 'evidence', sensate or otherwise, doesn't speak for itself. Whether or not the actions of Jesus are in some manner the actions of the triune God simply cannot be decided upon just by watching what went on. 'Jesus' Lordship', C.F. Evans has explained, 'is not the object of ordinary sight.'[18]

14. Geza Vermes, *The Religion of Jesus the Jew* (London: SCM Press, 1993) 4. The attitude is shared by E.P. Sanders who writes, 'I have been engaged for some years in the effort to free history and exegesis from the control of theology. I aim only to be a historian and an exegete.' E.P. Sanders, *Jesus and Judaism* (Philadelphia: Fortress Press, 1985) 333–4.

15. Vermes, *The Religion of Jesus the Jew*, 4.

16. Vermes, *The Religion of Jesus the Jew*, 5.

17. It does not matter here whether or not these reports of varying reactions to Jesus correspond exactly to what a particular historical figure said or thought. All we need for my point to stand is that varying assessments of the 'evidence' of Jesus' life have indeed been made.

18. Evans, *Resurrection and the New Testament*, 65.

The point being made here is precisely that to which G.E. Lessing eventually comes. Despite initially suggesting in 'On the Proof of the Spirit and of Power', that had he been able to see with his own eyes the miraculous events of Jesus' career, he would have been more inclined to believe, Lessing then goes on to admit that the theological claims of christological orthodoxy would not after all be proven even if he could be quite sure that he had seen Jesus alive and well and bearing the scars of crucifixion three days after his death.[19] The claim that Jesus is the only-begotten Son of God, Lessing finally admits, is not the kind of claim that can be verified by the eye-witness, nor by the best efforts of historical-critical enquiry. Stephen Evans explains:

> When Lessing objects to historical religious knowledge on the grounds that historical propositions are contingent, then his initial claims that his problems have to do with the character of historical evidence can't be taken seriously. Despite his claims that if he had been an eyewitness to the miracles of the New Testament he would have been a believer, it now appears that empirical propositions, however well attested, simply don't have the right kind of character to count as religious knowledge for Lessing.[20]

As Evans goes on to point out, Lessing is working here with a particular conception of religious knowledge. It is a rationalist conception according to which religious truths must be both necessary and certain. With that particular conception of religious knowledge, no historical truth is ever going to count as a basis for theological claims. Two things must be noted here: first, Lessing's conception of religious truth takes him outside the realms of Christian faith which has at its centre certain things that are confessed to have taken place in history. Religious truth, accordingly – at least as it is understood within Christianity – is bound up with historical events and is not, therefore, *necessary* but, rather, it is contingent. Nor, we may frankly admit, is it certain to us.

Secondly, however, we agree with Lessing that historical evidence as such – the evidence accessible to historical enquiry – cannot count as proof, both because it is approximate and provisional, as Lessing points out, but also because the assessment of such evidence relies on the beliefs and commitments of the observer.

In speaking of the quest of the historical Jesus, therefore, it is necessary to be clear that its practitioners are speaking of the 'Jesus' that historical enquiry can 'see'. It remains open to question, however, whether this mode of 'seeing' adequately apprehends the truth. It is my contention that a richer account of 'seeing' is needed, at least in this case, but arguably in all cases of historical reconstruction. This will be the kind of account that is implied when the

19. See Lessing, 'On the Proof of the Spirit and of Power', 54.

20. Evans, 'Empiricism, Rationalism and the Possibility of Historical Religious Knowledge', 145.

exclamation, 'I see' designates comprehension, rather than the mere appearance of something in one's perceptual field.

It is worth reiterating before we move on to consider such an account, that C.F. Evans's claim that Jesus' Lordship is not the object of ordinary sight does not require any special pleading on behalf of theological judgements. We commonly make claims about ordinary, everyday experience that entail an account of 'seeing' that is not reducible to mere visual perception. Take the claim, for example, 'I see that the milk has turned sour.'[21] As it happens there are no visual data that could support such a claim. Neither the event so designated – the milk turning sour – nor the ensuing state of affairs – the sour milk – provide us with any ocular evidence, even though we may have kept a close eye on the milk throughout the souring process. The reality we claim to see, therefore, is apprehended in some other way than through visual perception. If someone wants to know what they would have seen had they been a witness to the event in question, we would have to answer that they would have seen nothing supporting the claim that the milk had turned sour. That is also the answer to be given in respect of some of the claims the Gospel writers make about Jesus' career. 'The Spirit descended upon him like a dove', is a relatively straightforward case in point. That might be true reporting – the Spirit may well have come upon Jesus at his baptism – but it does not follow that those who were eye-witnesses to the event of his baptism could cite visual evidence for the pneumatological claim. Testifying to what really happened, in this case, is not simply – and may not be at all – a matter of recounting what one saw.

In the same way that the tools of visual perception are inadequate for the task of seeing that the milk has turned sour, the tools of historical-critical enquiry are inadequate for the task of seeing that God has come among us in the form of the man Jesus. Some other tools are required. Or, as Søren Kierkegaard expressed the matter, we need some other condition in order to apprehend this truth.[22] This condition, Kierkegaard calls faith. The God-man is seen, Kierkegaard further contends, by virtue of the *autopsy of faith*.[23]

II — Seeing as Understanding

When somebody listening to an argument or an explanation responds with the words, 'I see', we recognize that they are usually speaking metaphorically. They

21. The example is taken from Fred L. Dretske, who uses it in defence of an account of seeing rather different from my own. See Dretske, *Seeing and Knowing*, 32.

22. See Kierkegaard's *Philosophical Fragments*, ch. 1.

23. Kierkegaard, *Philosophical Fragments*, 102.

are indicating that the explanation being offered to them has afforded them new *insight* into the reality in question. Suppose that the reality is a work of art, a visual representation of some sort. The observer may 'see' perfectly well what is before her, if by that we mean that the visual data is being received by the properly functioning ocular apparati common to the human species. Suppose, however, that the observer doesn't know what to make of it. She is unable to make sense of it until the guidance of an experienced observer of art helps her to see what is there. We need not be detained here by the otherwise legitimate considerations of the philosophy of art concerning the subjective qualities of artistic perception. Our purposes are served well enough by the straightforward example of an expert guide pointing out to an unseasoned observer of Rublev's icon of the Holy Trinity, for instance, such simple matters as the connections the icon has to the story of the visitation to Abraham and Sarah at the oaks of Mamre, or the significance of the various colours that are used in the icon, or the suggestiveness of the reverse perspective used in the depiction of the table around which the three figures are seated, and so on. The three figures, the tree, the colours, and the table are seen well enough by the novice, prior to her instruction, as objects in her visual field, but the meaning of them escapes her untutored gaze. We may here recognise that the verb 'to see' can be applied not merely to the reception of incoming data but also to its interpretation. 'Seeing' is a sophisticated business that requires, as Kant made clear, the conceptual processing of perceptual data. Without such processing we do not 'see', Kant alleged. 'Percepts without concepts are blind.' He does not mean that we are literally blind, that we receive no visual data, but rather that without the organizing power of concepts – a framework of interpretation – we fail to comprehend what passes before our eyes. 'Seeing', on Kant's account, is inextricably bound up with judgement. It is a hermeneutical act, shaped by prior concepts and beliefs.

Some philosophers have denied this. Fred Dretske, for instance, claims that the visual differentiation of an object is quite independent of the beliefs or interpretations of the percipient.[24] Dretske does not deny that beliefs and interpretations can be applied to the visual data, as a second act, but on his account they are not intrinsic to the basic act of seeing. We can, for example, see a dark

24. Dretske, *Seeing and Knowing*, especially 29. Dretske's minimalist account of seeing allows that we can see things without registering that we have seen them. Again, one could concede the point perhaps, but nothing interesting comes from doing so. What we usually mean by the question, 'Did you see that?' is, 'Did you register what was there?' However infuriated we might be by the child who cannot see his socks plainly before his eyes on the bedroom floor, we have to concede that his 'seeing' them in the fashion that Dretske wants to allow, is no use to anybody. Dretske himself offers comment on such a scenario on pp. 18–19 of *Seeing and Knowing*.

semi-circular mass hovering over the lake without seeing that it is a swarm of insects. Even if we concede this point, no damage is done to my own view that we don't learn anything about the reality so perceived without judgement and interpretation. What would the basic experience of seeing without interpretation be like? The percipient could say no more than, 'There is something in my visual field.' If we then enquire what that something is; that is to say, if we want to learn even the most basic information about the object of perception, then we are asking for a judgement to be made. We are calling for an act of interpretation. If there is such a thing as basic seeing, in the way Dretske proposes, then it is epistemically uninteresting. So far as the life of Jesus is concerned, there is nothing of interest to be learned, even were it procurable, from an eye-witness report stripped bare of the percipient's interpretations. For those who are not eye-witnesses, therefore, the process of seeing what really happened involves a measure of trust in those who 'handed on to us' (Luke 1.2) their interpretation of the events that took place concerning Jesus. We will say more of this in the next chapter.

III — Seeing and Interpreting

We have contended above that the perception of historical reality is, irreducibly, a hermeneutical activity. There is no seeing of any epistemic worth without the interpretative judgements of observers who bring to the task a range of commitments, beliefs, experience, and so on, that inform the judgements made. And yet, despite widespread acknowledgement of this point,[25] the view persists in some circles that we can access the truth about Jesus without the 'interference' of personal interpretation. Such an assumption is common among those who advocate a literal reading of the Bible, but it is apparent also among more sceptical commentators whose efforts to identify what Jesus 'really' said and did are supposed to yield an array of uninterpreted data perceptible to any and all neutral observers. We hear from the Jesus Seminar, for example, that,

> The goal of the Seminar was to review each of the fifteen hundred items [the alleged sayings of Jesus] and determine which of them could be ascribed with a high degree of probability to Jesus. The items passing the test would be included in a database for determining who

25. N.T. Wright, for example, writes emphatically: 'There is no such thing as the "neutral" or "objective" observer; equally, there is no such thing as the *detached* observer.' N.T. Wright, *The New Testament and the People of God*, 36.

> Jesus was. But the interpretation of the data was to be excluded from the agenda of the seminar and left to individual scholars working from their own perspectives.[26]

The supposition that the authentic sayings of Jesus can be determined in isolation from any beliefs, theological commitments, and hermeneutical criteria that members of the Jesus Seminar may harbour is astonishingly naive, as the Seminar's own rules of evidence make abundantly clear.[27] Seeing the real Jesus is not a matter of isolating perceptual data, whether aural or visual, from the interpretative activity of those who first received it and now hand it on to us. Their seeing and hearing is already an interpretative activity and, joined with our similar activity, is the means by which we are afforded a true account of the reality of Jesus Christ. It is possible of course that some or all of those first witnesses and some or all subsequent enquirers are wrong in their judgements about Jesus. They will be wrong, however, not in virtue of their having allowed personal beliefs and commitments to shape their seeing, but in virtue of the particular beliefs they hold being somehow inadequate to the task, and in need, therefore, of modification, perhaps even of radical transformation.

One of the distinctive features of history writing, as is true indeed of all human engagement with the world, is selectivity. In offering their accounts of what has taken place in the past, historians sift and select from a vast array of data, much of it already sifted and selected by other writers, now counted among the historian's sources, who have recorded their own views on the events in question. Selection is itself an act of interpretation. The historian gathers evidence and pieces it together in formation and defence of a particular view of the meaning of events, of the causal relations between them, and even perhaps of particular lessons to be learned for our present and future habitation of the world. This viewpoint and interest of the historian need not undermine the historian's goal of telling the truth about the past. Individual historians may be more or less successful in accomplishing that goal. Of those who are more successful, however, we shall have to say, not that they have better eyesight, but that they are better interpreters. Their point of view will be judged more worthwhile than others, just as, for example, I might value the point of view of Desmond Tutu in reporting on the suffering of black people during the apartheid era in South Africa more highly than that of the notorious racist Stefan Terblanche. Both were eye-witnesses in the midst of that era and neither is a neutral observer, but the first holds beliefs which I find much more likely to yield a true telling of the story. It is readily apparent, however, that their seeing and their interpretation of what went on is radically shaped by the beliefs

26. Funk and Hoover, *The Five Gospels*, 35.

27. See Chapter 1 above, note 42.

they each hold about the world and about God. The belief-laden character of seeing and interpreting is a feature of every effort to tell what went on in history.

To claim that seeing is a belief-laden activity, radically shaped by the personal convictions and perspective of the observer, is not to say that the object to be seen is submerged into a mire of subjectivity, never to be seen again. The argument rather is that belief *helps us to see*. We quoted Kant above who said that percepts without concepts are blind, but Kant also said that concepts without percepts are empty. Such is often alleged against the concepts of christological orthodoxy and provides the impetus for theologians like Wolfhart Pannenberg quite properly to argue, as we have seen, that there must be something in the history of Jesus itself that provides a basis for the christological claims of the Church. This is not in dispute as far as I am concerned. What is in dispute is how that history is to be perceived.

Our conceptual ordering of the world is, in part at least, a response to what we see (and hear, smell, taste, etc.). In the case of the Bible the worldview commended by the texts contained therein is founded upon particular historical events to which those texts seek to bear witness, the establishment of Israel as the people of God, their liberation from slavery in Egypt, their exile from and return to the promised land, the emergence in their midst of the man Jesus, and the life he lived – all of these things constitute the foundations of a particular construal of the world, a construal in which God as creator brings the world into being as something other than himself, and is engaged throughout history in bringing the world to its fulfilment in loving communion with himself. It is true, of course, that not all the biblical material makes direct reference to history. There are prayers and parables and allegories in the mix as well. But these too contribute to and emerge from a construal of the world that has its basis in a series of historical events. The view of the world thus developed depends upon certain things having happened in history and cannot be sustained without them. Seeing these things involves interpretation, but the ongoing interpretative effort of generations of witnesses is directed toward getting clear about what has actually taken place. Even in embellishing the story, or 'inventing' speech to put into the mouths of the Bible's leading characters, the purpose always is to represent reliably who these people were and what their actions meant. Reliable representation, however, is not the same as reproducing what the eye-witness would have seen (or heard). Reliable representation involves directing our gaze to the significance of what was said and done.

IV — Re-presenting Reality

In his essay 'Seeing is Believing – Or is it?', Daniel C. Dennett offers an instructive discussion of Belotto's landscape painting of Dresden:

> I marvelled at the gorgeously rendered details of all the various people walking in bright sunlight across the distant bridge, in their various costumes, with their differences in attitude and activity. I remember having had a sense that the artist must have executed these delicate miniature figures with a magnifying glass. When I leaned close to the painting to examine the brushwork, I was astonished to find that all the little people were merely artfully positioned single blobs and daubs of paint—not a hand or a foot or head or hat or shoulder to be discerned. Nothing shaped remotely like a tiny person appears on the canvas, but there is no question that my brain represented these blobs *as* persons. Belotto's deft brushwork 'suggests' people crossing the bridge, and my brain certainly took the 'suggestion' to heart.[28]

Belotto's landscape is clearly a *rendering* of the scene that we may suppose he once saw with his own eyes. It is a rendering that enables us too to 'see' the same scene, to appreciate in it what Belotto saw in it. But that seeing is confounded if we take the magnifying glass to Belotto's painting. We are not supposed to read literally but rather, as Dennett suggests, to take his 'suggestion' to heart. It is in so doing that we see and understand the reality 'as it really was' on the day that Belotto captured the scene. We may draw an analogy with the reading of the Gospels. Let us suppose that the Gospel writers too render the reality of Jesus of Nazareth with daubs of paint. There is a way of perceiving their rendering which could conclude, 'that can't be what it looked like; these are just daubs of paint'; on the other hand, however, we may read the Gospels in a way that recognizes the rendering skills of the writers as precisely that which enables us to see truly what was really there.

To be more specific, one may read the 'I am' sayings of John's Gospel and conclude that it is improbable that Jesus ever said, 'I am the bread of life', or 'I am the resurrection and the life' and so on. These 'I am' sayings might be described as artfully rendered 'daubs'. Some will conclude on that basis that they do not belong to the historical reality of Jesus himself. For much of the twentieth century, for instance, it was supposed that the Gospel of John had little to offer the serious historian of the life of Jesus.[29] Another way of looking, however, will see this rendering of the Gospel writer, not in naively literalistic

28. Daniel C. Dennett, 'Seeing is Believing – Or is it?' in K. Akins ed., *Perception*, Vancouver Studies in Cognitive Science (Oxford: Oxford University Press, 1996) 158–72, 166–7.

29. Geza Vermes, for example, writes, 'The Christ of Paul and John on the way to deification, overshadows and obscures the man of Galilee.' *The Religion of Jesus the Jew*, 210.

terms, but as showing forth the reality of Jesus as he really was and is. Those 'daubs' really do depict the reality with which we are concerned, namely the person of Jesus Christ.

Dennett's example also helps to show the problematic character of that form of biblical study that reduces the text to a scattered array of distinct fragments. The Gospels as treated by the Jesus Seminar are a well-known example of this practice. As Dennett leans in closer to Belotto's painting to view the 'blobs' and 'daubs' he may marvel at the skill of the artist in rendering the subject matter so artfully, but he doesn't for a moment suppose that the truth value of the painting as a reference to a particular scene in Dresden sometime during the mid-eighteenth century may best be understood by focusing on the daubs themselves. Assessing the truth of Belotto's rendering involves making a judgement about the picture as a whole. That judgement will concern whether or not the impression given by the painting is 'true to life'.[30] And in that matter the discovery that the 'people' in the painting turn out to be no more than daubs of paint is utterly irrelevant. It makes no sense to say, 'these are not people; they have no arms and legs'. It likewise makes no sense, I suggest, to quibble over whether the words 'I am the resurrection and the life' ever passed Jesus' lips. The important question – if it is historical truth that we are concerned with – is whether John's rendering of Jesus thus, affords genuine insight into who Jesus really was and is. Gadamer offers helpful comment on this matter. Representation, he says – speaking particularly of art – is not mere repetition; it is rather a matter of 'bringing forth' the essence of the subject.[31] That is also true of the way in which the Gospel writers represent Jesus. They do not merely repeat his words; but seek to show forth the essential character of who Jesus was and is. The question for us is not whether their depictions of Jesus correspond in every particular to some empirical datum, but whether they are trustworthy representers of the reality of Jesus himself.

The example of Belotto's painting offers the further lesson that painting and texts, indeed all forms of representation, will not answer all the questions that we might have about the scenes and events they seek to depict. It would make no sense to upbraid Belotto for not providing us with information about who it was that was walking on the bridge at the hour he painted it. His selection of what was significant did not include that detail. Likewise with the Gospels; we cannot upbraid the writers for not selecting details that we might now be curious about, the psychology of Jesus for example, or the identity of the man who fled naked from the scene of Jesus' arrest. No representation includes

30. The example given here entails no prejudice against abstract art also being 'true to life'. Indeed it is precisely my point that the rendering of truth is not equivalent to naive realism.

31. Gadamer, *Truth and Method*, 103.

everything. To attempt to do so would be to obscure rather than to shed light on the meaning of the events in hand. Witnesses clear the scene for us of details that they don't count as significant. Of course, they may have failed to note something that is significant, and so we shall hope to pick up that detail from other witnesses, but the representation of *everything* seen and heard is neither possible nor helpful. A witness who did not exercise judgement in selecting what was significant for our understanding would leave us unable to see. I have found myself in that position when as a hapless father to be, I watched on screen the shifting array of smudges yielded by an ultra-sound scan of my child in his mother's womb. I had no clear idea of which smudge was a foot and which was a hand. Much less would I have been able to determine the gender of the child half-formed. The skilled witness, on the other hand, directs our gaze to the details of genuine significance, thus enabling us to see. In the case of the ultra-sound scan, the doctor who guided my seeing was able to bring to bear on the visual data a background of expertise and experience that made sense of the smudges on the screen. 'Making sense' here does not mean that the doctor fabricated something that was not there. The interpretation does not float free of but shows what is 'objectively' the case. Such guidance is also required if we are to see the truth of Jesus Christ.

V — Seeing the Risen Christ

An account of how that guidance comes about is offered in the Lucan account of the two disciples walking to Emmaus after Jesus' resurrection. As yet, though they had received reports of the empty tomb, the two disciples did not believe that Jesus had been raised from death. We have considered this story already in the previous chapter. I wish to draw attention now, however, to an aspect of the story that was passed over in the earlier discussion. As the two disciples were journeying together, Jesus himself came near and went with them, but, we are told, '*their eyes were kept from recognizing him*' (Luke 24.16, my emphasis).

Remember Lessing, now: 'Had I seen with my own eyes,' he said, 'I surely would have believed.' This story of the disciples on the road to Emmaus makes it clear that the matter is not as simple as that. The two disciples saw clearly enough that there was a man walking with them on the road. And they heard him tell of all the things that had happened among them and of their relation to the scriptures. But, to begin with at least, they did not believe. Let me reiterate the point. There is no fault with the sensory apparatus of the two disciples. They can see and hear just as well as they ever did. But they do not have the capacity to understand what is before them, and so, in another sense of the word, they have not really 'seen' at all. That is the situation, I believe, of those historians who attempt to recover a picture of Jesus stripped bare of any theological interpretation. They are presuming to do without the very categories through which alone truthful sense is to be made of the reality of Jesus himself. They presuppose, that is, that we must explain the world from within itself, without need of the God hypothesis. And in this way they determine in advance that the one visible to their way of seeing cannot be understood as the risen Son of God.

Notice that the disciples on the road to Emmaus were talking about all the things that had happened surrounding Jesus. Jean Luc Marion explains that it was not a sense of the facts that they lacked but rather the conceptual framework that would enable them to make sense of what they had seen and heard.[32] Well did they know, just as we do today, that dead men are not raised to new life, and, despite the women's testimony concerning their experience at the empty tomb, the two disciples stick by this certainty, just as we also are inclined to do. That is when the unlikely paradox takes place. Jesus overtakes them on the road. Drawing near, he began to travel with them, but their eyes were kept from recognizing him (v. 16). By what exactly? Marion asks.

> What concrete sign, what sensible perception, what intuition was lacking? None whatsoever, clearly. In fact, they kept themselves from recognizing him. Why were they denying the evidence? Not because it was deficient – it wasn't lacking in the slightest – but because it contradicts their entire comprehension (their miscomprehension, or at least, their pre-comprehension) of a phenomenon that is nevertheless patently beneath their eyes, and in their ears. They do not recognize him because they cannot even imagine that this is really him, Him, who has rejoined them, so far do their poor, cobbled-together, honest-to-goodness concepts find themselves outstripped by 'events' that leave them petrified within a matrix of irrefutable prejudices.[33]

It is their background beliefs that kept the disciples from recognizing the risen Lord, most especially their belief that dead men are not raised. They were kept from recognizing him because the reality before them contradicted their entire conception of how the world is constituted. But that is precisely the point. The resurrection is the beginning of a world *re-constituted* as the new creation of God. The two disciples could not be expected to see that on their own. Inevitably, they, as we also do, attempted to construe things in terms of what

32. Jean Luc Marion 'They Recognized Him; and He Became Invisible to Them', *Modern Theology* 18.2 (April 2002) 145–52, 147. Much of the following argument is drawn from Marion's article.

33. Marion, 'They Recognized Him', 147.

they already knew. It is for this reason that they were blinded to the new reality that had been brought about through the resurrection of Jesus himself.

The two disciples stood in need of guidance; they stood in need of one who could show them a new way of looking and a new conception both of God and of the world. Jesus becomes their guide. He listens to their story and by reference to God's dealings with his people throughout Israel's history, he begins to piece together for them a new way of seeing. It is when he breaks bread with them at the end of their journey that the miracle finally takes place. What miracle? Just the miracle of seeing aright the truth that was before their eyes. Why is it a miracle? Because the two disciples are incapable of seeing it without God's help.[34] Likewise with us; we learn to see with God's help. For the disciples on the road to Emmaus, it was Jesus himself who walked and talked with them on the road, until they learned to see. Elsewhere the biblical record testifies that Jesus sends the 'Spirit of truth' who will guide you into all the truth (John 16.13).[35]

It is noteworthy too that Jesus made himself known to the two disciples through the mediation of the scriptures.[36] 'Then beginning with Moses and all the prophets, he interpreted to them the things about himself in all the scriptures' (Luke 24.27). It is these same scriptures that God continues to use to make himself known. That subsequent generations, therefore, cannot see the risen Lord in the flesh as the first disciples saw him, does not preclude them from 'seeing that' he has been raised in accordance with God's purpose to redeem the world and to bring creation to its goal of abundant life in him.

34. C.F. Evans argues that the narratives of the resurrection appearances in the New Testament typically employ a linguistic construction that emphasizes the need of Jesus' help if those to whom he appeared are to see him aright. The Greek construction, Evans explains, indicates that Jesus 'let himself be seen'. The passive ὤφθη with the dative of the person to whom the appearance is made cannot be translated 'he was seen by…', which would require the preposition 'by' (ὑπο) with the genitive, and if the verb is used as a deponent, the emphasis lies not on the apprehension of the recipient but on the will and initiative of him who appears. It means 'he let himself be seen…' C.F. Evans, *Resurrection and the New Testament* (London: SCM Press, 1970) 63–4.

35. John 16:13 continues by saying that the 'Spirit of truth…will declare to you the things that are to come'. John Marsh sees here a specific reference to the events following on from the last supper. 'The Spirit will show the disciples what is to happen, i.e. what the real meaning of the events is, when Jesus is arrested, tried, condemned to death and crucified.' If Marsh is right, then the principle preserved in Luke through the Emmaus road story is echoed in John; namely, discerning the truth about Jesus' death and resurrection is contingent upon the help of God. See John Marsh, *Saint John* (Harmondsworth: Penguin Books, 1968) 541.

36. On which, see Watson, *Text, Church, and World*, 290.

VI — Conversion

Christian conversion is not the acceptance of a range of propositions into a worldview that otherwise remains unchanged. It is not a matter of squeezing the resurrection of Jesus, for example, into a Deistic view of history, the like of which we have traced in Western thought. The result of that procedure will always be a distortion of what the resurrection is – its reduction to a change in the minds of the disciples, for instance, or the revival of a weakened but not dead Jesus, or merely a story that shows forth the particular insight and power of Jesus' religious message. These procrustean accommodations of the resurrection, and indeed of the reality of Jesus himself, require no adjustment to the pagan conceptuality that governs them, and, just so, they do not afford insight into the reality of Jesus at all. The truth remains inaccessible to such a state of mind. What is required is conversion, a new way of seeing that takes its starting point from the reconfiguration of things brought about through the incarnation, and through the life, death, and resurrection of Christ.

The need of a new way of seeing is apparent in Luke's account of the resurrection appearances, especially so in the story of the journey to Emmaus, but it is evident too in John's report of the appearance of the risen Christ to Mary. In John's narrative, Mary apparently moves to embrace Jesus, but Jesus says, 'Do not hold on to me, because I have not yet ascended to the Father. But go to my brothers and say to them, "I am ascending to my Father and your Father, to my God and your God"' (John 20.17). Mary too had not, at first, recognized the risen Lord, but had mistaken him for a gardener. Again, this is not surprising. It is in the nature of things, so Mary believed, that those who have died do not emerge from the grave. Not until Jesus addresses her by name does she recognize who he is. But even then, as Denham Grierson has eloquently observed, the new world thus inaugurated dawns only gradually in Mary's mind.

> *Mary recognises the Resurrection event but misunderstands its meaning.* Her immediate assumption is that the old order is restored. By some miracle Jesus has survived death and all is as it was. Nothing has been lost. Jesus checks her, however, as she seeks to hold on to him. 'Do not cling to me', he says, and it has the force not only of 'don't touch me' but also 'don't cling to me as the one you have known'. The new has differences that take up the old into itself so that nothing is lost. But all is changed.
>
> The familiar, the taken-for-granted nature of the world and all the expectations associated with it are ruptured beyond repair. Yet at the same time the known becomes more precious because its promise is fulfilled, its very ordinariness transfused with a significance beyond telling.[37]

37. Denham Grierson, 'Resurrection and Personal Story' in Nigel Watson ed., *The Heart of the Matter: Reflections on the Resurrection Faith* (Melbourne: Joint Board of Christian Education, 1980) 43–9, 44.

When Jesus speaks further to Mary of 'my Father and your Father, my God and your God', Jesus' prior promise of reconciliation with God is fulfilled. Everything is as he said it would be.[38] It is a new world now that Mary inhabits, a world inconceivable within the limitations of the old.

Inhabiting that new world, or, more particularly, *seeing* the real world as the terrain in which the Creator is bringing the world to its fulfilment in communion with him, is made possible through encounter with the risen Christ, the one in and through whom the new creation comes about. In virtue of such an encounter, sustained over time through word and sacrament and through the continuing mediation of the Holy Spirit, the person of faith is one whose thinking and seeing and acting in the world is oriented to and guided by the logic of Christ's incarnation, his life, death, resurrection, and ascension, and by the redemption wrought through him.

The Christian account of conversion, and of the epistemic progress accompanying it, is irreducibly pneumatological. The transformation in one's thinking, seeing and acting, is brought about by the Spirit. This biblical view is attested to by Paul in his first letter to the Corinthians:

> But, as it is written, 'What no eye has seen, nor ear heard, nor the human heart conceived, what God has prepared for those who love him' – these things God has revealed to us through the Spirit; for the Spirit searches everything, even the depths of God. (1 Cor. 2.9–10)

This is not a claim that can be tested empirically; nor can it be demonstrated. It takes the form rather of a confession – a confession by the person of faith that what is spoken of in the Bible about the presence and impact of the Spirit has happened also for them. They have been given new eyes to see and a new way of understanding. It is as though the vital clue to the whole story of history has now been disclosed. Like the Gestalt shift in which, for example, a picture of a duck is now seen as a rabbit, this testimony of conversion will convince only those who also see. That is just the nature of things. It is important to recognize, however, that the testimony of faith is not defeated by the fact that there are others who do not see things this way. In just the same way, my judgement that the war in Iraq will exacerbate rather than curb the outbreaks of terrorism in the world, is not defeated by the fact that others do not see things as I do. Both I and they are estimating, in the meantime, a truth that remains to be seen. That is the position of each one of us with regard to the meaning and purpose of history. Christians are distinguished, in the meantime, by their belief that the vital clue to the whole has been disclosed to us in Christ.

38. Grierson, 'Resurrection and Personal Story', 45.

Seeing things that way is not the fruit of historical enquiry but rather of election, of that mysterious prerogative of God to make himself known to us one by one, as he who walks with us on the road. The matter is as Francis Watson has described it:

> According to the Gospels, the fact that the life of Jesus is at the same time the definitive act of God for the salvation of the world cannot merely be read off the surface of the story that they tell. The God who determines the life of Jesus is also the God who determines its *disclosure* as what it truly is...[39]

39. Watson, 'The Quest for the Real Jesus', 160.

6

Testimony and Tradition

I — The Disparagement of Testimony

Whatever Christian theologians may wish to say about the contemporary presence of Christ in the midst of his Church, the fact remains that the key formative events of the Christian story, the life, death and resurrection of Jesus of Nazareth, are no longer available for us to see. The passing of time renders them, as all past events, inaccessible as objects of immediate perception. Access to them is mediated now through the testimony of others, first conveyed orally among the followers of Jesus and then committed to written form in the texts of the New Testament and in a number of extra-canonical sources. Such testimony includes the interpretative efforts of some who were eye-witnesses and also of the communities which first heard and handed on the story of Jesus' career. Whatever else may be added to an account of how we now may know of the things that took place in and through Jesus, reliance upon such testimony will be an inescapable element of that epistemic process. It has been a standard view in Western epistemology, however, that reliance upon testimony renders deeply problematic any claim to *know*. Such a view has been encountered already in the work of G.E. Lessing who writes,

> The problem is that *reports* of fulfilled prophecies are not fulfilled prophecies; that *reports* of miracles are not miracles. These, the prophecies fulfilled before my eyes, the miracles that occur before my eyes, are immediate in their effect. But those – the reports of fulfilled prophecies and miracles, have to work through a medium which takes away all their force.[1]

Lessing's scepticism has a long and august pedigree. In Plato's *Theaetetus* Socrates contends that a jury hearing a case in court could not *know* the facts

1. Lessing, 'On the Proof of the Spirit and of Power', 52 (my emphasis).

about a robbery – in the case considered – because they are inescapably reliant on the testimony of others and have no means of verifying for themselves what in fact took place.[2] More recently, René Descartes and John Locke have set forth influential accounts of human knowing that eschew reliance on the testimony and opinions of others. Descartes determines, of course, to count as knowledge only that which he can verify through the operations of his own reason, while Locke writes dismissively,

> The floating of other Men's Opinions in our brains makes us not one jot the more knowing, though they happen to be true. What in them was Science is in us but Opinionatrety, whilst we give up our Assent only to reverend Names, and do not, as they did, employ our own Reason to *understand* those *Truths, which gave them reputation.*[3]

Such scepticism has not gone entirely unchallenged, but the rebuke to those who have sought to rehabilitate testimony has been swift and vehement. When Myles Burnyeat, at the 1980 meeting of the Aristotelian Society, questioned Socrates' scepticism, for example, and observed, quite correctly, that 'in normal contexts of communication, knowledge spoken is knowledge handed on to another',[4] his interlocutor, Jonathan Barnes, responded,

> He [Burnyeat] means that if x knows that p and x says to y that p, then (normally) y thereby comes to know that p. Now I think that that is quite false – it is a lot harder to acquire knowledge than Burnyeat imagines. No doubt we all do pick up beliefs in that secondhand fashion, and I fear that we often suppose that such scavenging yields knowledge. But that is only a sign of our colossal credulity: the method Burnyeat describes is a rotten way of acquiring beliefs, and it is no way at all of acquiring knowledge.[5]

It will be clear that such an attitude, if adopted, has a profoundly corrosive effect on the authority of the Bible, for the Bible is, in its fundamental character, a *testament* to the being and action of God and of his presence with his people. That the Bible is comprised of testimonies is problematic enough according to common philosophical consent, but that these testimonies also purport to speak of the action of God distances them still further from the

2. See Plato, *Theaetetus* 201b, trans. John McDowell (Oxford: Clarendon Press, 1973).

3. John Locke, *An Essay Concerning Human Understanding*, ed. Peter H. Nidditch (Oxford: Clarendon Press, 1975) Bk 1, Ch. 4, §23.

4. I.-M. F. Burnyeat, 'Socrates and the Jury: Paradoxes in Plato's Distinction Between Knowledge and True Belief I', *Aristotelian Society Supplementary Volume* 54 (1980) 173–91, 183.

5. Jonathan Barnes, 'Socrates and the Jury: Paradoxes in Plato's Distinction Between Knowledge and True Belief II', *Aristotelian Society Supplementary Volume* 54 (1980) 193–206, 200.

standard Western epistemology that privileges first-hand perception, individual memory and reasoned inference, especially as these epistemic tools are variously apparent in the standard verification techniques of modern science.

II — The Indispensability of Testimony

In contrast, however, to a tendency among theologians and biblical scholars to accept these strictures against the authority of their source material, there has recently been a growing philosophical interest in the epistemic value of testimony. Especially significant are C.A.J. Coady's book *Testimony: A Philosophical Study*,[6] and the collection *Knowing From Words* edited by Bimal Krishna Matilal and Arindam Chakrabarti.[7] In Coady's widely acclaimed book the author sets out to recover the role of testimony in the acquisition of knowledge and to provide philosophical support for the common practice of relying on the word of others. Coady's book advances the battle against scepticism on several fronts. He begins by surveying a range of arguments against the epistemic value of testimony, and notes, in particular, the individualistic account of the knowing process that typically accompanies such scepticism. Locke and Descartes are singled out here, since, for all that there are differences between their respective epistemologies, they are agreed in restricting the individual's field of knowledge to that which has been verified by the individual him or herself. Coady's principal argument against this restriction is the pragmatic one of pointing out how reliant we in fact are upon corporate support for our knowledge claims. Even the natural scientist, the paragon of epistemic virtue within Modernity, can't get along without heavy reliance upon the testimony of others. Coady helpfully illustrates the point by adducing Edmund Halley's reliance upon testimony in identifying his famous comet and predicting its return at 75-year intervals.

> It was while Halley was studying the comet of 1682 that he noticed the similarities between it and two other bright comets reported by earlier astronomers in 1531 and 1607. Noting the intervals of approximately seventy-five years he predicted the return of the comet in 1758 – which proved correct although he did not survive to see it... This is a good illustration of the way astronomy uses testimony from the past.[8]

6. C.A.J. Coady, *Testimony: A Philosophical Study* (Oxford: Clarendon Press, 1992).
7. Bimal Krishna Matilal and Arindam Chakrabarti, eds, *Knowing From Words* (Dordrecht: Kluwer Academic, 1994).
8. Coady, *Testimony*, 11.

Coady cites a number of examples across several spheres of scientific endeavour to show that science progresses in significant measure through an accumulation of testimony. Wherever, as they commonly do, scientists draw upon the experimental results of others and cite such work in support of their own, they violate the individualistic epistemologies that have dominated post-Enlightenment Western thought and contradict the claim that testimony is an illegitimate foundation for knowledge.

It is not news to the heirs of Descartes and Locke, of course, that, as a matter of fact, we do commonly rely on the testimony of others. Their argument is, however, that wherever testimony provides an apparent basis for knowledge it does so only because the testimony in question has been verified through the utilization of other *more basic* epistemic resources and principles, such as perception and inference. Such a procedure is commonly referred to as the reductive thesis of testimonial knowledge, but this view does not hold up under analysis. The reduction of testimonial knowledge to more basic epistemic foundations is shown by Coady to be neither necessary nor possible. The central plank of Coady's refutation of reductionism is his contention, identical to the one we have developed in the foregoing chapter, that perception is dependent upon a range of background beliefs that are themselves formed through acceptance of the testimony of others. Thus, for example, when I *perceive* the luxury yacht *Aurora* sailing up the harbour, I know that it is the *Aurora* because I have read the report in the morning paper announcing the scheduled arrival of the *Aurora* in port today. Furthermore, I can know that this particular configuration of matter is a yacht because I am in possession of the concept 'yacht' and, through the reliable testimony of my parents and other sundry witnesses, I have been taught in childhood to identify yachts successfully. Coady argues, accordingly, that our conceptual apparatus is socially constructed during the process of language acquisition and is irreducibly dependent, therefore, upon our uncritical acceptance of past testimony.[9] The process of inference is likewise saturated with background beliefs formed by

9. Agreement with Coady's view that global reductionism is impossible may be found in numerous recent discussions of testimony. Christopher Insole, for example, writes, 'Our very conceptualising framework is itself socially determined during our acquisition of language; so even perception, memory and reason are dependent on past testimony.' Christopher Insole, 'Seeing Off the Local Threat to Irreducible Knowledge by Testimony', *Philosophical Quarterly* 50.198 (January 2000) 44–56, 47. See also, Elizabeth Fricker, 'Telling and Trusting: Reductionism and Anti-Reductionism in the Epistemology of Testimony' in *Mind* 104 (April 1995) 393–411, and Steven Shapin, *A Social History of Truth: Civility and Science in Seventeenth-Century England* (Chicago: University of Chicago Press, 1994). Shapin notes that science has never in fact 'accomplished the rejection of testimony and authority' (xxv).

trusting in the testimony of others. It turns out to be impossible, Coady argues, to arrive at knowledge without reliance on testimony. Extending Coady's position, Arindam Chakrabarti considers the following argument compelling:

> No knowledge is possible without true belief. No belief is possible without some conceptual representation of a situation of the world. No conceptual representation is possible without some linguistic classification as to what is correctly called what. There is no other source of knowledge about what is correctly called what except testimony of the experts of a community. Thus testimony is *central* to all knowledge – including direct perception.[10]

What is the relevance of such an argument for biblical hermeneutics? I venture at this point only the modest claim that the bias against accepting biblical testimonies purely on the grounds that they are indeed testimonies must be re-examined. Coady himself comments, though he is not otherwise occupied with the defence of Christian faith, that the sceptical attitude to testimony 'has continued to exert a powerful (and, I venture to assert, a sometimes baneful) influence upon biblical exegesis'.[11] The bias against testimonial knowledge is, however, the product of highly questionable, and, indeed, unsustainable, epistemological commitments peculiar to a narrow, but nonetheless influential, strand of the Western intellectual heritage. If we insist on maintaining this bias we are left with next to nothing that we can call knowledge.[12] It is better, I think, to acknowledge frankly that such epistemologies have set an impossible standard, and, further, that they operate with a mistaken idea of what it is to know.

III — The Authority of Testimony

Accepting Coady's argument that our linguistic and conceptual socialization precludes us from eliminating altogether our reliance on testimony in the epistemic process, Elizabeth Fricker nevertheless argues that this does not

10. Arindam Chakrabarti in a review of C.A.J. Coady, *Testimony: A Philosophical Study*, in *Philosophy and Phenomenological Research* 54.4 (December 1994) 965–72, 969.

11. Coady, *Testimony*, 195.

12. It has been argued even of Descartes' Cogito, for example, that his self-consciousness is itself dependent upon the uncritical acceptance of a socially conditioned linguistic framework. Jenny Teichman, drawing on Wittgenstein, comments, 'A being without language could not entertain the thought encapsulated in Descartes' *Cogito*: nor indeed the doubts expressed by a Solipsist.' See Teichman, 'Wittgenstein on Persons and Human Beings' in Royal Institute of Philosophy, *Lectures*, vol. vii: *1972/73*: *Understanding Wittgenstein* (London: Macmillan, 1974) 133–48, 142.

remove from mature thinkers the obligation when confronted with particular instances of testimony to verify for themselves the competence and reliability of the testifier. We do not, in other words, have a presumptive right to trust the testimony of others. 'Acknowledging my general and irredeemable debt to past testimony', Fricker writes, 'I may nonetheless want to trust no new informants unless I have grounds to believe them trustworthy.'[13] Believing them to be trustworthy, Fricker further explains, is a matter of ascertaining that they are sincere in their utterance and that they are competent about the subject matter of their testimony. Fricker is willing to admit that,

> within the interpretative exercise sincerity is the default setting: it can be assumed unless there are signs of its lack. But... the hearer must always be scrutinising the speaker for telltale signs of its absence, and she must be alert to the presence of such signs. Similarly, competence may be assumed as default setting, but in this case with respect to a subclass of tellings only, viz. those with subject matters for which commonsense psychological knowledge licenses one to expect the speaker to be competent about them: such as her name, where she lives, what she had for breakfast, what is in clear view in front of her, and so forth. Again, the speaker must be sensitive to indicators of its lack.[14]

I think it is reasonable to assume competence in a broader range of cases than Fricker adumbrates here, including, for example, the testimony on medical matters of my doctor, or the testimony of an astrophysicist about the phenomena of our solar system, and so on. However large or small we may determine the group of reliable testifiers to be, Fricker's acknowledgement that, under certain conditions, trust in the testimony of others is a reasonable epistemic procedure, serves well my concern here to rehabilitate the authority of biblical testifiers. It is to be noted, of course, that the knowledge attained through testimony will not be absolutely certain, nor incorrigible. It is possible that we may be mistaken in judging the sincerity and competence of another. It is also possible that a competent testifier may, on occasion, be sincerely mistaken. Such things do happen, but not all the time, and so sometimes – I think, often – our trusting will yield true belief, even though we cannot eliminate all doubt. The result for biblical hermeneutics, let me repeat, is at this stage a modest one. We have no business dismissing the authority of biblical

13. Fricker, 'Telling and Trusting', 404.

14. Fricker, 'Telling and Trusting', 405. Coady thinks that Fricker wrongly supposes that 'the sort of evidence a person must have for the reliability of a witness if he is to be credited with knowledge of some reported fact has to be non-testimonial'. Coady, *Testimony*, 97, n. 9. I agree with Coady that it will usually be the case that ascertaining the competence and sincerity of the testifier will itself depend eventually on the acceptance of testimonial evidence, but I accept Fricker's caution, as distinct from out-and-out scepticism.

witness just because it has the character of human testimony. Chakrabarti puts it more boldly: 'We who assimilate knowledge', he says, 'from tutors, books and elders are not "scavengers" or "borrowers". We are just rightful claimants of an epistemic bequest of which sceptics and elitists are trying to deprive us.'[15]

Despite Chakrabarti's confidence, shared with Coady, in the epistemic value of testimony, neither proposes a straightforward presumptive right to trust the testimony of others. If total scepticism will not do, neither will blind credulity. It is necessary to accept Fricker's challenge to *do the best we can* to ascertain the trustworthiness of those who offer testimony. How should we go about this in the case of the biblical writers? It is important to note, to begin with, that ascertaining the trustworthiness of any witness, biblical or otherwise, involves personal judgements and is not reducible to a checklist of qualifications. Nor, as Coady points out, is critical judgement always a reflective process.

> What happens characteristically in the reception of testimony is that the audience operates a sort of learning mechanism which has certain critical capacities built into it. The mechanism may be thought of as partly innate, though modified by experience, especially in the matter of critical capacities. It is useful to invoke the model of a mechanism here since the reception of testimony is normally unreflective but is not thereby uncritical.[16]

Judgements of trustworthiness are informed, however, by a variety of factors, chief among which are what we know of the character and expertise of the witness, the absence of signs of insincerity, corroboration of the story from other sources, and the coherence and plausibility of what is said. Coady recognizes the importance of each of these:

> We may have 'no reason to doubt' another's communication even where there is no question of our being gullible; we may simply recognize that the standard warning signs of deceit, confusion or mistake are not present. This recognition incorporates our knowledge of the witness's competence, of the circumstances surrounding his utterance, of his honesty, of the consistency of the parts of his testimony, and its relation to what others have said, or not said on the matter.[17]

Judgements of the character and expertise of the witness may be arrived at in a variety of ways. In a court of law, for example, witnesses will be required to give an account of their credentials: formal qualifications and experience in the case of an expert witness, or such factors as proximity to the scene of the crime

15. Chakrabarti, 'Review of Coady', 972.
16. Coady, *Testimony*, 47.
17. Coady, *Testimony*, 47.

in the case of an eyewitness. Some witnesses may have their testimony discredited by their vested interest, by a history of dishonesty, by their sense of shock and confusion at the events witnessed, and the like. We should note here, however, that even in a court of law, judgements of trustworthiness, or otherwise, are themselves reliant on the unreflective acceptance of testimony. Members of the jury were not themselves present at the crime to verify that the eyewitness was present; nor do they require to see non-testimonial evidence of the expert witness's qualifications and experience.

In quotidian exchanges of testimony we typically trust those whom we know well and whose testimonies, more often than not, have been reliable in the past. We may be aware of their propensity to tell a good yarn now and again, but we have learned to detect the signs of jest – the hint of a grin or a twinkle in the eye – and so we are not for long deceived on such occasions.[18] So far as the testimony of strangers is concerned, we make judgements in that case too, about character and about expertise. I seek out a 'trustworthy-looking' local resident in order to seek directions in an unfamiliar city and may perhaps modify my, admittedly speculative, first judgement of trustworthiness when I hear the person testify, especially if she tells me that she too is a visitor to the city, or, perhaps, if her speech betrays recent over-indulgence in alcohol. We habitually and instinctively make such judgements in our everyday reception of the testimonies of others. While we are certainly not infallible, common sense accedes, I suggest, to the judgement that most of us are tolerably successful in making such assessments.[19]

What then of the biblical writers? We don't know them personally, and yet we are able to make some assessments of their character and expertise. The writer of Luke's Gospel offers us some assistance here:

> Since many have undertaken to set down an orderly account of the events that have been fulfilled among us, just as they were handed on to us by those who from the beginning were eyewitnesses and servants of the word, I too decided, after investigating everything carefully from the first, to write an orderly account for you, most excellent Theophilus, so that you may know the truth concerning the things about which you have been instructed. (Luke 1.1–4)

Aware that some account of his trustworthiness will be helpful to his audience he offers an account of his qualifications for the job of testifying concerning

18. Even if we miss such signs, the joking testifier will eventually want to reveal the deception in order that the joke may be enjoyed.

19. For a discussion of the 'prudential maxims' for assessing the trustworthiness of testimony as these were debated in the seventeenth century, see Shapin, *A Social History of Truth*, 211–42.

the things about which Theophilus has been instructed. He explains that he has investigated everything carefully and that he has honourable intentions in offering the testimony – he has no wish to deceive. We have to take his word for this, of course, but we do the same, both in a court of law in the case of an expert witness, and in numerous interactions of everyday life.

The apostle Paul is similarly concerned on numerous occasions to spell out his credentials as a testifier to the reality of Jesus. He has shared in the apostles' experience of the risen Christ (1 Cor. 15.3–9), he has consulted with those who were with Jesus and has gained their approval of the testimony he now offers (Gal. 1.18—2.10), he adduces his Jewish pedigree (2 Cor. 11.22), and he offers the evidence of his own character and personal history in support of the integrity and sincerity of his proclamation (2 Cor. 1.12; 6.2–10; 11.21–9).[20] Of course, none of these qualifications constitute irrefutable evidence that Paul will always speak the truth. Paul knows them to be, however, the kinds of thing that will need to be considered in any assessment of his trustworthiness. They are offered as evidence for what remains a personal judgement, a judgement of faith indeed.

The corroboration of others, or of other forms of evidence, is a second significant element in many assessments of the trustworthiness of witnesses. Such corroboration can be sought through established procedures, calling multiple witnesses, or accessing a range of documentary evidence, for example. Or, in less formal contexts, a somewhat unlikely story will be more readily believed if it enjoys corroboration from a variety of sources, especially if they are independent of one another. The investigation of corroborating evidence is well-established in biblical studies too, although debates inevitably continue about the relative value of corroborating evidence. Members of the Jesus Seminar, for example, favour the Gospel of Thomas, calling it 'a goldmine of comparative material'[21] whereas other scholars are more cautious about the value of Thomas's witness.[22] It is not always clear, furthermore, whether corroboration should be taken as independent verification or rather as indicative of collusion. As in daily life, we are required to exercise judgement in being more or less impressed by corroborating sources.

A third and crucially important aspect of the 'mechanism' by which we assess the trustworthiness of testimonial evidence is the criterion of coherence or plausibility. Here we may divide our concern between what we might call 'internal' coherence on the one hand, and 'external' coherence on the other. The

20. Paul also, on occasion, claims authority from God himself (1 Cor. 2.1–16; 2 Cor. 3.5). To this matter we shall return below.

21. Funk and Hoover, *The Five Gospels*, 15.

22. For a brief outline of this debate, see Tuckett, 'Sources and Methods', 128–30.

first is relatively straightforward, while the second is much more complex. By 'internal' evidence of coherence and plausibility I refer, simply, to the internal consistency of the story being told. A tale that my children are fond of telling nicely illustrates the point:

> One fine day in the middle of the night,
> Two dead men got up to fight,
> Back to back they faced each other,
> Drew their swords and shot each other.
> If you don't believe my story's true,
> Ask the blind man; he saw it too.

It is the internal inconsistencies and contradictions in the tale – deliberate, of course – that render it implausible without the need of any further checking. An analytic judgement will suffice for us to dismiss the truth value of testimonies that contradict themselves in this fashion, or, in less extreme cases, the discovery of such incoherence will oblige us to reserve judgement until the contradictions are resolved.

The assessment of external coherence and plausibility is, however, much more complex. Instinctively on encountering any new claim about the world, we ask about the extent to which the newly encountered story or proposition coheres with all else that we think we know. This may be a reflective process as, one hopes, in academic study, but it also happens, and much more commonly, on an instinctive basis. Assessment and assimilation of new information often takes place without conscious reflection. This need not diminish the epistemic value of the testimonial knowledge. Many testimonies are immediately recognizable as trustworthy and do not require reflective assessment. Caution and reflective assessment become obligatory only when we are alerted to possible defeaters of the testimonial proposition – defeaters such as signs of incompetence or dishonesty in the witness, a lack of coherence with other information that we have in our possession, and so on. On being alerted thus, our acceptance, or rejection, of the testimony will be conditional upon a more deliberate process of assessment.

Whether instinctive and instantaneous, or deliberate and reflective, however, the mechanism by which we accept testimonial knowledge draws heavily upon the array of background beliefs – many of them also accrued through testimony – that are constitutive of our basic view of the world. One's capacity to learn through testimony will be conditioned to some extent, therefore, by the truth and coherence of the background beliefs one holds. If I am a convinced believer that the earth is flat, then that belief renders me incapable of learning, if the newspaper reports are true, that the British sailor Ellen MacArthur, in February 2005, completed a solo circumnavigation of the globe in record time. Likewise, if I am a young-earth creationist who believes that the earth is a mere 7,000 years old, then I render myself incapable of learning, if it is true, that dinosaurs roamed the earth several million years ago. My background beliefs attend to that. One further example: if I am convinced that reality is constituted in such a way as to exclude the participation of God in the affairs of humankind, then I render myself incapable of learning, if it is true, that 'God was in Christ reconciling the world to himself' (2 Cor. 5.19).[23]

The epistemic incapacity referred to in each of these examples need not be chronic. It may be overcome in each case by a transformation of one's plausibility structure, to use a term introduced by the sociologist Peter Berger. Or, to put it otherwise, I can only come to learn each of the alleged truths set out above if I undergo a radical transformation of the paradigms that have hitherto governed my perception of reality. That sort of thing happens in science, we are told by Thomas Kuhn, whenever a revolutionary advance in knowledge takes place. Under pressure from a build-up of evidence that is anomalous within the previously conceived paradigm, scientific breakthroughs amount to a re-conception of the field, and open the way to new discovery. Such revolutions, or paradigm shifts, as they are called by Kuhn, are 'a reconstruction of the field from new fundamentals, a reconstruction that changes some of the field's most elementary theoretical generalisations as well as many of its paradigm methods and applications'.[24] The Copernican revolution is a Kuhnian case in point. Of interest here is that a body of evidence that is incomprehensible, or anomalous within one paradigm becomes comprehensible within another. A paradigm shift creates new structures of understanding that enable scientists to comprehend facets of reality that were previously enigmatic, paradoxical or simply unknown. What we can know, accordingly, is at once both facilitated and constrained by the paradigms to which we are committed. Although the acquisition of new knowledge can and does take place in a cumulative fashion within what Kuhn calls 'normal science', on occasion new knowledge is attained only by a revolution in which an old paradigm gives way to the new.

23. See Thomas Kuhn, *The Structure of Scientific Revolutions*, 2nd edn, enlarged (London and Chicago: University of Chicago Press, 1970). Kuhn's account of scientific enquiry has not gone uncontested but most critical comment is directed against Kuhn's alleged relativism and his account of the incommensurability of paradigms, rather than against the idea that science does sometimes progress through revolutionary paradigm shifts. The problem of incommensurability is helpfully addressed by Nicholas Jardine in *The Fortunes of Enquiry* (Oxford: Clarendon Press, 1986).

24. Kuhn, *The Structure of Scientific Revolutions*, 85.

Comparably, to adapt a further principle from Kuhn,[25] our readiness to accept testimonial evidence of hitherto unknown phenomena varies with our estimate of the extent to which the testimony violates paradigm-induced expectations. The business of assessing the external coherence and plausibility of testimony, therefore, is not a straightforward matter. It is a process that is conditioned by the hearer's background beliefs and plausibility structures so that something that sounds plausible to one hearer, might well appear to be wholly implausible to another, not because the first is more gullible, or has less well developed epistemic capabilities, but rather because his or her worldview may be better able to assimilate and make sense of the evidence at hand. It is possible, therefore, that in the event of two people being present to hear the same testimony, one person gets to know the reality to which the testimony is offered as evidence while the other does not.

An example will help to illustrate the point. Built into the floor of the viewing deck of the Skytower in Auckland, New Zealand, is a transparent glass panel through which one can see the life of the city going on several hundred feet below. Although visitors to the viewing deck are told that it is perfectly safe to walk out onto the glass panel, many visitors refuse the invitation to do just that. Such people reason, I suppose – though it may just as well be an instinct informed by a set of background beliefs – that it has always been the case before that when they have stepped out into what *appears* to be thin air, they fall to the ground. Even when registering the presence of the glass panel, they are unable to set aside the lesson of experience that glass commonly breaks when subjected to the impact of other solid bodies. The testimony of the Skytower staff that the strength of the glass is sufficient to bear their weight is not enough to convince them that things will be different in this case. Nor is the visual evidence of other visitors walking safely out onto the glass panel sufficient to reassure them. Their background beliefs and the paradigm that has served them so well thus far, preclude them from *knowing* that they would be safe if they were to attempt the feat of walking out onto the glass. Interestingly, young children are often unconcerned by the prospect of walking on glass at such a height. Their conceptual paradigms do not yet include, apparently, the 'knowledge' that glass often breaks when trodden upon, and so they do not see the threat to their safety that the errant plausibility structures of their parents have conjured up.

I have been attempting here to secure the point that the acquisition of knowledge through testimony depends crucially upon the hospitality of one's worldview to any new item of knowledge. In the case of biblical testimony it

25. See Kuhn, *The Structure of Scientific Revolutions*, 56.

is reasonable to argue, on this basis, that people with the requisite background beliefs will be more receptive to the testimonial knowledge offered in the Bible, just in case it is true. What might such background beliefs be? They are the sort of thing that was set out at length in Chapter 3, namely, belief in the God who is the creator and sustainer of all things, and who, through his Son and Spirit, is active in bringing creation to its fulfilment in reconciled relationship with him. These beliefs have themselves been arrived at through testimony, but in this regard, the believer is in just the same position as natural scientists who necessarily undertake their enquiries with heavy reliance on the testimony of those who have gone before them in developing the frameworks of intelligibility and enquiry within which a particular scientific community operates. Typically, therefore, in biblical interpretation as in the natural sciences we don't bear the weight of judgement on our own. Acceptance of testimony is often communally underwritten. This does not guarantee the truth of the testimony, but it does add rigour to critical assessments of the testimony's worth.

The account given so far of the epistemic value of testimony has offered very little by way of a theological consideration of the matter. I have attempted above only to show in general terms that, despite philosophical prejudices to the contrary, testimony is frequently and justifiably taken as a basis for human knowledge. The time has now come to offer a theological account of how readers of the Bible may come to trust the testimony of the biblical material.

On reading the Bible one encounters a different way of understanding, and ultimately of inhabiting, the world. Such an understanding is distinguished by the content of its theo-logic, that is to say, by its conviction that God is the Creator of the world and has constituted it as it is constituted in order to bring about his purpose of establishing a covenant relationality with his creatures—for their benefit and in order to show forth his love. This contrasts with the view, virtually obligatory in modern scholarship, that the world is constituted and must go its way without reference to God. To enter into the biblical view of the world, and to have one's life shaped and formed by this view, is to undergo what the Bible itself calls *metanoia*, a word variously translated into English as conversion or repentance. Its root meaning in Greek is the transformation of one's mind, but, according to J. Behm and E. Würthwein, the term is typically employed in the New Testament to designate a transformation of the whole person, 'first and basically the centre of personal life, then logically his conduct at all times and in all situations, his thoughts, words and acts...'.[26]

26. J. Behm and E. Würthwein, '*metanoeo* and *metanoia* in the New Testament' in Gerhard Kittel, ed., *Theological Dictionary of the New Testament*, vol. iv (Grand Rapids: Eerdmans, 1967) 999–1008, 1002.

They further explain that *metanoia*, as understood in New Testament usage, is both 'God's gift and man's task'.[27] Writing elsewhere, Johannes Behm notes that *metanoia* is conceived by Paul as a conversion to the knowledge of Truth (*Umkehr zur Wahrheitserkenntnis*) and is, as such, a gift of God.[28] Although there are distinctive features of the New Testament concept of *metanoia*, it involves, in common with Kuhn's paradigm shifts, an account of epistemic progress in which new understanding is effected only through a fundamental transformation of one's conceptual framework. The implications of this account of epistemic progress for the acquisition of testimonial knowledge are twofold.

In the first place, it is clearly the case that the acceptance of testimony, and the learning of what is true in it, is contingent upon the hearer having the requisite background knowledge and conceptual framework. Just as I will be unable to understand a proof of the existence of black holes in the universe, say, without the requisite mathematical knowledge and conceptuality, so also I will not be able to receive as knowledge those things to which the biblical writers testify unless I share their faith that the world is created by God and is the terrain within which God is bringing about his redemptive and perfecting purpose. We have seen already that one's conceptual framework, or worldview, to use the more common term, has a profound influence upon the processing of testimonial knowledge. Those who approach the biblical testimony apart from this faith therefore, and who tell us that this or that aspect of it cannot be believed, do not tell us anything that we could not have anticipated. They are simply confirming that Christian theism and methodological a-theism yield incompatible accounts of what is true. The question remains open, however, about which conceptual framework gives best access to the truth.

Second, it may be, however, that my reading of the testimony of the biblical writers is itself the occasion by which my worldview is transformed. This involves no special pleading for the biblical testimony, for the testimony of others about mundane matters may likewise be the occasion for a transformation of the hearer's worldview.[29] Presumably, such was the case as news of

27. Behm and Würthwein, '*metanoeo* and *metanoia* in the New Testament', 1001.

28. Johannes Behm, 'Metanoia: Ein Grundbegriff der neutestamentlichen Verkündigung', *Deutsche Theologie* 7 (1940) 75–86, 85.

29. Noting the widespread role of 'conversion' in human enquiries of all sorts, C. Stephen Evans writes, 'There are many beliefs, and many belief-forming processes, that require a transformation in the individual for their operation. People must be educated, must be trained and socialized into communities, in order to do science, history, and many other things. The fact that in this [theological] case God himself is involved in the education and transformation of the individual does not seem to me to imply that the result cannot be knowledge.' Evans, *The Historical Christ and the Jesus of Faith: The Incarnational Narrative as History* (Oxford: Clarendon Press, 1996) 274.

Copernicus' heliocentric model of the solar system spread and gained acceptance. To this day most people have not worked through for themselves the scientific proofs for Copernicus' theory furnished successively by Kepler, Galileo and Newton, but have simply accepted the testimony of the scientists against the evidence of their own senses. Our view of the universe has changed dramatically from that accepted by pre-Copernican inhabitants of this world and it has done so for the most part, simply, and justifiably, on the basis of the scientific community's testimony.[30] This readiness to have one's conception of things transformed under the impact of testimonial evidence, might well be set forth as one of the marks of critical enquiry, and contrasts with the closed-minded presupposition that things cannot be otherwise than we have so far believed them to be. J.M. Robinson astutely observes that,

> the objectivity of modern historiography consists precisely in one's openness for the encounter, one's willingness to place one's intentions and views of existence in question, i.e. to learn something basically new about existence and thus to have one's own existence modified or radically altered.[31]

As we have seen in our earlier discussion of the resurrection, the author of the Gospel of Luke was well aware – in common with all four evangelists – that his testimony called forth a radical re-conception of the way things are.

What is *distinctive* about the biblical conception of *metanoia*, and of the conversion called forth by biblical testimony, is that the transformation of one's worldview occasioned by the hearing of such testimony comes about not as a feat of human prowess but rather under the impact of God's action. Whatever else may be the content of the biblical proclamation about God, it includes, centrally, the conviction that God makes himself known. Both on account of our creatureliness and because of human sin, God is beyond our epistemic reach. He is known only as he gives himself to be known. Christian conversion, as the New Testament presents it, therefore, cannot be separated from a proper understanding of the divine economy. It is not flesh and blood or the resourcefulness of human enquiry that enables Simon Peter to see that Jesus is the Messiah, the Son of the Living God. Rather it is, Jesus says, 'my Father in heaven' who has disclosed this truth (Matt. 16.17).

The application of this theological statement to the question of biblical hermeneutics leads properly to the position recently advanced by John Webster

30. Copernicus' heliocentric model of planetary motion was not without precedent, of course, it being proposed as early as *c.*270 BC by Aristarchus of Samos.

31. J.M. Robinson, *A New Quest of the Historical Jesus*, Studies in Biblical Theology 25 (Chicago: Allenson, 1959) 77.

who explains that because 'the Bible as text is the *viva vox Dei* addressing the people of God and generating faith and obedience' the situation of biblical hermeneutics is 'in the last analysis' without analogies.[32] None of what I have said above about the analogous dependence upon testimony in other spheres of human enquiry must be allowed to obscure this distinctive feature of biblical hermeneutics. Christian interpretation of Scripture is 'in the last analysis' attentiveness to the speaking of God. It is the hearing of God's Word addressed now to humankind. The hermeneutical tools that may be applied to this task have value for Christian life only as they are applied to *this* task in response to the call of Christ and under the guidance of the Spirit of God. Thus, as John Webster further claims, 'the hermeneutical situation is... an episode in the history of God's relation to humanity in his works of creation, salvation and perfection'.[33] It is an episode, furthermore, that belongs within the continuing story of God's 'appointment, calling and commissioning' of a people to be his witness in the world, and of his 'appointment, calling and commissioning'[34] of the apostolic testimony itself. Reading the Bible is not, on this account, primarily a matter of technique – though the techniques of scholarship may certainly be brought to bear; it is first and foremost, as Trevor Hart has put it, 'a matter of being in the presence and open to the handling of the One who, in some sense, is the final "author" of its message, because he is the one whose story it tells'.[35]

For the Christian hearer of biblical testimony, therefore, the authority of its witness rests with God. None of what has been said above about testimony in general serves as proof that the biblical witness is authoritative. My aim there was the modest one of showing that, in purely human terms, the news of God's presence and purpose for the world as it is proclaimed in the Bible cannot be discredited simply by virtue of the fact that it comes to us by way of testimony. In this respect it is analogous to many other spheres of discovery. The truth and the authority of Scripture, however, is secured by God's action in calling forth this testimony and by his continuing faithfulness to these thoroughly human words as the medium through which his own Word may be sounded and heard.

32. John Webster, *Word and Church: Essays in Christian Dogmatics* (Edinburgh: T&T Clark, 2001) 58–9.

33. Webster, *Word and Church*, 64.

34. See Webster, *Word and Church*, 74, n.65.

35. Trevor Hart, 'Tradition, Authority and a Christian Approach to the Bible as Scripture' in Joel B. Green and Max Turner, eds, *Between Two Horizons: Spanning New Testament and Systematic Theology* (Grand Rapids: Eerdmans, 2000) 183–204, 204.

IV — Tradition

Although we have been speaking above of the conversion of the individual and the transformation of his or her worldview, the conversion of individuals must not be conceived *individualistically*, for what takes place through conversion is the incorporation of the individual into a community, the community of Jesus Christ extensive in time and space. An important result of this is that human knowing is to be understood as a corporate practice. This is true of all communities of enquiry. The scientist, for example, knows what he or she knows not just on account of what has been verified by the individual, but rather on account of his or her participation in a community of knowledge.

The example is often cited of a scientific paper recently published in the *Physical Review of Letters* under the names of 99 authors, no one of whom had command of all the data brought to bear upon the research findings, but each of whom contributed his or her particular expertise to the experiment in particle physics described therein.[36] This example merely makes explicit what is the case on many occasions of epistemic success. Epistemic progress is built upon trust in the testimony of others. The Church is not different in this, but it has been more ready to recognize that acceptance of its Scripture, and assent to its credal formulations, is not the outcome of individual epistemic prowess but of one's belonging to a community that knows more than any single individual has grasped. We shall say more of this in the following chapter. In the meantime, however, this recognition of the corporate nature of human knowing will enable a positive assessment of the process whereby the knowledge gained through testimony is received, reflected upon, developed and handed on.

Again, to take an easily accessible statement of the prejudice with which we are here concerned, Robert Funk and Roy Hoover write in the Introduction to *The Five Gospels* that,

> the evidence provided by the written gospels is hearsay evidence. Hearsay evidence is secondhand evidence. In the case of the gospels, the evangelists are all reporting stories and sayings related to them by intermediate parties; none of them was an ear or eyewitness of the words and events he records. Indeed, the information may have passed through several parties on its way to the authors of the first written gospels. Those initial transmitters of tradition are, of course, anonymous; they cannot speak for themselves and we cannot interrogate them about the source of their reports. We don't even know who they were. The authors of the written gospels are also anonymous; the names assigned

36. For a fuller account of this case, see John Hardwig, 'Epistemic Dependence', *Journal of Philosophy* 82 (1985) 335–50, 346–8.

> to the gospels are pious fictions... Because the evidence offered by the gospels is hearsay evidence, scholars must be extremely cautious in taking the data at face value.[37]

The tone and intent of this passage are clearly disparaging: as if it were not bad enough, it seems to say, that the Gospel narrative is testimonial in character rather than 'hard evidence' for the life of Jesus, it is rendered even more unreliable by virtue of its having passed through several stages of tradition. Here we encounter a second bias against the biblical testimony, namely that it is 'second, and third, and fourth... hand', or, to use the pejorative term: it is 'hearsay'. Worse still, Funk and Hoover elsewhere suggest,[38] it has undergone considerable modification in the process of transmission. Funk and Hoover are repeating here a frequently made case. John Locke states the matter clearly:

> *any testimony, the further off it is from the original truth, the less force and proof it has.* The being and existence of the thing itself, is what I call the original truth. A credible man vouching his knowledge of it is a good proof; but if another equally credible do witness it from his report, the testimony is weaker: and a third that attests the hearsay of an hearsay is yet less considerable. So that in traditional truths, each remove weakens the force of the proof: and the more hands the tradition has successively passed through, the less strength and evidence does it receive from them.[39]

Such a view is common, but is it really the case that tradition, the process of 'handing on' the testimonial narratives of past witnesses and communities, is likely to be corrosive of the truth? It is not at all clear that this is so; indeed, it is arguable that such a process can both secure and bring into clearer relief the truth once given to our forebears. This is the point noted in Chapter 1 above when citing Gadamer:

> The important thing is to recognise the distance in time as a positive and productive possibility of understanding. It is not a yawning abyss but is filled with the continuity of custom and tradition, in the light of which all that is handed down presents itself to us.[40]

Despite the persistence of an official creed that promotes empirical verification and distrust of authority as unassailable epistemic virtues, tradition clearly plays an indispensable role in the conservation of truth in scientific communities.

37. Funk and Hoover, *The Five Gospels*, 16.

38. They speak approvingly, for example, of Thomas Jefferson's effort to 'separate the real teachings of Jesus, the figure of history, from the encrustations of Christian doctrine', and of D.F. Strauss's project to distinguish the 'mythical' from the historical, and so on. See, *The Five Gospels*, 2–3.

39. Locke, *An Essay Concerning Human Understanding*, Bk IV, Ch. xvi, §10.

40. Gadamer, *Truth and Method*, 265.

Although it does not thereby lose its provisional character, the truth discovered by earlier generations of scientists (as opposed to their errors) is confirmed rather than undermined by its acceptance and transmission by the tradition. The acceptance and refinement of scientific truths by succeeding generations enhances rather than diminishes its authority for the contemporary generation. Indeed, as Coady has demonstrated,[41] there are occasions when, by passing through more hands in a chain of transmission, the testimony has become more reliable not less. That is especially the case where the members of the transmission chain are expert in the relevant field of enquiry, can smell a rat when there is one about, and can vouch for the coherence of the testimony in question with a much greater sphere of knowledge than a single testifier could manage. It is very commonly the case, furthermore, that it is only through a process of sustained critical reflection that a community may work out what to make of the data that a, perhaps naive, first testifier makes available for scrutiny.

Karl Popper, likewise, contends that reliance on tradition is an indispensable feature of scientific progress. Popper writes,

> It is a very simple and a decisive point, but nevertheless one that is often not sufficiently realized by rationalists – that we cannot start afresh; that we must make use of what people before us have done in science. If we start afresh, then, when we die, we shall be about as far as Adam and Eve were when they died (or, if you prefer, as far as Neanderthal man). In science we want to make progress, and this means that we must stand on the shoulders of our predecessors. We must carry on a certain tradition.[42]

Given these positive potentialities of tradition, it is not clear why the deliverances of tradition should be treated with such scepticism in some circles of biblical study. A 'neutral enquiry', if that is considered possible, would surely demand that we approach tradition with a degree of openness to what it might teach us about the reality with which we are concerned. No enquiry is purely neutral, of course, but *a priori* decisions against the veracity of tradition constitute a quite unnecessary compromise of critical scholarship. Critical openness to the value of tradition has the added feature of being a more modest stance than that which supposes that our own interpretative and critical judgements will always be superior to those made by others in the relevant tradition of enquiry. The project of Enlightenment rationalism to eliminate prejudice by the subjection of all authority to the test of human

41. Coady, *Testimony*, 218–19.

42. Karl Popper, 'Towards a Rational Theory of Tradition' in *Conjectures and Refutations: the Growth of Scientific Knowledge* (London: Routledge & Kegan Paul, 1963) 120–35, 129.

reason involves glaring prejudices of its own, notable among which is the supposition that the individual with his or her own reason is a more secure authority *across the full range of human knowledge*(!) than generations of critical thinkers who have gone before.[43] The individualism of modern epistemology is remarked upon by Coady and again by Stephen Shapin, who writes: 'both seventeenth-century and present-day "moderns" celebrate proper science as a culture which has indeed rectified knowledge by rejecting what others tell us and seeking direct individual experience'. Pointing out the delusion of this view, Shapin argues that 'no practice has accomplished the rejection of testimony and authority and that no cultural practice recognizable as such could do so'.[44] An enquiry that lets itself be addressed by tradition, by contrast, is, as Gadamer points out, very far from blind obedience, but is rather a reasoned act of knowledge in which the individual recognizes his or her own limitations and accepts that others have a better understanding.[45]

What might such acceptance, and thus a critical appreciation of the value of tradition, entail in biblical studies? First of all, it involves treating successive generations of tradents as collaborators in the task of discerning the nature, meaning and significance of the realities to which the biblical writers bear witness. The biblical writers are themselves tradents of course, who have gathered, organized and reflected upon previous layers of tradition that are no longer available to us. For this reason their testimony functions, for us, as the first layer of tradition and so constitutes an authority behind which, for the most part, we cannot go.[46]

To treat as collaborators those who have added their interpretative efforts to the various sources that we have inherited from them and that we now use in seeking to understand the realities of which the Bible speaks requires nothing more from us than an acknowledgement, first, that other people might know more than we do, and, second, that a community of readers might be more capable of interpreting the biblical texts than any one of us on our own. We can certainly retain the right to think otherwise about the texts than other readers have done; but to mistrust the tradition as a matter of principle, and to treat the texts themselves with 'extreme caution' in the way that Funk and Hoover urge us to do, constitutes a return to the individualistic epistemology of earlier generations that rather overestimates the investigative capacities of any single individual. By contrast, we must let ourselves be addressed by the

43. On which, see Gadamer, *Truth and Method*, 247.

44. Shapin, *A Social History of Truth*, xxv.

45. Gadamer, *Truth and Method*, 248.

46. Odd bits of earlier evidence here and there, certainly so far as the New Testament's testimony concerning Jesus is concerned, constitute an exception to rather than a refutation of this rule.

tradition, in hope that our own prejudices and blind spots will be questioned and exposed. There is no good reason to suppose that we see the truth about Jesus more clearly than do the biblical authors, or Athanasius, or Cyril of Alexandria, or Luther, or Calvin, and so on. We may see things that they don't, and see other things more clearly, but so might they see where we don't and thus offer correction to our misunderstandings.

A second feature of a biblical hermeneutic that recognizes the value of tradition, will be an increased respect for those features of the biblical narrative that do not appear to correspond precisely to something that actually happened or that was actually said – by Jesus, or indeed by any other of the biblical characters. The reported words of Jesus have repeatedly been subjected, of course, to the corrosive acids of scepticism. Respect for the tradition, however, will enjoin a less sceptical attitude and will involve the recognition that the truth about Jesus is not to be discerned by eliminating everything that does not correspond precisely to some thing that Jesus himself actually did or said. If we were to agree with the claim of the Jesus Seminar, for example, that the 'I am' sayings of John's Gospel are unlikely to have been uttered by Jesus himself, it does not follow that we should exclude such sayings from the database of information about Jesus, as the Seminar counsels us to do. We might judge, rather, that these features of the Johannine narrative, while not emanating from the mouth of Jesus himself, nevertheless bear faithful witness to the reality with which we are concerned. As a matter of fact, we might say, the 'I am' sayings do shed light on who Jesus really was. Such a judgement involves trust in the evangelist's interpretative skill, of course, but we may well have good reasons to trust. There is no good reason to suppose that mistrust is the more scholarly stance or that those who trust should be lumbered with the burden of proof. As Ludwig Wittgenstein remarks, 'What kind of grounds have I for trusting text-books of experimental physics? I have no grounds for not trusting them...'[47] Until we have such grounds, our trust, for the time being, seems to me to be a perfectly respectable position to adopt.

The example of the 'I am' sayings from the Gospel of John illustrates more generally the character of the four Gospels. They are historical narratives, not chronicles (in Hegel's sense of the word)[48] and thus offer an account of the meaning and the implications of what took place. What is involved in trusting the

47. Ludwig Wittgenstein, *On Certainty*, ed. G.E.M. Anscombe and G.H. von Wright (New York: Harper Torchboooks, 1972), §600, p. 79e.

48. As noted in Ch. 1 above, Hegel applies the term chronicle to the report of bare uninterpreted data. We need not revisit here the question of whether interpretation can ever be eliminated from historical reporting. The point, for our purposes, is that historical writing proper can have no such pretensions.

Gospel writers, therefore, is not the supposition that their own post-resurrection faith along with their own ecclesial interests have made no impact on their telling of the story, so that we have it in 'pure' form. What is involved, rather, is confidence that the evangelists are reliable and successful interpreters of the reality with which we are concerned, that of Jesus himself.

Likewise with those who come later in the tradition – our collaborators in the task of understanding who Jesus is. They are to be trusted – or not – as more or less reliable and successful explorers of the logic and implications of the gospel. In a recent exploration of the place of tradition in theology, Stephen Holmes has explained that there is often a cumulative case in favour of trusting the tradition in theology as in any field of enquiry, in defence of which he writes:

> A first point might be the general esteem in which a book or teacher is held; if most of those who have had opportunity to pass judgement regard it as generally successful, then that is a presumption in its favour. Many people attempting to discern what it means to be faithful to Scripture in a particular context, and all agreeing that a particular exposition provides a helpful and convincing account, are more likely to be right than wrong, in the absence of other considerations. This point is strengthened if the consensus extends to those who themselves may be regarded as having some expertise in the work of theology, as the agreement of experts on a topic within their sphere of expertise always carries a certain weight.
>
> This agreement is again more weighty if it extends to widely differing contexts, or across time. A particular context will have its own presumptions or blind spots, which may lead to a great deal of agreement on points which actually have nothing to do with the gospel, or are in fact a denial of it. If, however, an argument is judged to be successful by Christians from different cultures, places and times, it is more likely that the agreement is a result of a shared commitment to the gospel, rather than something else that they share, simply because less else is shared. I suggest then that where there is general agreement on a particular point amongst Christian believers from a wide variety of intellectual and historical contexts, then that agreement itself is evidence for the correctness of the point.[49]

Holmes is referring specifically here to the theological interpretation of Scripture but the principle can be applied more generally. There is a presumption in favour of the authority of the New Testament accounts of the meaning and significance of the events that took place in and around Jesus of Nazareth because their logic and coherence has been upheld by generations of critical readers.

This is not to say, of course, that there has been no dissent within the tradition, or among those who have read the biblical testimonies. But, over time, dissenting

49. Stephen R. Holmes, *Listening to the Past: The Place of Tradition in Theology* (Carlisle: Paternoster Press, 2002) 157–8.

voices are heard and examined and the tradition either adjusts itself so as to take account of the dissenting opinion, or it judges such opinion to be mistaken and thus repudiates it. This a rule of all communities of enquiry, and produces, in the main, reliable but not infallible results. It is a strength of a healthy tradition that, in this way, it tests rather than suppresses dissenting views. Of course, there have been times in the history of Christian theology when the community of critical enquirers has not worked successfully, when enlightened views have been suppressed, and dissenting voices silenced. But it is precisely the strength of tradition that local disputes and failings are subject to the evaluation and authority of a community of enquiry extended in space and time. That broader community has judged the inquisitions, for example, to be a failure in faithfulness to the gospel, or the oppression of women, likewise, to be at odds with the gospel that Christian tradition seeks to conserve, and so on... Tradition, over time and across cultures, generally does a good job of securing the truth of the matter against error.

All of this means that at any particular time, the Church may succumb to error. It is one of the tasks of theology, therefore, to set the present proclamation of the gospel alongside Scripture and the wider tradition and to assess, as best it can, the faithfulness and truthfulness of the present age. Again, the comparison with science is apposite. The scientific community has its own stories to tell of times when, within its own ranks, scientific truth was rejected or suppressed, but, over time, the wider tradition has corrected these errors and seen to it that the truth has emerged.[50]

A third feature of a methodological dependence on tradition in biblical studies is the due recognition it gives to our locatedness as historical human beings. Part of Kierkegaard's polemic against Hegel involved a critique of Hegel's rationalistic presumption to see the world *sub specie aeternitatis*.[51] That kind of 'god-like' knowledge is not proper to, nor possible for human beings

50. Laplace's refusal to accept the evidence that stones fall to earth from the heavens, as aerolites do on a daily basis, is a case in point. The case is discussed by C.S. Peirce in 'The Century's Great Men in Science' in P.P. Wiener, ed., *Selected Writings: Values in a Universe of Chance* (New York: Dover, 1966) 269, and is cited in Coady, *Testimony*, 195. A more recent example is that of Alfred Wegener's theory of continental drift which received a very hostile reaction from the scientific community when first proposed. 'Utter, damned rot!' said the president of the prestigious American Philosophical Society, while a British geologist responded to Wegener's proposals with the claim that anyone who 'valued his reputation for scientific sanity' would never dare support such a theory. These reactions are cited by Patrick Hughes, 'The Meteorologist Who Started a Revolution', *Weatherwise* 47 (April/May 1994) 29–35, 29. I am grateful to John Stenhouse for alerting me to the Wegener case.

51. See, especially, *Concluding Unscientific Postscript to Philosophical Fragments*, ed. and trans. Howard V. Hong and Edna H. Hong (Princeton: Princeton University Press, 1992) 171, 301–9.

constrained as we are by historical locatedness and finitude. Gadamer, likewise, observes that all human existence is limited and qualified in various ways. 'If this is true', Gadamer goes on, 'then the idea of an absolute reason is impossible for historical humanity.'[52] It belongs to the way we are constituted as human beings that our experience and knowledge of the world is shaped by our historical locatedness. We can no more escape this contingency than we can jump out of our own skins. Attempts to transcend the historical mediation of knowledge – through testimony and tradition – are vain attempts to view the world *sub specie aeternitatis*. From Lessing, through Kant, Hegel and Troeltsch and on to modern-day despisers of tradition, there is a consistent failure to recognize the historical constitution of our humanity and the consequent propriety of learning the truth through historical mediation. Stephen Holmes is correct in observing, therefore, that, '[t]o attempt to engage with the scriptural witness in any other way than as that which has been handed on is simply theologically improper, a refusal to accept the way in which God has created us'.[53]

One further feature of a reliance on tradition in biblical studies requires consideration here. It was argued above that the authority of biblical testimony rests finally with God. The same is also true of the Christian theological tradition. What has been described above as the very human process of tradition – handing on the knowledge and wisdom of generations of enquirers – attains authoritative status for the Christian reader of the biblical material by virtue of the fact that God calls forth, empowers, and sides with the tradition's testimony to his presence and purpose. Indeed, it is part of the divine economy and purpose itself that there should be this vital human testimony to the being and act of God. God's calling forth, empowering of, and siding with the tradition does not mean that the tradition is infallible, or that it does not on occasion succumb to error. The promise of the Spirit who will 'guide you into all truth' (John 16.13), however, means, we may faithfully hope, that God will not abandon the Church in its stumbling efforts to bear witness to him, but will, over time, form and reform the Church in order to safeguard and uphold the truth of the gospel. We can thus proceed, as Holmes has eloquently put it,

> patient of our own infirmities and dullness, and confident in both our own work and in the coming future knowing that in all the confusion and messiness of our life and our thoughts we are not abandoned to our own slender resources but upheld by the Spirit. One day we shall know fully; the theological task will be accomplished. Until then, we

52. Gadamer, *Truth and Method*, 245.

53. Holmes, *Listening to the Past*, 13.

> can be sure that it at least will not fail. God will not abandon his Church to error. That is the fundamental content of the promise...[54]

Determination to trust in our own resources alone – be they the resources of reason or of historical enquiry – and to set aside the tradition and testimony of those who have gone before constitutes a refusal to avail ourselves of the provision God has made for our knowing of him. We may safeguard our pride in doing so, but at the considerable cost of sacrificing the truth.

V — Conclusion

It has been my purpose in this chapter to confront the widespread contemporary prejudice in theology and biblical studies against the reliability of testimony and the authority of tradition. Such prejudice did not originate within theology or biblical studies but has been taken over from rationalism,[55] itself a fashion in Western intellectual history that is now, I think, on the wane. According to Gadamer, 'It is the tyranny of hidden prejudices that make us deaf to the language that speaks to us in tradition.'[56] In opposing this prejudice, I have not suggested that either testimony or tradition should be accepted uncritically, or that citing what others have said is enough to settle the truth of any matter. Neither of these sources is infallible and citation of them does not constitute a proof of the claims we seek to make. I have argued, however, that the claims of the biblical writers about Jesus of Nazareth and about God's purposes for and involvement in history should not be dismissed merely because they are testimonial in character or because they have been mediated to us through a tradition. The latter fact may just as well have strengthened and enriched the authority of the original testimony, while the 'original' testimony itself – that of the biblical writers – is already the fruit of sustained critical reflection upon and exploration of the meaning and implications of the career of Jesus of Nazareth. To reject such critical exploration in favour of our own judgements is not improper, but much better reasons for doing so must be offered than is typically the case.

54. Holmes, *Listening to the Past*, 156.

55. In his essay cited above, 'Towards a Rational Theory of Tradition', Karl Popper, though claiming to be a 'rationalist of sorts', offers a powerful critique of rationalism's hostility toward tradition.

56. Gadamer, *Truth and Method*, 239.

7

The Ecclesial Reading of Scripture

In his recent work, *Engaging Scripture*, Stephen Fowl contends that, 'for Christians, scriptural interpretation should shape and be shaped by the convictions, practices and concerns of Christian communities as part of their ongoing struggle to live and worship faithfully before God'.[1] It is my purpose in this chapter to support this contention, though not in the same way that Fowl does,[2] and to argue, further, that the ecclesial reading of Scripture is not just one hermeneutic among many, but is normative. Whatever else may be done outside the ecclesia with the various texts that comprise the Christian Bible, the reading of the Bible, as such, is *essentially* an ecclesial practice.

I — The Meaning of a Text

Fowl himself proposes an 'underdetermined interpretation' of Scripture, a proposal that contrasts with determinate interpretation on the one hand – that form of interpretation that seeks a single meaning inherent in the text – and indeterminate or anti-determinate interpretation on the other, that form of interpretation that seeks to upset, disrupt, and deconstruct interpretive certainties in the name of the excluded or obscured 'other'.[3] Fowl's third alternative,

1. Stephen E. Fowl, *Engaging Scripture* (Oxford: Blackwell, 1998) 62.

2. One way in which I will defend the claim differently from Fowl is to give more attention to the theological character of biblical interpretation. A theological reading of Scripture, as I understand it, should be concerned not merely to highlight the theological content of Scripture but to give an account of how we are to read with God's help. A similar concern is expressed by Donald Wood in his critique of the book *Reading in Communion* (Grand Rapids: Eerdmans, 1991) that Fowl co-authored with Greg Jones. See Donald Wood, 'Theological Hermeneutics', *International Journal of Systematic Theology* 4.2 (July 2002) 156–71, 164.

3. Fowl takes Ben Witherington III as an exemplar of the determinate interpreter, and Jacques Derrida as representative of anti-determinate interpretation. See his discussion in ch. 2 of *Engaging Scripture*.

underdeterminate reading, begins, following Jeffrey Stout,[4] with the recommendation that we abandon the idea that the text has a meaning. It is the indeterminate meaning of the word 'meaning' itself that leads Stout and Fowl to this recommendation. We would do better, they argue, to isolate from the notion of the 'meaning' of a text the particular function that we want to perform. Thus, for example, we might say that we are interested in the author's communicative intentions. 'Alternatively', says Fowl, 'we might want to display a text's contextual connections to the material or gender-based means of its production', and so on. The recommendation, then, is to articulate precisely what we are looking for and 'not cloud the issue further by calling the result of this interpretive activity "meaning" at the expense of other interpretive interests one might pursue'.[5]

I take from Fowl his suspicion of determinate meaning, especially where that is conceived narrowly and restrictively as the author's intended sense discoverable by leaving aside one's own doctrinal or ideological commitments. I agree too with his rejection of anti-determinate interpretation that, despite a commendable concern to resist both the presumption that a text can be 'mastered', and the tendency to exclude or override readings that differ from one's own, nevertheless fails to provide any safeguards against errant readings of a text, or any control upon interpretation.[6] I also accept Fowl's recommendation that we be precise about the task and particular goals of interpretation. But I am not persuaded that we should abandon the category of meaning in our reading of biblical texts. In my view, the challenge to be precise is a challenge to be precise about what we mean by 'meaning'. This can be done, I think, in ways that do not reduce to authorial intention, although they may include it, do not result in a single determinate reading, do not exclude the other, and do not preclude a range of interpretative interests being brought to the biblical text. The account of meaning considered below holds promise, I believe, for a hermeneutic that recognizes and utilizes a range of interpretative tools and concerns and, most importantly, preserves the conception shared by both Jews and Christians that Scripture is the Word of God.

Before venturing an account of the meaning of the text, however, a word needs to be said about the Church's incorporation of Jewish texts in its Bible. I will be arguing below that the community of faith is the primary and

4. Fowl draws on Jeffrey Stout's article 'What is the Meaning of a Text?' in *New Literary History* 14 (1982) 1–12.

5. Fowl, *Engaging Scripture*, 58.

6. I recognize that there are advocates of indeterminate or anti-determinate interpretation who deny this result, but it is difficult to see, and it has not been demonstrated, how a method that starts out by refusing all suggestion of semantic limits can conclude by reintroducing them without undermining itself.

normative locus for the interpretation of the Bible. At various points I will specify the community of faith as the Church, thereby appearing to exclude the Jewish community of faith. If that were the case then the objection could properly be advanced that I am wresting from the hands of Jews their own Scripture, and imposing upon it a hermeneutic that does violence to the integrity of the texts themselves. Such an objection presumes, however, a supersessionist account of the relation between Israel and the Church. We should see the matter, rather, as Paul does when he explains to the Gentiles in the church in Rome that they are as a wild olive that has been grafted onto the rich root of a cultivated tree, that of Israel (Rom. 11.11–24). The Church cannot be detached from Israel without losing its own life, any more than the Church's Bible can be wrested from the hands of the Jews. When speaking of the community of faith, therefore, I mean the covenant community of God encompassing both Jew and Gentile, painfully rent asunder at present, but in need of each other in order to interpret the Word of God aright. It is clear that there are disagreements about the meaning of the biblical texts shared between Israel and the Church, but the account I give below allows us, within particular limits, to speak of 'meanings' in the plural and to recognize the legitimacy of such plurality. Both branches of the divided covenant community seek through reading Scripture to hear the Word of God. But God gives his Word differently on occasion, according to our need.

Let us return to the question of the meaning of the text. We begin with a general account of what 'meaning' means. The meaning of X is the role X plays in its context. Understanding the context and determining the role of X thus become the twin tasks of interpretation. This usually involves an investigation of several layers of context. To ask after the meaning of a word, for instance, is to ask after the role it plays, in a community of discourse – to refer, or to exclaim, or to greet, for example. We may ask further about the role that a word plays in a particular sentence, and about that sentence in a broader discourse, and so on. Take the following as example: 'I am the resurrection and the life' (John 11.25). The role of the word 'I', in this case, is to designate the one who purportedly utters the sentence as the subject of the sentence's claim. Extending our enquiries to the surrounding textual context we find that the one so designated is Jesus. 'I' means, in this context, Jesus – he it is who is the resurrection and the life. This semantic judgement survives – as a truth claim – even if the sentence is thought not to have been uttered by Jesus himself but to be an interpretive gloss by the evangelist. Extending still wider our contextual appraisal, we learn from John's Gospel that this Jesus is confessed to be the Christ, the one who is sent by the Father to give life, and to inaugurate the new creation.

At various points in this appraisal of the context the question of authorial intention will be of interest, so far as it may be discerned,[7] as will also, possibly, the question of the text's contextual connections to the material or gender-based means of its production. In these tasks, the redaction critics, and the social theorists, the linguists and the literary critics will undoubtedly be of assistance. We may go on to ask about the role the sentence plays within the wider canon of Scripture and in the community to which the text was directed. Here the canonical critics, the rhetorical critics, and the historical critics will help. But the meaning of the text is not exhausted by what these experts may say, either singly or severally. The context extends further to the continuing community of God's people whose story these texts tell, and so the major part of the interpretative task will be to ask after the role of this text within that community, or, as preachers typically put it, we may ask: 'What is the meaning of this text for us today?' These multi-layered interpretive concerns are not excluded by but are embraced within the intention to uncover the role a word, a sentence, or a text plays in its *con*text. The point here is to recognize that there are multiple layers of context that are in some way integrated and thus interdependent.

A further feature of this account of meaning is that we are not restricted by it to a single determinate meaning. Authorial intention along with other features of a text's origins will undoubtedly contribute a part of the semantic story, but so too will the history of the text's reception. The underdetermined character of a text's meaning, which Fowl is concerned to safeguard, is afforded by virtue of the fact that the context is not circumscribable. To ask after the meaning of a text, where meaning is defined as the role of a text in its context, is to enquire after authorial intention and original setting, certainly; but equally, it is to enquire into the role it now plays in the canon, the role it plays in the biblical narrative of God's call upon Israel, of his presence with us in Jesus Christ, and in the ongoing story of God's dealings with his people. All of these constitute the meaning of the text, which is not reducible, therefore, to a single determinate meaning. As already noted, God gives his Word differently on occasion, according to our need. Rowan

7. The debates about whether or not authorial intention can be discerned have little bearing on the account of meaning I offer here. If authorial intention can be discerned then it will legitimately inform our judgement about the role a text plays in its context, but, if it can't, then we shall happily make do with such knowledge of the text and its context as we have to hand. For further discussion of the problems attending an appeal to authorial intention, see Stephen Fowl, 'The Role of Authorial Intention in the Theological Interpretation of Scripture' in Joel B. Green and Max Turner, eds, *Between Two Horizons: Spanning New Testament Studies and Systematic Theology* (Grand Rapids: Eerdmans, 2000) 71–87.

Williams, similarly, observes that 'the hearing of God at any one point does not exhaust God's speaking'.[8]

The meaning of a text, thus outlined, implies, when we are dealing with a witness to events in history, that the meaning of the text is bound up with the significance of the events themselves. To ask what a text means, when it says, for example, that God brought the Israelites out of slavery in Egypt, is to ask not merely about literal meaning and literary context, as Spinoza would have it, but also about God and about Israel and about history. The text means to direct our attention to the exodus and to make a claim about its significance. Significance, like meaning, is not circumscribable. The significance of the events is brought out over time as they successively give rise to and shape subsequent events. The significance of the exodus is brought out by Israel's subsequent experience as God's people and by God's continuing creative and redemptive work. In the light of that ongoing history, brought to a climax in the life, death and resurrection of Jesus, the *meaning* of the text bearing witness to the exodus is understood and enriched in ways not envisaged by the author or redactor himself. It is on account of the continuing and unfolding significance of the exodus that the witness is read and reappropriated by the people whose life continues to be shaped by it. In an unending process, the meaning of the text – its role in the context of the divine economy – is constantly being broadened and reconfigured under the impact of that economy itself.

The question arises, of course, whether there are any limits to the context and thus to the meaning of the text. What safeguards are there against the misreading of the biblical texts, such as has occurred, for instance, in the crusades and the Inquisition, in the Dutch Reformed Church's misreadings of the text under apartheid in South Africa, or in patriarchal abuse of scriptural texts in defence of the oppression of women? If the meaning is the role a text plays in its context, why are these readings not legitimate? Here the multilevelled nature of context is of the utmost importance. Any reading of a text, any effort to speak of its meaning, is validated precisely through its relation to the multiple levels of context. Those who ask after the meaning of a scriptural text in the midst of apartheid, for example, are answerable to the role played by the text in question within the book from which it is taken, within the collection of books that is the canon, within the community that has bound these books into its Bible, and within the worldwide community that is constituted precisely by its acceptance of and participation in the biblical story of God's dealings with his people. The context, on this account, is,

8. Rowan Williams, 'Historical Criticism and Sacred Text' in David F. Ford and Graham Stanton, eds, *Reading Texts, Seeking Wisdom* (Grand Rapids: Eerdmans, 2003) 217–28, 226.

again, the divine economy. The divine economy is the singular reality that constitutes the unity of the Bible, and it is the divine economy that establishes the conditions for the meaningfulness of the text. All the many contexts in which the divine economy is worked out – historical, geographical, cultural and so on – are layers of the single context that is the creative and redemptive purpose of God. The role the text plays in service of and in witness to this reality is the meaning of the text. Interpreters go astray precisely as they ignore this multi-layered context and the unity given to it by God. The interpretive resources and context of the community as a whole, whose story the Bible tells, are the safeguard against errant readings.

This conception of the multi-layered context of Scripture accords with what Stephen Fowl says about context:

> Despite [the] variety of contexts in which Christians interpret scripture, their primary aim in all of these different settings and contexts is to interpret scripture as part of their ongoing struggles to live and worship faithfully before the triune God in ways that bring them into ever deeper communion with God and with others.[9]

The continuing story of God's dealings with his people constitutes an overarching context in which the 'otherness' of the multiple contexts is subordinate to the commonality that is shared in communion with God and with one another. The meaning of Scripture becomes evident within that communion which is itself generated by the hearing of God's Word.

Fowl is no doubt correct in asserting that there can be no *guarantee* against errant readings. We 'cannot produce a method', he writes, 'that will, if properly followed, rule out Christians from interpreting the Bible to confirm and underwrite their sinful practices'.[10] We need a frank acknowledgement of the fact that readers within the community of faith have frequently misread the text and used it improperly. My proposal is not a method for avoiding errant readings, therefore, but rather for identifying them when they occur. That task, of 'vigilance', to use Fowl's term, falls to the *whole* Church, to that community of faith whose story the Bible tells. Whoever determines to stand outside of this multi-layered context, and recognizes no accountability to it, is likely to do violence to the meaning of the text. Here, then, is a first reason why the ecclesial reading of Scripture is normative, rather than just one among many options.

Several features of this account of the meaning of a text require further comment. First, Stephen Fowl, we have noted, is concerned that meaning

9. Fowl, *Engaging Scripture*, 2–3.
10. Fowl, *Engaging Scripture*, 74.

should not be restrictive. That is to say, he resists any hermeneutic that delivers a single determinative account of the meaning of a text, and which construes that meaning as a property of the text itself. In this he sides with Derrida and other anti-determinate interpreters who speak on behalf of the excluded other. The proposal I have offered likewise resists the imposition of a single determinate meaning, and offers an account of meaning not reducible to a property of the text independent of its relation to context. What Trevor Hart says of the *authority* of a text applies equally to the *meaning* of biblical texts, namely,

> I would prefer to construe the authority [likewise the meaning] of the text, or the 'presence' upon which it reposes, not as a property of the texts themselves (although their various properties are certainly not irrelevant) but rather as a 'property' or aspect of the event in which the text and reader together are drawn into a relatedness to the living God whereby God 'speaks' or is known through the reading.[11]

The role a text played in drawing the community for which it was written into relation with the living God is of vital interest to later interpreters, but this original relation need not exhaust the meaning of the text. The text may well play different roles as the relatedness of God and his people continues to unfold across diverse geographical, cultural and historical settings. The Suffering Servant passages of Isaiah, directed first to Israel's situation in exile, but later heard by the Church as referring to the one Word of God now incarnate among them, provide a case in point. We don't have to choose between nor exclude either of these readings. Rather, we should see them together as witness to the continually emergent story of God's purpose for the world. So too might these texts be the means of God speaking to his people today. With this interest in the text as word of God, the question of the role a text plays in its context becomes focused especially on the role given a text by God himself. The community of faith therefore attends in its reading of Scripture not just to the ways in which God's word has been heard and understood in the past, for which task the critical tools of biblical scholarship are of undoubted assistance, but also to the ways in which the text becomes the instrument of God's speaking afresh.

Jesus' celebration of the Passover meal with his disciples provides a clear example of the reinterpretation of Scripture in service of the divine economy. Without in the least denying the meaning of the Passover celebration as it is understood within Judaism and mediated through the texts of the Old Testament,

11. Trevor Hart, 'Tradition, Authority, and a Christian Approach to the Bible as Scripture' in Joel B. Green and Max Turner, eds, *Between Two Horizons: Spanning New Testament and Systematic Theology* (Grand Rapids: Eerdmans, 2000) 183–204, 202.

the new context of Jesus' own death enables him to read this tradition in a very different way, not discontinuous with, but in profound continuity with God's deliverance of his people from bondage in Egypt. Exodus 12 provides the conceptual framework within which to understand the divine deliverance now to be effected through the death and resurrection of God's Son. At the same time, the new act of God – the salvation wrought through his Son – allows Jesus to shed previously undreamt-of light upon the story of the Passover itself.

In seeking to discern whether it hears God's voice afresh in the texts of Scripture, the community of faith will attend to the other layers of context that have been set in place through the course of history and in diverse geographical settings. They will attend to them with the conviction that there is an intelligible unity to the story of God, born of the steadfast love of God himself. Contemporary readings must be coherent, then, with earlier readings, where those readings have themselves been judged to cohere with the story as a whole, or, to put it otherwise, to bear faithful witness to the one God who is the same yesterday, today and tomorrow. The 'rule of faith' has been the usual means by which the Church has tested this coherence. We will say more of this matter below.

What about the excluded other – women, or the poor, or readers from non-Western cultures, to take some examples of which the Church has lately been made more aware? By identifying the meaning of a text with the role it plays in its context, the meaning of the text is opened to new exploration and application within the contexts inhabited by such excluded others. There is a proviso, however – the same one that applies to all readers: the multiple levels of context – the original *sitz im leben*, the canon, the community of God's people whose story the Bible tells – must all be attended to in every new context of reading.[12] Here is the place to note the privilege that must be accorded to the canonical context. If it can be shown, as has often been done, by women readers of the Bible, or by Liberation theologians, for instance, that traditional readings of a particular text have failed to take sufficient note of the biblical story as a whole, then coherence with the canonical context will be a decisive argument in favour of any new reading. A reading that more

12. I acknowledge that there is some looseness in my use of the term 'context'. In some respects it makes sense to speak of *contexts* in the plural when referring to the different places and people in which and among whom the Bible is read, but in another sense, it is better to recognize these diverse settings as different levels of a single context, that of the unfolding story of God's dealings with his people across a vast array of times, cultures and places. I hope that the respective reference to one or other of these two senses will be apparent as I use the term variously in this chapter. The important point is that my earlier identification of the meaning of a text as the role it plays in its context picks up both aspects of the 'context' and requires that they be held together.

clearly identifies the role a text plays in the canon will take priority over one that tears it from its context. This latter practice has clearly been the case in the attempts often made to deny ordination to women on the basis of selected texts in the Pauline epistles. There is enough evidence in Paul himself, let alone in the rest of the New Testament, to deny the legitimacy of such use. Intra-canonical coherence then becomes a key criterion of legitimate reading. This does not mean that every text must be harmonised with every other. Rather, it means that texts are to be read in the light of the biblical story as a whole.

Another way of putting this is that the different contexts in which the text is interpreted – original community, early Church, contemporary Church, women readers, third-world readers, and so on, do not constitute separate spheres isolated from one another. They are related to each other, rather, as layers in the overarching context of the divine economy. The readings offered within widely divergent local contexts are to be understood as episodes in a single story and gain their legitimacy in that way or not at all. Precisely because of this the texts are properly read in diverse local contexts only when readers recognize their responsibility to each other. They cannot cut loose from the wider community of interpretation. Male readers are responsible, therefore, to women readers of Scripture; first-world readers are responsible to third-world readers; rich readers are responsible to the poor; contemporary readers are responsible to the tradition, and so on, and vice versa (as temporal constraints permit), so that each reads in collaboration with a wider community to which he or she is responsible. It is in virtue of such responsibility and collaboration that Dutch Reformed readings in defence of apartheid, or National Socialist readings by the German Christians, are found to be errant, either by prophetic voices in the midst of the errant community, or by the wider Church. An anti-determinist hermeneutic, by contrast, has no such controls and is to be rejected precisely because it allows no limits to the role the text may play, and cannot offer a secure basis, therefore, upon which to say that the use of the Bible in defence of such atrocities was wrong.

The model suggested above, of multiple layers of context within which the meaning of a text may vary, does not give licence for a limitless pluralism. The various local 'contexts' of interpretation are not in fact distinct from one another. They should not be conceived as separate spheres of enquiry, and indeed not even as different contexts, but rather as different levels of an ever-broadening context, that of the unfolding story of the relation between God and his world. There is a primary and a final answerability across all levels, therefore, to the God whose story this is. In the end, God defines himself through this story, and supremely so through the incarnation of his Word. It is in the event of incarnation worked out through the life, death, resurrection and ascension of Jesus of Nazareth that the meaning of the story, and thus of the diverse partial tellings of the story, is once and for all disclosed. This is because in Jesus Christ the context of the text, from creation to new creation, is laid out in its fullness. This is seen especially in the Gospel of John, which begins with an echo of the opening words of Genesis and ends with a reference to the parousia (John 21.23), 'until I come'![13] The meaning of the text is thus a matter of the role it plays in this story of the God who goes his way among his people and who, through his Word and Spirit, gathers all things and successively embraces countless 'others' into reconciled communion with himself. This story is the overarching context in which the meaning of the text is to be discerned.

II — The Community of Readers

To say that errant readings of biblical texts are possible is not contentious. Despite offering no consistent criteria for identifying errant readings, even the most ardent anti-determinist is not commonly to be found tolerating the use of biblical texts in defence of anti-Semitism or in the oppression of women, for example.[14] The question then arises, how are errant readings to be identified and true readings preserved? I have suggested above that such decisions are facilitated primarily through the recognition that readers of Scripture ought not to retreat, either to the privacy of their own homes, or to the relative isolation of their studies. Good reading takes place, rather, in humble recognition that one belongs within and is answerable to a community of readers extended through space and time. All communities of enquiry, whether they be focused on texts or not, have a moderating and corrective function in relation to the claims of their members. The claims of an individual, or indeed of a sub-group within the community, are received and tested by public scrutiny. So far, that should be uncontroversial, despite the individualistic ideologies that have been so prevalent in Western epistemology. Even Cartesian or Kantian epistemologists typically endorse the idea of the university, a forum for the communal assessment and development of claims to truth.

13. I owe the point to Richard Bauckham, 'Reading Scripture as a Coherent Story' in Ellen F. Davis and Richard B. Hays, eds, *The Art of Reading Scripture* (Grand Rapids: Eerdmans, 2003) 38–53, 41.

14. Two main options are open to anti-determinate readers in such cases. Either they reject the interpretation of the oppressor, in which case it is evident that not all interpretations are equally to be respected, or they reject the text, which decision implies that there *is* a determinate meaning that cannot be got rid of.

Less agreeable to many, however, is the claim that in the case of the interpretation of the Bible, the community that is best equipped to scrutinize the fruit of hermeneutical activity is not the university but the Church. This does not mean that scholars who have no allegiance to the Church should be ignored or excluded – no one should be excluded from reading and responding to the Bible – but their results should not be accorded an authority beyond that of the Church or binding upon it.[15] But why should the Church be the community to which biblical hermeneutics is primarily answerable?

The first answer to be given is that the Christian Bible is the Church's book. It was assembled by the Church under the twofold conviction, first, that these particular texts tell the Church's own story, the story of God's dealings with his people for the sake of bringing to completion his purposes for creation as a whole, and, second, that it is in reading these texts that we can expect to hear the voice of God. There is no other reason for the Bible to exist. Thus, as Robert Jenson rightly points out, 'Where the church's calling to speak the gospel is not shared, the binding of these particular documents between one cover becomes a historical accident of no hermeneutical significance.'[16] It is therefore not surprising, as Jenson further points out, that

> when folk who do not follow the gospel turn their attention to the Bible, the one book immediately disintegrates into its component parts, splitting first into Hebrew Scripture and New Testament and then into traditions, redactions, and so forth...[17]

The Church has a presumptive claim on the meaning of Scripture because it is in the context of the Church's own life that the Bible, as Bible, came to exist at all. When Philip Davies asks, therefore, 'Whose Bible is it anyway?',[18] the answer is quite clear: it belongs to the Church. No other community has any

15. N.T. Wright offers a characteristically lively and illuminating comment on this matter: 'It is, of course, open to anyone to do what he or she likes with this or any book. A volume of Shakespeare may be used to prop up a table leg, or it may be used as the basis for a philosophical theory. It is not difficult, though, to see that using it as the foundation for dramatic productions of the plays themselves carries more authenticity than either of these.' N.T. Wright, *The New Testament and the People of God*, 5–6.

16. Robert Jenson, 'Hermeneutics and the Life of the Church' in Carl E. Braaten and Robert W. Jenson, eds, *Reclaiming the Bible for the Church* (Edinburgh: T&T Clark, 1995) 89–105, 89–90. See also Jenson's chapter, 'Scripture's Authority in the Church' in Ellen F. Davis and Richard B. Hays, eds, *The Art of Reading Scripture* (Grand Rapids: Eerdmans, 2003) 27–37.

17. Jenson, 'Hermeneutics and the Life of the Church', 90.

18. Philip R. Davies, *Whose Bible is it Anyway?*, 2nd edn (London: T&T Clark, 2004). (Originally published as JSOT Supplement 204, Sheffield Academic Press, 1995).

reason to place these texts together and to read them as a single story.[19] The efforts of Davies to argue that textual variants and disputes over the canon, along with the uncontroversial fact that the texts of the Bible did not come into being as books of the Bible, fail to undermine, as he hopes, the reality of the Bible as the Church's book. Only the most naive inerrantist is likely to be troubled by textual variants, while differences of opinion among the various branches of the Church about the precise make-up of the canon does not threaten their common conviction that the texts commonly agreed upon – by far the majority – are properly to be read together as constitutive of a single story. Even those texts excluded from some canons but included in others are acknowledged as worthy of study by most branches of the Church. Finally, that particular texts were not 'born' into the canon, as it were, does not preclude them from being properly understood alongside other texts as part of the continuing story of God's people. If that is the story they set out to tell in the first place, it makes a great deal of sense to set them alongside, and to interpret them in the light of other texts that seek to tell the same story, not least because inter-textual references, both explicit and allusive, are frequently to be found. Such references and allusions, quite apart from the common subject matter of the texts – the working-out of the covenant relationality between God and his people – constitute a demand that the biblical texts be read together. Davies protests that 'no ancient writer should have his or her text accorded a retrospective meaning dictated by the dogmatic requirements of an institution that chose to "canonize" it'. It is by no means clear, however – indeed it is highly implausible – that the dogmatic requirements of 'non-confessional' readers who, as Davies himself puts it, 'do not accept the reality of the deities [the texts] refer to'[20] should provide a better framework in which to read the texts. The ancient writers, I suggest, would probably take far less offence at the thought of having their texts included in a story that continues beyond their own context than they would at being subjected to a hermeneutical method that turns suspension of belief into a methodological requirement. Yet, remarkably, Davies contends that only the second set of readers with their non-confessional methodology should be allowed to ply their

19. In support of the view that the Bible is the Church's book and has no reason to exist as Bible outside the Church, R.W.L. Moberly comments, 'There is thus a nice irony in the fact that the recurrent rhetoric on the part of biblical scholars about freeing the Bible from ecclesiastical and dogmatic presuppositions, so that it can speak for itself, tends to coexist largely uncomplainingly with the preservation of that ecclesiastical and dogmatic construct, the Bible itself.' See Moberly, *The Bible, Theology and Faith: A Study of Abraham and Jesus* (Cambridge: Cambridge University Press, 2000) 13–14.

20. Davies, *Whose Bible is it Anyway?*, 12.

trade within the university.[21] There is a whiff here of the discredited myth of the neutral reader.[22] The dispute should not be about confessional and neutral readers, however, because none of the latter exist. The important question rather is whether insight into the meaning of the texts is better served within a conceptual framework formed by the texts themselves, such as we have outlined in Chapters 3 and 4, or by one that takes its bearings elsewhere. If, as Davies suggests, we are to speculate about the way the original authors might have preferred their texts to be handled, then a methodology that is characterized by sympathy for rather than antipathy towards what the texts are saying would seem to have much to commend it.

The conceptual world of the texts themselves is best understood, not as a set of intellectual propositions to which one assents or not, but as a form of life shaped by and in turn shaping one's thinking about and reading of the Bible. Here we come back to the claim from Stephen Fowl with which we began this chapter: 'for Christians, scriptural interpretation should shape and be shaped by the convictions, practices and concerns of Christian communities as part of their ongoing struggle to live and worship faithfully before God'. The biblical texts themselves commend, exhort, and call us forth to a particular form of life that we might broadly describe as one of faithfulness to God. The one place where that call and exhortation is taken seriously is in the community of God's people. It is in that community, furthermore, that the reality of which the Bible speaks, the reality of God's creative purposes for the world, is accepted, explored, and wrestled with, not merely as an intellectual exercise but in the ongoing struggles and challenges of daily life. For this community, the biblical writers are not citizens of an alien world from which we are separated by a vast temporal gulf and an even more vast conceptual one.

21. It is quite astonishing to observe the attempts of Davies to *exclude* confessional interpretation of the Bible from the university on the grounds that confessional reading is exclusive. Note, that I am not proposing the exclusion of anyone from the university, nor from reading the Bible. My contention, rather, is that the Church constitutes the primary and normative context for the reading of the Bible. If others want to read the Church's Bible as well, then they are very welcome, but it does seem rather unpromising to begin by requiring it to be accommodated within a framework of interpretation other than its own.

22. Davies is inconsistent on this matter. Sometimes he claims that for practitioners of biblical hermeneutics in the university he does not require any kind of belief except in the usefulness of universally agreed rules of evidence and argument (53), while elsewhere he claims to recognize that no discourses are neutral (26). If this latter principle is upheld, however, then his case for the exclusion of confessional hermeneutics from the university reduces to the assertion that his atheistic convictions are better able to serve the truth than theistic convictions, unless, of course, he supposes that universities are not in the business of seeking truth, but rather of supporting a modernist secular ideology.

They are, rather, cohabitants in a single community of God's people. It is among this community that the reality of which the Bible speaks has begun to be borne out. It is among this people that the grace and forgiveness of God are fashioning new life from old, and it is in the midst of this community that the promise of God to dwell with his people is claimed and experienced. That is why this community of people can lay claim to a certain privilege in hearing the texts of the Bible aright; it is because they are participants in the reality of which the Bible speaks. Discerning the meaning of the text, for this community, is bound up with the role these texts continue to play in mediating to them the Word of God.

It is this continuing role of the texts as the vehicle of divine self-disclosure that constitutes the primary reason why the Church has a certain privilege in reading them. Only if it were not true that God speaks his Word through these texts would it be legitimate to take them from the hands of the community that reads them with that expectation and to demand acceptance of an alternative means of discerning their meaning. Thus, as Francis Watson observes,

> The biblical texts are to be read as Christian holy Scripture not primarily because of sociological facts about their traditional roles but because, in all their imperfections, oddities and contingencies, they together constitute the inspired and normative testimony to a universally- and ultimately-significant history of divine self-disclosure. A Christian theological interpretive practice cannot do otherwise than claim that it alone can accommodate itself to the true reality of these texts in their constitutive relation to the history of divine self-disclosure that has called them into being and that continues to occur through them.[23]

It is wrong to assume, as Philip Davies unfortunately does,[24] that reading the texts with the expectation of hearing God's Word should entail disinterest in, or renders incidental the contextual, literary and historical studies that are customarily undertaken within the university. Christian readers of the Bible are interested in the role a text plays in its context, and the context, for them, includes the whole narrative of the people of God. The context is not limited

23. Francis Watson, 'Bible, Theology and the University: A Response to Philip Davies', *Journal for the Study of the Old Testament* 71.1 (1996) 3–16, 13.

24. See Davies, *Whose Bible is it Anyway?*, 20. Davies's claim is ironically refuted by his observation, explored in ch. 2 of his book, that many scholars writing within the university address historical-critical questions while at the same time appealing to canonical criteria of interpretation. Davies thinks this is problematic in some way, but it would only be so under the (false) presumption that confessional readers have no interest in the kinds of questions that non-confessional readers restrict themselves to. Francis Watson, again, correctly points out that Davies has manufactured the confusion himself. See Watson, 'Bible, Theology and the University', 15n.

to the original author's or the redactor's immediate community, but it does not exclude it either. All that can be known about the circumstances and nature of a text's composition will be of interest in discerning the meaning of the text, but so too will the reception history and the new ways in which God might use the text to speak afresh today.

Speaking afresh does not mean saying something divorced from what the text meant originally or in its reception history. It means rather that the community hears afresh the call to participate – undoubtedly in ways appropriate to its own time – in the reality to which the text bears witness. Since that is the call of the text in all times and places, the Church reasonably expects a high degree of coherence across the various levels of context in which the text is interpreted.[25] The expectation of coherence does not mean that all readers will arrive at the same meaning; their different levels of context will preclude that. The text will play a different role at different levels of context and call forth different forms of action within the community of faith. But since the Bible bears witness as a whole to the singular reality of God's unfolding purpose in creation and redemption, we may properly expect a high degree of coherence between the varying forms of participation in that reality. That is to say, the new Word of God that is heard through the text, is not incidentally but essentially related to the Word as it has been variously heard throughout the history of God's dealings with his people. Where that essential relation is lacking, such as has been evident in the use of the Bible in defence of apartheid, to oppress women, to prohibit inter-racial marriage, and so on, the Church may rightly judge that the Bible has been misread and its meaning obscured. Again, however, it is the ecclesia as a whole, under the guidance of the Spirit, that regulates the reading of Scripture, preserves the meaning of the text, and thus seeks to hand on the gospel with which it has been entrusted. As Stephen Fowl puts it, 'In countless, and often subtle, ways, Christians' engagements with Scripture are (and should be) shaped by the successes, failures, debates, discussions and prayers of previous generations of Christians.'[26] Success in this enterprise depends finally, however, not principally on human resources, but on the faithfulness of God to the Church. Reading Scripture aright is not finally a matter of technique but of grace.

25. This is not to say, of course, that there have not been and will not continue to be divergences in interpretation that are simply and straightforwardly incompatible. Because of its confidence in the unity of truth, however, a unity established in the one Word of God, the Church cannot ultimately rest content with *incompatible* meanings of the text but will strive towards greater understanding in hope and in prayer.

26. Fowl, *Engaging Scripture*, 7.

III — The Rule of Faith

To recognize the regulative role of the ecclesia in the reading of Scripture is to allow one's reading to be shaped by the convictions, practices and creedal formulations of the Church. It is to recognize, as John Webster has put it, that 'the Bible has its place in that sphere of human life and history which is generated by God's revelation'.[27] That 'sphere of human life', manifest in worship, in doctrine and in mission, now constitutes the context for the text. There is, of course, a dialectical process at work here: the worship, the doctrine and the mission of the Church emerge and develop through engagement with Scripture, and then those same doctrines and practices successively constitute a hermeneutical guide to the reading of Scripture itself. This accords with what has been said earlier about the meaning of the text. Meaning is simply the role a text plays in its context. A conversation goes on between text and context, and precisely through that conversation, the meaning of the text emerges.

The story of the Church's life is long and complex of course, but it is possible to offer a brief description of this life and of its place in the divine economy. That brief description is known as the rule of faith. It is an account of God's action from creation to new creation and centred around Jesus Christ, in the course of which the community of faith is called into being as witness to and fruit of the action of God. Put another way, the rule of faith is the plot of the Bible that cannot therefore be read according to some other plot without disintegrating the Bible itself.

It can be alleged of the claim that the Bible is to be read according to the rule of faith that this is a circular process. It is! But this is as it should be in any field of human enquiry. Each time we go to the object of our enquiry we learn more from it, and what we learn then shapes the way in which we go back to it again. Other disciplines will give their own account of how this circularity fosters rather than inhibits a genuine openness to the reality with which they are concerned. In the case of theology and the reading of Scripture, openness to the reality of Scripture itself is expressed in the prayer, 'Come Holy Spirit'. That prayer, always accompanying the ecclesial reading of Scripture, asks that we should hear in Scripture, not our own voice reflected back at us, but rather the voice of God. The rule of faith provides a guide to such reading; it is a summary of what the Church has learned hitherto when it has gone to the Bible to hear the Word of God. It is in this way appropriate that the rule of faith should light our way when we go back to the Bible again.

27. Webster, *Word and Church*, 100.

IV — Narrative Unity

More needs to be said about the narrative unity and singular plot of the Bible to which I have appealed above. It is clear enough that the books of the Bible do not constitute a single narrative with beginning, middle and end. Nor do they all take the form of narrative; they include prayers, songs, doctrinal explorations, prophecies, interpretations of the narrative itself, and so on. To appeal to narrative unity, therefore, is not to insist that as arranged in the canon all the books of the Bible are successive parts of a story that begins in Genesis and ends in Revelation. It is to recognize, rather, that all these texts have their place within an overarching narrative of God's purpose for the world. None of the texts tell the whole narrative from creation to new creation but each plays a part within it, constituting together a people's reception and exploration of God's word, their faithfulness and failure, their insights and their misconceptions. The principle of unity in this complex and meandering story is God himself. He it is who calls people into relation with himself, who inspires their insight and their obedience, who judges, forgives and redeems their failures and who, by means of the Israelite people and through his own presence in Jesus Christ, makes himself known as author[28] of the story and as the one who will bring it to completion in the final victory of Christ and the pervasiveness of the new creation. John Goldingay observes that,

> It is not by chance that the bulk of Scripture is narrative. This characteristic corresponds to the nature of Christian faith. The fundamental Christian message is not an ethic, such as the challenge to humanity to live by the law of love, a challenge Christianity shares with some other religions. Nor is it a theology, a collection of abstract statements such as 'God is love' – statements that it also shares with some other religions. It is a gospel, an account of something God has done, a concrete narrative statement: 'God so loved the world that he gave his only Son...'[29]

It is precisely because there is a complexly braided yet single story to which the texts in their various ways bear witness, that the texts not only may, but *must* be read together.

In defence of the narrative unity of the Bible, Richard Bauckham explains that we do not need to rely solely on the existence of the canon or the Church's reading of it in order to claim such a unity; nor need we make a simply arbitrary decision to read the Bible in this way. We can appeal also to significant features of the texts

28. The human act of writing is one of attentiveness and response to the *author*ity of God.

29. John Goldingay, *Models for Scripture* (Grand Rapids: Eerdmans, 1994) 23.

themselves.[30] Among those Bauckham adduces are the numerous ways in which the texts themselves recognize and assert the unity of the story they tell, the summaries that are given in the Bible itself of the story as a whole, and the way in which the book of Revelation presents itself as the summation of the whole biblical tradition of prophecy. We might adduce, too, the multitude of inter-textual references, and the simple observation that the texts are concerned with the same subject matter, namely, the people of Israel and their dealings with God, the development of that story through the life, death and resurrection of Jesus of Nazareth, and the subsequent gathering of the Gentiles into the body of God's people. Attempts by Davies and others to construe the obvious diversity of the biblical texts in ways that are subversive of their unity simply ignore, for their own dogmatic reasons, far too much of the evidence within the texts themselves.[31]

A compelling account of the interrelatedness of the biblical texts has recently been offered by Christopher Seitz.[32] In an examination of the phrase, 'in accordance with the scriptures', used by Paul in 1 Corinthians 15 to account for both Christ's death and his resurrection, Seitz draws attention to the fact not always explicitly recognized that Paul is referring here to the Old Testament scriptures, and is arguing therefore that the death and resurrection of Jesus has its place within the single story of God to which the Old Testament bears witness. That is the context in which the meaning of Jesus' death and resurrection is made known.

Although Seitz does not make the point explicit, the implication of his argument is that we cannot understand Paul's text without the canon. The canon, accordingly, is not an arbitrary imposition upon the texts, doing violence to their meaning and integrity. The canon is, rather, an arrangement of diverse texts that are intrinsically related to one another.

30. Richard Bauckham, 'Reading Scripture as a Coherent Story', 42. Attempts have recently been made to speak of a unity behind the canon. Nicholas Wolterstorff, for example, has argued that texts may be given a hermeneutically significant unity by virtue of the fact that they have been 'authorized', by virtue, that is, of someone or some community having arranged them together under the conviction that together they satisfy the demands for completeness and coherence. Such is certainly the process by which the Church formed its canon, but one hopes to find evidence within the texts, too, that such authorization was in keeping with the content of the texts themselves. Wolterstoff's discussion can be found in 'The Unity Behind the Canon' in Christine Helmer and Christof Landmesser, eds, *One Scripture or Many? Canon from Biblical, Theological and Philosophical Perspectives* (Oxford: Oxford University Press, 2004) 217–32.

31. It is beyond the scope of this work to lay out that evidence in detail. See, however, Richard Bauckham's article cited above. The common appeal among biblical exegetes to 'inter-textuality' provides further evidence of the hermeneutical merits of reading the Bible as canon.

32. Christopher R. Seitz, 'In Accordance with the Scriptures' in *Word Without End: The Old Testament as Abiding Theological Witness* (Grand Rapids: Eerdmans, 1998) 51–60.

V — Reading With God's Help

I have claimed in note 2 above that a theological reading of Scripture should be concerned not only to highlight the theological content of Scripture but to give an account of how we are to read with God's help. These two concerns belong together. The theological content is not understood properly if it is reduced to a series of theological propositions arousing curiosity of various kinds and to which we may give or withhold assent; it is understood rather as we are drawn to participate in the reality to which Scripture bears witness. The logic of this form of understanding is rather like that of the person who comes to understand the statement, 'I love you', when it is addressed to them. The meaning of the statement, reducible, if we like, to something that can be investigated with a range of critical tools, is truly understood only as the person to whom it is addressed learns to participate in the reality to which the statement testifies. Whatever value there may be in the deliverances of scholarly appraisal – and I do not wish to deny such value – there is a semantic privilege and normativity attaching to the hermeneutic efforts of the one who learns what the statement means by dwelling within the reality the statement helps to reveal.[33] One cannot expect this normativity to be acknowledged, however, except by the person who has been gripped by the reality to which the text bears witness.[34] Such acknowledgement is contingent upon one's acceptance that the witness of Scripture is true.[35]

There is a further parallel to be drawn between understanding Scripture and understanding the word of one who loves us. Our participation in the reality is made possible by the one who gives his or her word. The Johannine affirmation, 'We love because God first loves us' (1 John 4.19) expresses the logic of the matter. Dwelling within the reality to which the word bears witness is not a possibility grounded in our own resources, shaped as they are by finitude and sin, but solely in what is given. It is because God gives *his* Word to us that, despite our limited understanding and despite our sin, we may hear and understand. The Church expects to hear that Word whenever it reads the Bible. It

33. In an extension of the metaphor, Søren Kierkegaard compares the reading of Scripture to reading a letter from one's beloved. Without 'disparaging scholarship', Kierkegaard insists that the point of reading – the primary point of reading – is to participate in the life to which the letter invites us. See Kierkegaard, *For Self-Examination*, 26–33.

34. The point is adapted from G.C. Berkouwer, who writes that one cannot 'be compelled to accept the revelation of Scripture on the basis of its God-breathed quality before being gripped by the message to which its words testify'. G.C. Berkouwer, *Holy Scripture*, ET (Grand Rapids: Eerdmans, 1975) 166–7.

35. The point is taken from Goldingay, *Models for Scripture*, 28.

expects to hear not by virtue of possibilities grounded in the text itself, but by virtue of the faithfulness of God who has entrusted his Word to these earthen vessels.

The properly Christian way to talk about the dynamic of reading Scripture is through the language of justification. To be justified is to be given a place in God's story; it is to be embraced within the triune communion of his love. God's story, furthermore, is itself the power by which those who hear it are brought to salvation (Rom. 1.16). That is to say, the Word of God, incarnate in Jesus Christ and sounded again in Scripture as testimony to him, accomplishes what it says: 'I will be your God and you will be my people; Lo, I am with you always; Your sins are forgiven…' There is nothing in us that deserves this Word, or that renders us capable of hearing it. Indeed, on account of human sinfulness, we stand against the Word and render ourselves incapable of hearing it. It is only as God himself creates the conditions for hearing that we do hear. Precisely as we do hear and accept the role thus given us in God's story, we are justified; we are set in right relation to God and to one another. Thus, as John Webster has put it,

> Christian acts of reading Holy Scripture are… episodes in the history of God's gracious, communicative encounter with the redeemed sinner. Christian reading is, therefore, not within the range of human competence, for the reader's capacities are distorted by sin – by choice of wrong ends to which to put the text; by desire to fashion that which the text says into something which pleases, rather than something which disturbs or judges or commands or calls to repentance; by dominance of interests. Reading Scripture is therefore a microcosm of the history of judgement and salvation, a point at which that history is realized in the process of God's communication.[36]

Then follows the grace-laden irony: although they have little worthiness in themselves, God accepts and renders fruitful *our* efforts to hear his Word. That includes our efforts to read Scripture – even our very sophisticated hermeneutical efforts, so long, only, as they are offered as 'acts of consent to the text as an instrument for the speaking of God'.[37]

None of this can be accommodated to a general theory of reading because general theories are predicated upon one or another human capacity or upon some feature of texts themselves. Reading Scripture aright, by contrast, is predicated upon the grace and faithfulness of God. If this is true, then nothing seems more likely to misguide our reading than the decision to begin by leaving God out. We should begin rather with prayer, 'resigning ourselves

36. Webster, *Word and Church*, 79.

37. Webster, *Word and Church*, 82.

wholly to the direction of the Divine Spirit'.[38] That principle is commended by the biblical texts themselves. We find in the Psalms, for example, the oft-repeated refrain: 'The fear of the Lord is the beginning of wisdom, all those who practise it have a good understanding' (Ps. 111.10; cf. Job 28.28; Prov. 1.7; 2.6; 9.10; Js. 1.5). According to the Gospel of John, we are told by Christ himself that the Spirit will teach all that is necessary concerning Christ (John 14.25). To pray for the Spirit's guidance, therefore, and to study Scripture with the expectation that wisdom and understanding are gifts of God, is simply to read Scripture on its own terms. The posture of openness to God's guidance in the reading of Scripture is personally involving. It is an act in which our methodological presuppositions, our scholarship, and indeed our whole being, is genuinely tested and subjected to criticism and re-formation. Against Philip Davies's claim that only a non-confessional reading of Scripture truly permits and stimulates criticism of its own practices and beliefs,[39] Christian readers of Scripture go to the Bible with the clear and precise aim of subjecting all their practices and beliefs to the judgement and the transforming power of God's Word. It is not the university but the prayerful reading of Scripture that offers the most radical critique of ideological presuppositions available to human beings.[40]

VI — The Church as Hermeneutic of Scripture

The title of this concluding section will be recognized as an adaptation of Lesslie Newbigin's claim that the Church, or, more precisely, the believing congregation, is the hermeneutic of the gospel.[41] Newbigin means by this claim that the most compelling testimony to the truth of the gospel is the community that lives it. The gospel, and indeed Scripture, makes a claim about the way the world is constituted. The world it presents is constituted very differently than the one that we customarily perceive ourselves to inhabit. At its centre is the risen Christ, the firstborn of God's new creation, the one through whom all things came to be and in whom all things will be brought to completion. The world of Scripture is a world created by God, loved by God, redeemed from its fallenness by God, reconciled and perfected by God. The world's history is this history even though, for the most part, we go our way in defiance of it. It

38. John Calvin, *Institutes of the Christian Religion*, trans. John Allen (Philadelphia: Presbyterian Board of Christian Education, 1936) III.7.1, p. 752.

39. Davies, *Whose Bible is it Anyway?*, 48.

40. I owe the point to Donald Wood's exposition of Barth in his 'Theological Hermeneutics' 169.

41. Lesslie Newbigin, *The Gospel in a Pluralist Society* (Grand Rapids: Eerdmans, 1989) ch. 18.

is commonly asserted that the world of the Bible is very different from our own, and, further, that understanding of the Bible's message and appropriation of its truth requires a reframing of the biblical conception of the world within our own plausibility structures. That is a half-truth tragically misapplied. The Bible does present a different world, but its difference from our own is not shown forth in the primitivity of its science – a merely relative assessment – but rather through its orientation to God. The Bible does not invite us to de- (or re-) mythologize its world, but rather to inhabit it, and to participate thus in the coming kingdom of God.[42] It offers by way of testimony to its world, the raising to life of the one who our world put to death. The plausibility of the Bible's testimony, the plausibility of the creative and redemptive purpose of God, rests on him. If he is not raised, then faith is in vain (1 Cor. 15.17).

Then comes Newbigin:

> Almost everything in the 'plausibility structure' which is the habitation of our society seems to contradict this Christian hope. Everything suggests that it is absurd to believe that the true authority over all things is represented in a crucified man. No amount of brilliant argument can make it sound reasonable to the inhabitants of the reigning plausibility structure. That is why I am suggesting that the only possible hermeneutic of the gospel is a congregation which believes it.[43]

Perhaps it is overstated to say that the *only* possible hermeneutic is such a congregation, for God is free to give himself as he chooses, but the invitation to inhabit the world of the Bible is surely made more plausible by a community that does inhabit it and among whom the new creation is a present reality. The gospel says, after all, that in Christ God has reconciled the world to himself (2 Cor. 5.19). We should therefore expect to see some signs of the reconciliation God has wrought. The signs are not moral perfection. They are, rather, forgiveness and gratitude, love and hope. These are signs of the kingdom and essential characteristics of the Church's life. Where these characteristics are evident, the biblical message of new creation centred on the crucified and risen one becomes believable – the world of the Bible comes into view as the real world constituted thus by God.

42. The tendency in modern times to fit the Bible in procrustean fashion into the prevailing plausibility structures is, as we have seen in Chapter 2, the hermeneutical reversal identified by Hans Frei in *The Eclipse of Biblical Narrative*.

43. Lesslie Newbigin, *The Gospel in a Pluralist Society*, 232.

Epilogue: Theology and History Once More

The discipline of historical study has frequently been undertaken, not least in the sphere of biblical hermeneutics, in ways that have left us 'theologically speechless'.[1] No less commonly, theology has sometimes been done in ways that render the particularities of history incidental to the gospel. Neither approach can tell the truth, for in the person of Jesus Christ – the one who is the Truth – history and theology are given together.

That Jesus Christ is himself the Truth – as Christian faith confesses – justifies an account of history that takes its bearings from him. Because he is the alpha and the omega, the first and the last, the beginning and the end (Rev. 22.3), the origin and the goal and thus also the content of history, requires theological description. Consistent with the logic of Hans Frei's account of the reversal that took place in Modern hermeneutics,[2] Christ is not to be understood in the light of all else we think that we know about history. All else, rather, is to be understood in the light of Christ. Of course, to make this claim and to accept it, is to dwell within the interpretive paradigm of the Bible, especially as that paradigm takes christocentric shape in the New Testament. Joel Green puts the matter well:

> [A]s with other biblical narratives, the essential truth-claim with which we are concerned in our reading the Gospels and Acts lies above all in the claim of these narratives to speak, as it were, on God's behalf – that is, to interpret reality in light of God's self-disclosure of God's own character and purpose working itself out in the cosmos and on the plain of human events.[3]

1. The phrase is taken from Gerhard von Rad, who is said to have used it of W.F. Albright and his school. Cited in Christopher R. Seitz, 'What Lesson Will History Teach?' in Craig Bartholomew, C. Stephen Evans, Mary Healey and Murray Rae, eds, *'Behind' the Text: History and Biblical Interpretation* (Carlisle: Paternoster Press, and Grand Rapids: Zondervan, 2003) 443–67, 445.

2. See Chapter 2 above.

3. Joel Green, 'Which Conversation Shall We Have?' in Craig Bartholomew, C. Stephen Evans, Mary Healey and Murray Rae, eds, *'Behind' the Text: History and Biblical Interpretation* (Carlisle: Paternoster Press, and Grand Rapids: Zondervan, 2003) 141–9, 148.

How it should come about that we accept the claim of the biblical narratives is not easy to say in general. The process of becoming a Christian, of accepting the gospel, does not conform to a rule such that following certain steps of enquiry or of devotion will lead inevitably to faith. Learning to indwell the paradigm of the Bible has to do, rather, with God's act of revelation and reconciliation by which men and women are gathered into the community of faith. Once there, however, the world looks different and all history with it. For now it appears as the space and time given to humankind to grow into the fullness of covenant relationship with God.

That should yield a different historiography and a different historical discourse from that established by the canons of secular reason. Surprisingly perhaps, in light of much that has been said above, its difference will not result in the abandonment of the tools of critical enquiry as they have been developed in biblical studies. The critical processes of sifting evidence, evaluating testimony, and so on will continue in much the same way that they have done in the past except that the categories of explanation available to the enterprise of making sense of the evidence will now include theological ones. The theological historian will have at his or her disposal, for instance, the category of sinfulness. Such a category might well have far greater explanatory power in accounting for a particular stretch of human history than anything available to the secular historian. Or she might utilize the category of divine grace in accounting for *extra-ordinary* acts of forgiveness and reconciliation that may be evident in human affairs. That such categories don't permit of empirical verification in the way that some others might doesn't settle the matter of whether or not they are valid categories to use. It just means that their utilization is a very skilled affair that draws upon uncommon resources of wisdom and insight. Again, the test of their validity will be the explanatory power afforded by their use.

The thinking of theology and history together will even allow for the utilization of Troeltsch's three principles of historical enquiry, namely, criticism, correlation and analogy,[4] but their employment will be shaped now not by the presumption of Deism, agnosticism or atheism, but rather by faith in the revelation of God in Christ. Criticism, for example, the first of Troeltsch's principles, will be applied to all claims about the action of God in history. No witnesses should be regarded as absolutely authoritative, but, as Wittgenstein reminds us,[5] good reasons need to be supplied for not trusting the testimony of those through whose witness we gain access to the events. In the case of

4. I am very grateful to Tim Cooper for suggesting to me the possibility of rehabilitating the Troeltschian principles within a theological account of history.

5. See Chapter 6 above.

theological judgements about history, more authority should quite properly be accorded to those whose lives manifest qualities of Christ-likeness and wisdom, than to those who offer no such evidence of their trustworthiness.

The principle of correlation, Troeltsch's second, will likewise be employed in doing theology and history together. In this case the complex of causes giving rise to an event – of the Truth and Reconciliation Commission in South Africa, for example – might well include God's equipping of particular people to be the agents of a non-violent revolution by means of which the structures of oppression and injustice were dismantled. This is the kind of thing that accords with the divine economy as it is set forth in the Bible. The world of the Bible provides, then, a framework for understanding our world, much along the lines that Hans Frei suggests.

The principle of analogy, finally, might also be used to test the claims of God's involvement in the affairs of humankind. When claims are made about sin and forgiveness and the inspiration of God's Spirit – as they are commonly enough in the stories people tell about their history – those who consider it legitimate to do theology and history together will test such claims by analogy with what else they have learned of God's dealings with the world. The political leader who sends armies into battle claiming that God is on his or her side might well have a difficult job convincing the theological historian that such an account finds analogous support in God's self-disclosure in Jesus Christ, whereas the claim of Mother Teresa that God assisted her daily in the tasks of healing and comfort offered to the poor enjoys the support of a much clearer analogy with what God has done in Christ. The principles of analogy and correlation may serve also in the case of miracles. Within a conception of history understood as the terrain upon which God is bringing about his purpose of reconciliation and new life, we should not be surprised to see the signs of new life transforming our present reality as indeed was suggested by Jesus when he directed the attention of John the Baptist to the lame who walk, to the blind who now see, and to the poor who have heard the good news.

These principles, of criticism, correlation and analogy, do not yield infallible judgements, of course, but neither do they do so in the hands of secular historians. They do provide, however, some guidelines for responsible historical and theological judgements that serve well most of the time to weed out the claims of charlatans, the deluded, and even the innocently mistaken.

Utilizing these principles in the way that I have suggested does not permit us to subject the Word of God to the same test. It is the Word made flesh who establishes and constitutes through his own history the framework for doing theology and history together. The Christian gospel invites people to dwell with him, to embrace his story as their own, and to look with new eyes upon the world as created, redeemed and shaped by the promise that in due time all things will be brought to fulfilment in him.

Bibliography

Althaus. P., *Fact and Faith in the Kerygma Today* (Philadelphia: Muhlenberg Press, 1959)

Augustine, *City of God*, trans. J. Healey (London: J.M. Dent & Son, 1945)

Barnes, Jonathan, 'Socrates and the Jury: Paradoxes in Plato's Distinction Between Knowledge and True Belief II', *Aristotelian Society Supplementary Volume* 54 (1980) 193–206

Barth, Karl, *Der Römerbrief*, 2nd edn (Munich: Christian Kaiser Verlag, 1922)

—— *Church Dogmatics*, translation edited by G.W. Bromiley and T.F. Torrance (Edinburgh: T&T Clark, 1957–69)

Bauckham, Richard, 'Reading Scripture as a Coherent Story' in Ellen F. Davis and Richard B. Hays, eds, *The Art of Reading Scripture* (Grand Rapids: Eerdmans, 2003) 38–53

Bebbington, David, *Patterns in History: Christian Perspectives in Historical Thought*, 2nd edn (Leicester: Apollos, 1990)

Behm, Johannes, 'Metanoia: Ein Grundbegriff der neutestamentlichen Verkündigung', *Deutsche Theologie* 7 (1940) 75–86

Behm, J., and Würthwein, E., '*metanoeo* and *metanoia* in the New Testament' in Gerhard Kittel, ed., *Theological Dictionary of the New Testament*, vol. iv (Grand Rapids: Eerdmans, 1967) 999–1008

Berkouwer, G.C., *Holy Scripture*, ET (Grand Rapids: Eerdmans, 1975)

Braaten, Carl E., 'The Reality of the Resurrection' in Christopher R. Seitz, ed., *Nicene Christianity: The Future for a New Ecumenism* (Grand Rapids: Brazos Press, 2001) 107–18

Brown, Colin, 'History and the Believer' in *History, Criticism and Faith*, ed. Colin Brown (Downers Grove: Intervarsity Press, 1976) 147–218

Bultmann, Rudolf, *Theology of the New Testament*, vol. i, trans. Kendrick Grobel (London: SCM Press, 1952)

—— 'New Testament and Mythology' in *Kerygma and Myth*, trans. Reginald H. Fuller (London: SPCK, 1953) 1–44

—— 'Liberal Theology and the Latest Theological Movement' in *Faith and Understanding*, 6th edn, trans. Louise Pettibone Smith (London: SCM Press, 1966) 28–52

Burnyeat, I.-M.F., 'Socrates and the Jury: Paradoxes in Plato's Distinction Between Knowledge and True Belief I', *Aristotelian Society Supplementary Volume* 54 (1980) 173–91

Chakrabarti, Arindam, Review of C.A.J Coady, *Testimony: A Philosophical Study*; *Philosophy and Phenomenological Research* 54.4 (December 1994) 965–72

Coady, C.A.J., *Testimony: A Philosophical Study* (Oxford: Clarendon Press, 1992)

Collingwood, R.G., *The Idea of History*, ed. T.M. Knox (London: Oxford University Press, 1946)

Cullmann, Oscar, *Christ and Time* (London: SCM Press, 1951)

—— *Salvation in History* (London: SCM Press, 1967)

Daniélou, Jean, *The Lord of History*, trans. Nigel Abercrombie (London: Longmans, 1958)

Davies, Philip R., *Whose Bible Is It Anyway?*, 2nd edn (London: T&T Clark, 2004)

Davis, Stephen T., *Risen Indeed: Making Sense of the Resurrection* (Grand Rapids: Eerdmans, 1993)

Dawes, Gregory W., ed., *The Historical Jesus Quest: Landmarks in the Search for the Jesus of History* (Louisville: Westminster John Knox Press, 1999)

De Lubac, Henri, *Medieval Exegesis*, trans. E.M. Macierowski (Grand Rapids: Eerdmans, 2000)

Dennett, Daniel C., 'Seeing is Believing – Or is it?' in K. Akins, ed., *Perception*, Vancouver Studies in Cognitive Science (Oxford: Oxford University Press, 1996) 158–72

Denton, Donald L. Jr, *Historiography and Hermeneutics in Jesus Studies: An Examination of the Work of John Dominic Crossan and Ben F. Meyer*, JSNT Supplement 262 (London: T&T Clark, 2004)

Derrida, J., *The Gift of Death*, trans. David Wills (Chicago: University of Chicago Press, 1995)

Descartes, R., *Discourse on Method and the Meditations*, trans. F.E. Sutcliffe (Harmondsworth: Penguin Books, 1968)

Dilthey, Wilhelm, *Introduction to the Sciences of the Mind* in *Gesammelte Schriften*, vol. i (Stuttgart, Teubner, 1927)

Downing, F. Gerald, *Cynics and Christian Origins* (Edinburgh: T&T Clark, 1992) 167

Dretske, Fred, *Seeing and Knowing* (London: Routledge & Kegan Paul, 1969)

Ebeling, Gerhard, *Theology and Proclamation*, trans. John Riches (London: Collins, 1966)

Eichrodt, W., 'Offenbarung und Geschichte im Alten Testament', *Theologische Zeitschrift* 4 (1948) 321ff.

Evans, C.F., *Resurrection and the New Testament* (London: SCM Press, 1970)

Evans, C. Stephen, 'Empiricism, Rationalism and the Possiblity of Historical Religious Knowledge', in C.S. Evans and M Westphal, *Christian Perspectives on Religious Knowledge* (Grand Rapids: Eerdmans, 1993) 134–60

—— *The Historical Christ and the Jesus of Faith: The Incarnational Narrative as History* (Oxford: Clarendon Press, 1996)

Evans C.S. and Westphal, M., *Christian Perspectives on Religious Knowledge* (Grand Rapids: Eerdmans, 1993)

Fichte, J.G., *Die Anweisung zum seligen Leben*, ed. Fritz Medicus (Hamburg: Felix Meiner, 1954)

Fitzmyer, Joseph A., *The Gospel According to Luke X–XXIV* (Garden City, NY: Doubleday, 1983)

Fowl, Stephen E., *Engaging Scripture* (Oxford: Blackwell, 1998)

—— 'The Role of Authorial Intention in the Theological Interpretation of Scripture' in Joel B. Green and Max Turner, eds, *Between Two Horizons: Spanning New Testament Studies and Systematic Theology* (Grand Rapids: Eerdmans, 2000) 71–87

Frei, Hans, *The Eclipse of Biblical Narrative: A Study of Eighteenth and Nineteenth Century Hermeneutics* (New Haven and London: Yale University Press, 1974)

—— 'Theological Reflections on the Accounts of Jesus' Death and Resurrection' (1975) reprinted in *The Identity of Jesus Christ* (Eugene, Oreg.: Wipf & Stock, 2000) 1–49

—— *The Identity of Jesus Christ* (Eugene, Oreg.: Wipf & Stock, 2000)

Fricker, Elizabeth, 'Telling and Trusting: Reductionism and Anti-Reductionism in the Epistemology of Testimony', *Mind* 104 (April 1995) 393–411

Fukuyama, Francis, *The End of History and the Last Man* (New York: Free Press, 1992)

Fuller, Daniel P., *Easter Faith and History* (London: Tyndale Press, 1968)

Funk, R., and Hoover, R., eds., *The Five Gospels* (New York: Macmillan, 1993)

Gadamer, H., *Truth and Method*, 2nd edn (London: Sheed & Ward, 1975)

Goldingay, John, *Models for Scripture* (Grand Rapids: Eerdmans, 1994)

Goldmann, L., *The Hidden God: A Study of Tragic Vision in the 'Pensées' of Pascal and the Tragedies of Racine* (London: Routledge & Kegan Paul, 1964)

Green, Joel, 'Which Conversation Shall We Have?' in Craig Bartholomew, C. Stephen Evans, Mary Healey and Murray Rae, eds, *'Behind' the Text: History and Biblical Interpretation* (Carlisle: Paternoster Press, and Grand Rapids: Zondervan, 2003) 141–9

Grierson, Denham, 'Resurrection and Personal Story' in Nigel Watson, ed., *The Heart of the Matter: Reflections on the Resurrection Faith* (Melbourne: Joint Board of Christian Education, 1980) 43–9

Gunton, Colin E., *Christ and Creation* (Carlisle: Paternoster Press, 1992)

——*The One, the Three and the Many: God, Creation and the Culture of Modernity* (Cambridge: Cambridge University Press, 1993)

—— *The Triune Creator: A Historical and Systematic Study* (Edinburgh: Edinburgh University Press, 1998)

Hamilton, W., *A Quest for the Post-Historical Jesus* (London: SCM Press, 1993)

Hardwig, John, 'Epistemic Dependence', *Journal of Philosophy* 82 (1985) 335–50

Harrisville, Roy A., 'The Loss of Biblical Authority and its Recovery' in Carl E. Braaten and Robert W. Jenson, eds, *Reclaiming the Bible for the Church* (Edinburgh: T&T Clark, 1996) 47–61

Harrisville, Roy A., and Sundberg, Walter, *The Bible in Modern Culture: Theology and Historical-Critical Method from Spinoza to Käsemann* (Grand Rapids: Eerdmans, 1995)

Hart, Trevor, 'Tradition, Authority and a Christian Approach to the Bible as Scripture' in Joel B. Green and Max Turner, eds, *Between Two Horizons: Spanning New Testament and Systematic Theology* (Grand Rapids: Eerdmans, 2000) 183–204

Hays, R.B., 'The Corrected Jesus', *First Things* 43 (May 1994) 43–8

Hegel, G.W.F., 'The Positivity of the Christian Religion' in *Friedrich Hegel on Christianity: Early Theological Writings*, trans. T.M. Knox (New York: Harper Torchbooks, 1961) 67–181

—— *Lectures on the Philosophy of World History*, trans. H.B. Nisbet, Introduction by Duncan Forbes (Cambridge: Cambridge University Press, 1975)

—— *Lectures on the Philosophy of Religion*, 3 vols, trans. P.C. Hodgson and R.F. Brown (Berkeley: University of California Press, 1984–6).

Hengel, Martin, 'Salvation History' in David F. Ford and Graham Stanton, eds, *Reading Texts, Seeking Wisdom: Scripture and Theology* (Grand Rapids: Eerdmans, 2003) 229–44

Holmes, Stephen R., *Listening to the Past: The Place of Tradition in Theology* (Carlisle: Paternoster Press, 2002)

Hughes, Patrick, 'The Meteorologist Who Started a Revolution', *Weatherwise* 47 (April/May 1994) 29–35

Hume, David, 'An Enquiry Concerning Human Understanding' in *Enquiries Concerning the Human Understanding and Concerning the Principles of Morals*, ed. L.A. Selby-Bigge (Oxford: Oxford University Press, 1962)

Insole, Christopher, 'Seeing Off the Local Threat to Irreducible Knowledge by Testimony', *Philosophical Quarterly*, 50.198 (January 2000) 44–56

Ive, J., 'Robert W. Jenson's Theology of History' in *Trinity, Time and Church: A Response to the Theology of Robert W. Jenson*, ed. Colin E. Gunton (Grand Rapids: Eerdmans, 2000) 146–57.

Jaki, S.L., *The Saviour of Science* (Edinburgh: Scottish Academic Press, 1990)

Jardine, Nicholas, *The Fortunes of Inquiry* (Oxford: Clarendon Press, 1986).

Jeanrond, W., *Theological Hermeneutics: Development and Significance* (London: SCM Press, 1994)

Jenson, Robert, 'Hermeneutics and the Life of the Church' in Carl E. Braaten and Robert W. Jenson, eds, *Reclaiming the Bible for the Church* (Edinburgh: T&T Clark, 1995) 89–105

—— 'Scripture's Authority in the Church' in Ellen F. Davis and Richard B. Hays, eds, *The Art of Reading Scripture* (Grand Rapids: Eerdmans, 2003) 27–37

Kähler, Martin, *The So-called Historical Jesus and the Historic, Biblical Christ*, ed. and trans. by Carl E. Braaten (Philadelphia: Fortress Press, 1964)

Kaiser, C.B., *Creation and the History of Science* (Grand Rapids: William B. Eerdmans Publishing Co., 1991)

Kant, I., *Religion Within the Limits of Reason Alone*, translated with an Introduction and Notes by Theodore M. Greene and Hoyt H. Hudson (New York: Harper & Row, 1960)

Käsemann, Ernst, 'The Problem of the Historical Jesus', first published in *Zeitschrift für Theologie und Kirche* 51 (1954) 125–53, and reprinted in Gregory W. Dawes, ed., *The Historical Jesus Quest: Landmarks in the Search for the Jesus of History* (Louisville: Westminster John Knox Press, 1999) 279–313

Kesich, Veselin, *The First Day of the New Creation: The Resurrection and the Christian Faith* (Crestwood, NY: St Vladimir's Seminary Press, 1982)

Kierkegaard, S., *Philosophical Fragments*, ed. and trans. Howard V. Hong and Edna H. Hong (Princeton: Princeton University Press, 1985)

—— *For Self-Examination*; and *Judge for Yourself!*, ed. and trans. Howard V. Hong and Edna H. Hong (Princeton: Princeton University Press, 1990)

—— *Practice in Christianity*, ed. and trans. Howard V. Hong and Edna H. Hong (Princeton: Princeton University Press, 1991)

—— *Concluding Unscientific Postscript to Philosophical Fragments*, ed. and trans. Howard V. Hong and Edna H. Hong (Princeton: Princeton University Press, 1992)

Kuhn, Thomas, *The Structure of Scientific Revolutions*, 2nd edn, enlarged (London and Chicago: University of Chicago Press, 1970)

Künneth, Walter, *The Theology of the Resurrection*, trans. James W. Leitch (London: SCM Press, 1965)

Lessing, G.E., 'On the Proof of the Spirit and of Power' in *Lessing's Theological Writings*, ed. Henry Chadwick (London: Adam & Charles Black, 1956) 51–61

Locke, John, *An Essay Concerning Human Understanding*, ed. Peter H. Nidditch (Oxford: Clarendon Press, 1975)

Marion, Jean Luc, 'They Recognized Him; and He Became Invisible to Them', *Modern Theology* 18.2 (April 2002) 145–52

Marsh, John, *Saint John* (Harmondsworth: Penguin Books, 1968)

Matilal, Bimal Krishna, and Chakrabarti, Arindam, eds, *Knowing from Words* (Dordrecht: Kluwer Academic, 1994)

May, Gerhard, *Creatio ex Nihilo: The Doctrine of 'Creation out of Nothing' in Early Christian Thought*, trans. A.S. Worrall (Edinburgh: T&T Clark, 1994)

McDowell, Josh, *Evidence that Demands a Verdict* (San Bernardino: Campus Crusade for Christ International, 1972)

Moberly, R.W.L., *The Bible, Theology and Faith: A Study of Abraham and Jesus* (Cambridge: Cambridge University Press, 2000)

Moltmann, Jürgen, *Theology of Hope*, trans. James W. Leitch (London: SCM Press, 1967)

—— *The Way of Jesus Christ: Christology in Messianic Dimensions*, trans. Margaret Kohl (London: SCM Press, 1990)

Newbigin, Lesslie, *The Gospel in a Pluralist Society* (Grand Rapids: Eerdmans, 1989)

Niebuhr, Richard R., *Resurrection and Historical Reason: A Study of Theological Method* (New York: Charles Scribner's Sons, 1957)

Novak, D., *The Election of Israel: The Idea of the Chosen People* (Cambridge: Cambridge University Press, 1995)

O'Collins, Gerald, 'The Resurrection: The State of the Questions' in Stephen T. Davis, Daniel Kendall and Gerald O'Collins, SJ, eds, *The Resurrection: An Interdisciplinary Symposium on the Resurrection of Jesus* (Oxford: Oxford University Press, 1997) 5–28

Pannenberg, W., *Revelation as History: A Proposal for a More Open, Less Authoritarian View of an Important Theological Concept*, trans. David Granskou (London: Macmillan, 1968)

—— *Jesus – God and Man*, trans. Lewis L. Wilkins and Duane A. Priebe (London: SCM Press, 1968)

—— *Basic Questions in Theology*, vol. i (Philadelphia: Fortress Press 1970)

—— 'Did Jesus Really Rise from the Dead?' *Dialog* (Spring 1965), reprinted in Richard Batey, ed., *New Testament Issues* (London: SCM Press, 1970) 102–17

—— *Systematic Theology*, vol. ii, trans. Geoffrey W. Bromiley (Edinburgh: T&T Clark, 1994)

Peirce, C.S., 'The Century's Great Men in Science' in P.P. Wiener, ed., *Selected Writings: Values in a Universe of Chance* (New York: Dover, 1966)

Plantinga, A., *Warranted Christian Belief* (New York: Oxford University Press, 2000)

Plato, *Theaetetus*, trans. John McDowell (Oxford: Clarendon Press, 1973)

Popper, Karl, 'Towards a Rational Theory of Tradition' in *Conjectures and Refutations: The Growth of Scientific Knowledge* (London: Routledge & Kegan Paul, 1963) 120–35

Provan, Iain, 'Knowing and Believing: Faith in the Past' in Craig Bartholomew, C. Stephen Evans, Mary Healey and Murray Rae, eds, *'Behind' the Text: History and Biblical Interpretation* (Carlisle: Paternoster Press, and Grand Rapids: Zondervan, 2003) 229–66

Rae, Murray A., 'The Forgetfulness of Historical-Talkative Remembrance in Kierkegaard's "Practice in Christianity"' in *International Kierkegaard Commentary: Practice in Christianity*, ed. Robert L. Perkins (Macon, Ga.: Mercer University Press, 2004) 69–94

Reimarus, H.S., 'Concerning the Intention of Jesus and His Teaching' in *Reimarus Fragments*, ed. Charles H. Talbert (London: SCM Press, 1971)

Richardson, A., *History Sacred and Profane* (London: SCM Press, 1964)

Ritschl, Albrecht, *The Christian Doctrine of Justification and Reconciliation* (Edinburgh: T&T Clark, 1902)

Robinson, J.M., *A New Quest of the Historical Jesus, Studies in Biblical Theology* (Chicago: Allenson, 1959)

Sanders, E.P., *Jesus and Judaism* (Philadelphia: Fortress Press, 1985)

Schweizer, Albert, *The Quest of the Historical Jesus*, trans. W. Montgomery (London: A&C Black, 1954).

Seitz, Christopher R., 'In Accordance with the Scriptures' in *Word Without End: The Old Testament as Abiding Theological Witness* (Grand Rapids: Eerdmans, 1998) 51–60

—— 'What Lesson Will History Teach?' in Craig Bartholomew, C. Stephen Evans, Mary Healey and Murray Rae, eds, *'Behind' the Text: History and Biblical Interpretation* (Carlisle: Paternoster Press, and Grand Rapids: Zondervan, 2003) 443–67

Shapin, Steven, *A Social History of Truth: Civility and Science in Seventeenth-Century England* (Chicago: University of Chicago Press, 1994).

Spinoza, B., *Ethics*, trans. Andrew Boyle (London: J.M. Dent & Co., 1959)

—— *Tractatus theologico-politicus*, trans. Samuel Shirley (Leiden: E.J. Brill, 1991)

Stanton, Graham, *The Gospels and Jesus*, 2nd edn (Oxford: Oxford University Press, 2002)

Steinmetz, David C., 'Uncovering a Second Narrative: Detective Fiction and the Construction of Historical Method' in Ellen F. Davis and Richard B. Hays, eds, *The Art of Reading Scripture* (Grand Rapids: Eerdmans, 2003) 54–65

Stout, Jeffrey, 'What is the Meaning of a Text?' *New Literary History* 14 (1982) 1–12

Strauss, D.F., *The Life of Jesus Critically Examined*, ET (Philadelphia: Fortress Press, 1972)

Taylor, Charles, *Sources of the Self: The Making of the Modern Identity* (Cambridge: Cambridge University Press, 1989)

Teichman, Jenny, 'Wittgenstein on Persons and Human Beings' in Royal Institute of Philosophy Lectures, vol. vii, *1972/73: Understanding Wittgenstein* (London: Macmillan, 1974) 133–48

Theissen, Gerd, 'Historical Scepticism and the Criteria of Jesus Research or My Attempt to Leap Across Lessing's Yawning Gulf', *Scottish Journal of Theology* 49.4 (1996) 147–76

Torrance, T.F., *Theology in Reconstruction* (London: SCM Press, 1965)

Troeltsch, E., 'Historical and Dogmatic Method in Theology' in *Religion in History: Ernst Troeltsch* (Edinburgh: T&T Clark, 1991) 11–32.

Tuckett, Christopher, *Reading the New Testament: Methods of Interpretation* (London: SPCK, 1987)

—— 'Sources and Methods' in Markus Bockmuehl, ed, *The Cambridge Companion to Jesus* (Cambridge: Cambridge University Press, 2001) 121–37

Turner, H.W., *The Roots of Science: An Investigative Journey Through the World's Religions* (Auckland: DeepSight Trust, 1998)

Vanhoozer, Kevin J., *Is There a Meaning in This Text?* (Grand Rapids: Zondervan, 1998)

Vermes, Geza, *The Religion of Jesus the Jew* (London: SCM Press, 1993)

von Rad, G., *God at Work in Israel*, trans. John H. Marks (Nashville: Abingdon Press, 1980)

von Ranke, Leopold, *Geschichte der romanischen und germanischen Völker, 1494–1535* (Berlin: Reimer, 1924)

Watson, F., *Text, Church, and World: Biblical Interpretation in Theological Perspective* (Edinburgh: T&T Clark, 1994)

—— 'Bible, Theology and the University: A Response to Philip Davies', *Journal for the Study of the Old Testament* 71.1 (1996) 3–16

—— *Text and Truth: Redefining Biblical Theology* (Edinburgh: T&T Clark, 1997)

—— 'The Quest for the Real Jesus' in Markus Bockmuehl, ed, *The Cambridge Companion to Jesus* (Cambridge: Cambridge University Press, 2001) 156–69

Webster, John, *Word and Church: Essays in Christian Dogmatics* (Edinburgh: T&T Clark, 2001)

Wilder, Amos N., *Otherworldliness and the New Testament* (London: SCM Press, 1955)

Williams, Rowan, 'Historical Criticism and Sacred Text' in David F. Ford and Graham Stanton, eds, *Reading Texts, Seeking Wisdom*, (Grand Rapids: Eerdmans, 2003) 217–28

Wittgenstein, Ludwig, *On Certainty*, ed. G.E.M. Anscombe and G.H. von Wright (New York: Harper Torchboooks, 1972)

Wolterstorff, Nicholas, *Until Justice and Peace Embrace* (Grand Rapids: Eerdmans, 1983)

—— 'The Unity Behind the Canon' in Christine Helmer and Christof Landmesser, eds, *One Scripture or Many? Canon from Biblical, Theological and Philosophical Perspectives* (Oxford: Oxford University Press, 2004) 217–32

Wood, Donald, 'Theological Hermeneutics', *International Journal of Systematic Theology* 4.2 (2002) 156–71

Wright, N.T., *The New Testament and the People of God* (London: SPCK, 1992)

—— 'Five Gospels but No Gospel: Jesus and the Seminar.' in W.R. Farmer, ed., *Crisis in Christology: Essays in Quest of Resolution* (Livonia, Mich.: Dove, 1995) 115–57

—— *Jesus and the Victory of God* (London: SPCK, 1996)

—— *The Resurrection of the Son of God* (London: SPCK, 2003)

Index